"This is an appealing and engaging narrative for those who seek to make connections between the art and conduct of war, at a particular time in modern history, and the challenges that modern organisations face in an uncertain world, as seen through the lens of resilience and organisational theory."

— Sandra Eaton, UK Ministry of Defence MOD Strategic Change Leader

"This is an extremely interesting approach to looking at Organisational Resilience. The use of historical events is very clever and I believe would be appealing to many people, students and interested readers alike. I believe this approach is unique and makes the learning experience far more enjoyable."

— Rebecca Harnet, Squadron Leader, SO2 Defence Movements Policy in ACDS (Log Ops)

THE ART OF ORGANISATIONAL RESILIENCE

The battlefield of the past is an opportunity for the future commander, the future manager, to reflect. The book's rationale for translating military concepts into management speak is the author's impression in the classroom that managers in commercial organisations tend to follow 'outdated' models of management without reflecting on military science that is believed to provide thought leadership.

The case study of the Fall of France in 1940 is a contest between two archetypes of organisational resilience, with one prevailing over the other. The resulting insights shaped military science: concepts such as *Auftragstaktik* have found their way into doctrinal thinking of modern armies and framed contemporary management literature.

This book provides a compelling analysis of the monumental events in May 1940 and provides rudimentary answers from a military and management perspective true to the premise of history. *The Art of Organisational Resilience* is a highly distinctive and readable book that explores the strategy, operations and tactics of modern business, and the role of resilience in sustaining business in increasingly complex, often fast-changing and adverse conditions.

ELMAR KUTSCH is a Senior Lecturer in Risk Management, Cranfield School of Management. His passion for the management of risk and uncertainty in projects led him to pursue a career in academia. He served as a Lecturer in Operations Management at the University of Surrey and has been at Cranfield since 2007.

THE ART OF ORGANISATIONAL RESILIENCE
REVISITING THE FALL OF FRANCE IN 1940

Elmar Kutsch

LONDON AND NEW YORK

First published 2018
by Routledge
2 Park Square, Milton Park, Abingdon, Oxon OX14 4RN

and by Routledge
711 Third Avenue, New York, NY 10017

Routledge is an imprint of the Taylor & Francis Group, an informa business

© 2018 Elmar Kutsch

The right of Elmar Kutsch to be identified as author of this work has been asserted by him in accordance with sections 77 and 78 of the Copyright, Designs and Patents Act 1988.

All rights reserved. No part of this book may be reprinted or reproduced or utilised in any form or by any electronic, mechanical, or other means, now known or hereafter invented, including photocopying and recording, or in any information storage or retrieval system, without permission in writing from the publishers.

Trademark notice: Product or corporate names may be trademarks or registered trademarks, and are used only for identification and explanation without intent to infringe.

British Library Cataloguing-in-Publication Data
A catalogue record for this book is available from the British Library

Library of Congress Cataloging-in-Publication Data
Names: Kutsch, Elmar, author.
Title: The art of organisational resilience: revisiting the fall of France in 1940 / Elmar Kutsch.
Description: Abingdon, Oxon; New York, NY: Routledge, 2019. | Includes bibliographical references and index.
Identifiers: LCCN 2018014830 (print) | LCCN 2018018182 (ebook) | ISBN 9781315164014 (eBook) | ISBN 9781138058750 (hardback: alk. paper) | ISBN 9781138058767 (pbk.: alk. paper)
Subjects: LCSH: Organizational change. | Organizational behavior. | Strategic planning. | Leadership. | Strategy. | World War, 1939–1945—France. | France—History—German occupation, 1940–1945.
Classification: LCC HD58.8 (ebook) | LCC HD58.8 .K885 2019 (print) | DDC 658.4/06—dc23
LC record available at https://lccn.loc.gov/2018014830

ISBN: 978-1-138-05875-0 (hbk)
ISBN: 978-1-138-05876-7 (pbk)
ISBN: 978-1-315-16401-4 (ebk)

Typeset in Minion Pro
by codeMantra

CONTENTS

Preface	xi
Timeline	xiii

CHAPTER 1 THE NEED FOR ORGANISATIONAL RESILIENCE — **1**

Von Clausewitz and De Jomini: the art of war	3
Organisational resilience	6
The need for resilience in 1940	10
Von Clausewitz and De Jomini: the surprise	14
De Jomini: grand tactics and battles	17
Offensive battles	18
Order of battle	20
Common explanations	24
Technical specifications of the tank	30
Competing concepts of resilience	34
Limitations of the book	38
Armageddon	40
Notes	43
References	44

CHAPTER 2 STRATEGIC RESILIENCE — **47**

The story: pre-May 10th 1940	48
La Bataille Conduit versus Bewegungskrieg	53
The challenge: 'surprising' an enemy	54
Deciding factors: imagination, sensitivity, adaptability	59
Von Clausewitz and De Jomini: strategy	62
Translation and explanation: linear versus adaptive strategy	64
Towards organisational resilience: the fallacy of determinism	67

CONTENTS

Battle of Kursk	70
Outlook	77
Notes	79
References	79

CHAPTER 3 OPERATIONAL RESILIENCE — 81

The story: May 10th–May 12th 1940	82
Schwerpunkt *versus* La Colmatage	85
De Jomini: assembly of forces in space	86
Von Clausewitz: assembly of forces in space	88
The challenge: crossing a river	88
Deciding factors: redundancy, determination, agility	94
Centre of gravity determination	95
Translation and explanation: dispersion versus concentration	98
Towards organisational resilience: the fallacy of protecting everything at minimal cost	102
Battle of the Bulge	107
Outlook	112
Notes	115
References	115

CHAPTER 4 TACTICAL RESILIENCE — 117

The story: May 10th–May 11th 1940	118
Auftragstaktik *versus* La Bataille Conduit	120
Allied Joint Doctrine – mission command	121
The challenge: capturing Fort d'Ében-Émael	124
Deciding factors: autonomy and sensitivity	130
Von Clausewitz: information in war	134
Translation and explanation: centralisation versus decentralisation	135
Towards organisational resilience: the fallacy of centralisation	138
Communicating intent	143
Battle of Leyte Gulf	144
Doctrinal principles in operations planning	150
Outlook	151
References	154

CHAPTER 5 LEADERSHIP **155**

The story: May 13th–May 17th 1940	156
Adaptive versus administrative leadership	159
Limitations of Von Clausewitz and De Jomini: leadership as a trait	160
The challenge: breaking out	168
Deciding factors: direction, alignment and commitment	174
Command philosophy	175
Importance of a cohesive staff team – command of the German Africa corps	177
Von Clausewitz: boldness	180
Translation and explanation: adaptive leadership versus administrative leadership	181
Towards organisational resilience: the fallacy of order	184
Battle of Hürtgen forest	186
Wargaming	191
Outlook	194
Notes	196
References	196

CHAPTER 6 LOGISTICS **197**

The story: May 18th–May 25th 1940	198
Logistical independence versus dependence	201
De Jomini: a few remarks on logistics in general	202
North Atlantic Treaty Organization (NATO): logistics planning	206
The challenge: racing to the channel	207
Deciding factors: abundance of resources, operational availability and logistical autonomy and cohesion	213
Continuous logistics	214
Translation and explanation: JIT versus JIC	217
Towards organisational resilience: the fallacy of 'pure' just-in-time	219
The Africa campaign	222
NATO: logistic planning considerations	228
Outlook	230
Notes	232
References	232

CONTENTS

CHAPTER 7   ROADS TO RESILIENCE — **233**

The story: May 26th–June 20th 1940	234
Roads to resilience	240
Why and what can be learned?	241
Erosion of resilience	243
The fallacy of hindsight	249
The five fallacies: some thoughts on British military thinking	250
Reversing the erosion of resilience	252
Red Teaming	254
Epilogue	262
Comment on De Jomini and Von Clausewitz	262
Notes	265
References	265
Index	267

PREFACE

The Second World War (WWII) is a fascinating historical chapter for me. As a German, born in the 1970s, I did not hear it talked about openly. Guilt and German society's longing to move on triggered my curiosity and desire to understand the 'why' and the 'how'. Why was a nation capable of 'living' an ideology as abhorrent as Nazism and willing to do so? How did it come to this?

Despite a mass of literature, I am still struggling to understand. I am even more perplexed and concerned to notice the recent rise of populism and nationalism in Europe, expressed to some extent by the very post-Second World War generation that grew up in the shadows of the trauma of 1939–1945.

The answer to the political 'why' question is not the focus of this book. Instead, the book embarks on a discourse of 'why' the military apparatus of Nazi Germany was so successful in subduing most of Europe in 1940–1942. Resource strapped and reeling from the economic turmoil of the Weimar Republic, Germany nevertheless defeated Poland in five weeks and brought France, a juggernaut in military terms, to its knees in just six weeks.

The battlefield of the past is an opportunity for the future commander, the future manager, to reflect. My rationale for translating military concepts into management speak is my impression in the classroom that managers in commercial organisations tend to follow 'outdated' models of management without reflecting on military science that I believe provides thought leadership. In my classes, I often repeat that we have a lot to learn from the military as they tend to be progressive in their thinking. They have to be, as their thinking on how to wage war determines the survival (and supremacy) of whole nations.

The primary aim of this book is to enable you, the reader, to reflect upon the Fall of France in 1940 and to question how the French and their Allies, as well as the Germans, conducted their operations and why one managerial path of thinking prevailed over the other. In this book, you will step into the role of commander, although the battlefield you manage is one of competition with other organisations, with the aim of prevailing. In this regard, history is

> meant to educate the mind of the future commander, or, more accurately, to guide him in his self-education, not to accompany him to the battlefield; just as a wise teacher guides and stimulates a young man's intellectual development, but is careful not to lead him by the hand for the rest of his life.
>
> (Von Clausewitz, quoted in Kennedy and Neilson, 2002, 26)

Nevertheless, managers use different languages, and some military concepts may not seem applicable to managers in commercial organisations. This book bridges that gap with a compelling case study, one in which two fundamental archetypes of management – one French and the other German – are in opposition to each other. I aim to analyse the Battle of France in May/June 1940, breaking it down into historical snippets and translating military speak into language that managers can more easily relate to.

Such translation and transformation have at times been difficult, and the alignment between military and management concepts is not perfect. The book has its limitations, some derived from the uneasy alignment of historic military concepts with those of contemporary management. You are free to disagree with the ideas put forward in these pages.

TIMELINE

September 1st 1939 – June 24th 1940

September 1st 1939	Germany invades Poland with 39 divisions.
September 3rd 1939	France and England declare war on Germany. The start of the 'Phoney war', which saw an eight-month period of little military activity on all sides.
September 10th 1939	The British Expeditionary Forces (BEF) start arriving in France.
September 27th 1939	Poland surrenders.
February 24th 1940	Hitler approves *Fall Gelb* (Operation Yellow), the invasion of France and the Low Countries.
May 1st 1940	Swiss military intelligence informs the French High Command that an attack is imminent. The French Forces are put on highalert.
May 3rd 1940	More intelligence indicates a massing of German troops at the borders with Belgium and the Netherlands.
May 6th 1940	Armoured columns are spotted on roads leading to the Ardennes.
May 9th 1940	After numerous postponements, the invasion is set for May 10th.

TIMELINE

May 10th 1940	Three Army groups push into the Low Countries. In the North, the invasion is preceded by airborne troops to secure vital bridges over the Albert Canal and disable key fortifications surrounding the 'Dutch' corridor. British and French Forces enact the Dyle-Breda Plan, moving some of their mobile forces to a prepared defensive line towards the Dyle river and the city of Breda in Belgium.
May 11th 1940	In the North, a key fortification covering the Albert Canal – Fort d'Ében-Émael – is assaulted by 78 airborne soldiers using gliders and quickly rendered inoperable. At the centre, at the French town of Sedan, the river Meuse is crossed by troops from the 9th Panzer Division in rubber boats at around noon.
May 12th 1940	At the Centre, further crossings over the Meuse succeed at Dinant and Monthermé. Pontoon bridges are established to allow armoured vehicles to get across. French and British air forces continuously attack those crossings but with little success. In the North, at Hannut in Belgium, the first tank battle results in the destruction of large parts of the German armoured Forces. The Germans lose around 160 tanks compared to 105 on the French side. Nevertheless, the French Forces are forced to retreat to the Belgian town of Gembloux.
May 13th 1940	At the Centre, bridgeheads across the Meuse are reinforced by armoured divisions, with the intention of attempting a break-out and linking all bridgeheads.

TIMELINE

May 14th 1940	The Netherlands surrenders.
May 16th 1940	In the North, the Germans break through the Dyle Line. British Forces retreat towards Brussels.
	The first 'Halt Order' is issued but largely ignored.
May 17th 1940	In the North, the French and British decide to straighten their front and prevent the Germans from outflanking them by retreating to the Scheldt river. Brussels is captured soon after by the German Forces.
May 18th 1940	In the North, the deep-sea water port Antwerp is captured.
May 22nd 1940	The centre of the attack starts to swing around to the North.
May 23rd 1940	In the North, the Germans cross the Scheldt in Belgium.
	The BEF is ordered to retreat to Dunkirk.
May 24th 1940	Adolf Hitler demands that further offensive actions be halted. The second 'Halt Order'.
May 26th 1940	The second 'Halt Order' is lifted.
May 27th 1940	The Germans resume their pressure on the encircled Allied forces. Dunkirk is shelled.
May 28th 1940	Belgium surrenders.
June 4th 1940	Operation Dynamo, the evacuation of the Allied Forces, is completed. Approximately 400,000 Allied soldiers have been evacuated.
June 5th 1940	*Fall Rot* (Operation Red) begins with the move of 142 divisions south towards the Weygand line, a defensive line of strongpoints.
June 10th 1940	Italy declares war on France.
June 14th 1940	German troops march into the open city of Paris.
	German forces break through the Maginot Line. Out of the 58 major fortresses of the Maginot Line, only 10 are captured in battle.

TIMELINE

June 21st 1940	Negotiations between French and German representatives commence.
June 22nd 1940	Franco-German Armistice is signed.
June 24th 1940	Franco-Italian Armistice signed.

ALLIED ORDER OF BATTLE

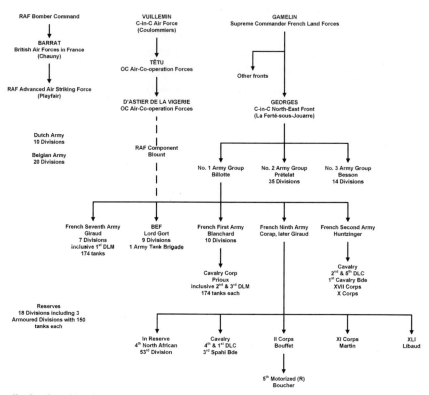

Allied order of battle (Horne 1990)

TIMELINE

GERMAN ORDER OF BATTLE

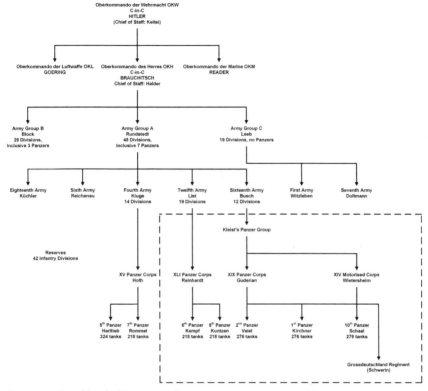

German order of battle (Horne 1990)

REFERENCES

Horne, A. (1990). *To lose a battle: France 1940*. London: Penguin Books.
Kennedy, G., & Neilson, K. (2002). *Military education: past, present, and future*. United States of America: Praeger.

CHAPTER ONE
The need for organisational resilience

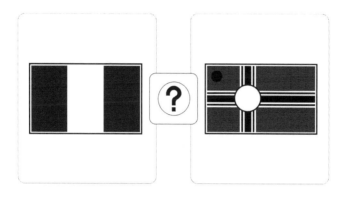

*War is
a grave affair of state;
It is a place
Of life and death.
A road
To survival and extinction,
A matter
To be pondered carefully.*

(Tzu 2008, 1)

CONTENTS

Von Clausewitz and De Jomini: the art of war	3
Organisational resilience	6
The need for resilience in 1940	10
Von Clausewitz and De Jomini: the surprise	14
De Jomini: grand tactics and battles	17
Offensive battles	18
Order of battle	20
Common explanations	24
Technical specifications of the tank	30
Competing concepts of resilience	34
Limitations of the book	38
Armageddon	40
Notes	43
References	44

On May 15th 1940, the British Prime Minister Sir Winston Churchill, while he was still in bed, was called by Paul Reynaud, his French counterpart:

> He spoke in English, and evidently under stress. 'We have been defeated'. As I did not immediately respond he said again: 'We are beaten; we have lost the battle.' I then remarked: Surely it can't have happened so soon? But he replied: 'The front is broken near Sedan; they are pouring through in great numbers with tanks and armoured cars.'
>
> (Jackson 2003, 9)

On May 10th, Nazi Germany commenced its offensive in the west, with the invasion of Holland, Belgium, Luxembourg and France. On May 13th, German forces crossed the river Meuse and broke through the French defences. The author of the 'Little Prince', who was a pilot at that time, set off on a reconnaissance on May 22nd 1940:

> We stand against the enemy as one man against three, one plane against ten or twenty, since Dunkerque, one tank against a hundred. We have no time to meditate upon the past. We are engaged in the

present. The present is as it is. No sacrifice, ever, anywhere, can possibly slow the German advance.

(Antoine de Saint-Exupéry 1942, 46)

The Fall of France in May/June 1940 at the hands of Nazi Germany is one of the great surprises of the twentieth century. The disparity of strength between the French and German disposition of forces favoured the Allies[1]; yet the weaker party prevailed. Germany inflicted one of the 'strangest' defeats in military history. The reason for the defeat of France in 1940 lends itself to renewed analysis from a management perspective.

The purpose of this book is not to replicate history or to improve its accuracy. It seeks to evaluate this piece of history through the eyes of management, a function that enables modern organisations to accomplish goals and objectives using available resources efficiently and effectively in the face of a range of adversities. In this respect, as Von Clausewitz suggested, history is

> meant to educate the mind of the future commander, or, more accurately, to guide him in his self-education, not to accompany him to the battlefield; just as a wise teacher guides and stimulates a young man's intellectual development, but is careful not to lead him by the hand for the rest of his life.

(quoted in Kennedy and Neilson 2002, 26)

VON CLAUSEWITZ AND DE JOMINI: THE ART OF WAR

This book will provide excerpts from two groundbreaking works on theories of war: *On War* (Von Clausewitz 2011) and *The Art of War* (De Jomini 2008). Both theories appeal to military planners and organisational strategists alike, although Von Clausewitz is more well known to both.

Carl von Clausewitz was born in 1780 and rose through the ranks of the Prussian army, with an interlude with the Russian army that led him to experience the Napoleonic Wars at Borodino. The Battle of Borodino, fought on September 7th 1812, during the invasion of Russia by Napoleonic forces, pushed the Russian army back from its positions, but the only gain was a tactical victory. With no capitulation of the Russian army in sight and the French forces ill-prepared for a prolonged stand-off, it marked the beginning of the end of the Russian campaign for Napoleon Bonaparte.

Von Clausewitz rejoined the Prussian army, mesmerised but also disillusioned by the Napoleonic way of thinking. He commented on Borodino that in the whole battle there was *not a single trace of an art or superior intelligence.*

He was transferred to an administrative post in the Prussian army and found time to write down his impressions and reflections on this remarkable period of warfare. The book *On War* remained unfinished when Von Clausewitz died in 1832, but his works were published in 1835 by his widow.

De Jomini was born in 1779, joining the French army in 1797. He held staff positions under Napoleon and Ney but was only promoted to *general de division* when he joined the ill-fated campaign against Russia on June 28th 1812. He gained first-hand experience of the Napoleonic method and its failure during the retreat from Moscow, which concluded in December 1812, with the loss of around 300,000 French, 70,000 Poles, 50,000 Italians, 80,000 Germans and 60,000 from other nations. His thoughts about strategy were originally published in 1830, with a revised edition eight years later.

Since then, Von Clausewitz and De Jomini have been seen as the cornerstones of military science and yet not without substantial criticism of their work. One aspect of the criticism of Von Clausewitz relates to his preoccupation with the political sphere as a strategic variable in war, whereas De Jomini is said to focus his attention on operational and tactical details, lacking a 'bigger picture' understanding.

Both theories were developed with an understanding of the current context, not with an imaginative, futuristic one. Military technology did not, in the Napoleonic era, provide military planners with opportunities to kill over a great distance, in stealth, and to the far greater extent that it does now. Logistics were constrained by the means available for transporting men and materials (e.g. ammunition) over distance. The opportunity to exploit the sky was in its infancy, with some early attempts to use hot-air balloons for observation.

Nevertheless, the art of war feeds on human ingenuity to develop novel ways of subduing hostile forces. This does not make those past theories redundant. They serve rather as a point of reflection, one that makes one think about their usefulness in the current context. Hence, general principles cannot be a blueprint to be taken for granted and applied universally. Instead, they should trigger a thought process. Like the concept of Organisational Resilience as a translation of military concepts, evolved over centuries, any theory is an expression of human creative skills, it is an art. Von Clausewitz argued,

> All thinking is indeed Art. Where the logician draws the line, where the premises which are the result of cognition stop – where judgement begins, there Art begins. But, more than this, the mind's perception is judgement again, and consequently Art; and at the last, even the perception of the senses is also Art. In a word, if it is impossible to imagine a human being possessing merely the faculty of cognition, devoid of judgement or the reverse, so also Art and Science can never be completely separated from each other. The more these subtle elements of light embody themselves in the outward forms of the world, so much the more separate appear their domains; and now once again, where the object is creation and production, that is the province of Art; where the object is investigation and knowledge Science holds sway. Because of all this it is self-evidently more fitting to say Art of War than Science of War.
>
> (Adapted from Von Clausewitz 2011, 50)

ORGANISATIONAL RESILIENCE

History is most useful when explored through the eyes of those who contributed to the development of the art of war, such as Von Clausewitz and De Jomini. Depth of study is achieved by examining a campaign or battle in detail. In this respect, we will focus in depth on the German campaign in the west in May/June 1940 but will also add insights into other campaigns and battles in the Second World War (WWII). All attempt to be thought-provoking in their own right, resonating with many of today's challenges about how to be resilient.

Organisational Resilience is a state to be established and maintained to counter the effects of two key environmental conditions: uncertainty and complexity.

UNCERTAINTY

Uncertainty is associated with a lack of knowledge about how the future will unfold, leading to the inability to pursue an appropriate organisational response. We cannot establish with confidence how an environment may change or what impact that may have on the function of our own organisation, and thus we cannot define a response to it to either prevent it from happening or bounce back from it.

COMPLEXITY

As shown in Figure 1.1, in a tightly-coupled system, interdependencies between elements mean that incidents can build upon each other and escalate rapidly, triggering a sudden crisis. Loose coupling implies that points of failure are relatively independent, and buffers or slack between them can limit the effects of interconnectivity. Loose coupling provides 'breathing space' to contain a creeping crisis, thereby preventing them from gradually destabilising the whole.

CHAPTER ONE: THE NEED FOR RESILIENCE

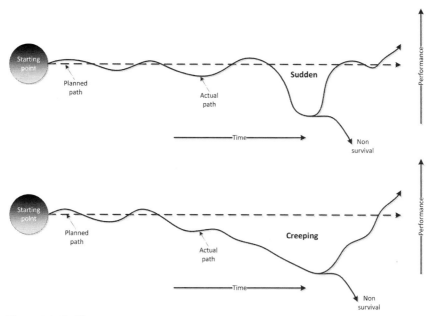

Figure 1.1 *Sudden versus creeping crisis*

To address the challenges of uncertainty and complexity, organisational resilience is often referred to as an ability to bounce back from adversity (Burnard and Bhamra 2011). Originally, the resilience literature emerged from studies of ecological systems noted for having a persistent absorptive capacity to deal with disturbances, followed by a reconfiguration of the system (Holling 1973; Gunderson 2000; Warner 2011).

From a socio-ecological perspective, resilience is associated with the ability of a system to retain function when perturbed (Carpenter et al. 2001). The concept of disaster management (Paton et al. 2000), for example, focusses primarily on recovering from a crisis, largely ignoring the pre-crisis incubation phase (Turner 1976).

Another strand is one of Organisational Resilience (Home and Orr 1997; Hamel and Välikangas 2003; Pagonis 2003) – not dissimilar to the body of literature on resilience engineering (Hollnagel 2006; Woods 2006) – which sees resilience as the fundamental property of an organisation to adapt to the requirements of the environment's variability. From a socio-psychological view, a further body of literature has emerged which considers Resilience as an outcome, based on an attentional state of mindfulness (Weick and Sutcliffe 2006, 2015). Mindfulness is

> the combination of on-going scrutiny of existing expectations, continuous refinement and differentiation of expectations based on newer experiences, willingness and capability to invent new expectations that make sense of the unprecedented events, a more nuanced appreciation of context and ways to deal with it, and identification of new dimensions of context that improve foresight and current functioning.
>
> (Weick and Sutcliffe 2001, 32)

What these bodies of literature have in common are the principal properties of resilient organising (see Figure 1.2). Resilient organisations may choose to be defensive, to protect their organisations from anything bad happening. They may be progressive in an opportunistic manner, pursuing consistency in goals, processes and routines as well as being flexible in their ideas, views and actions.

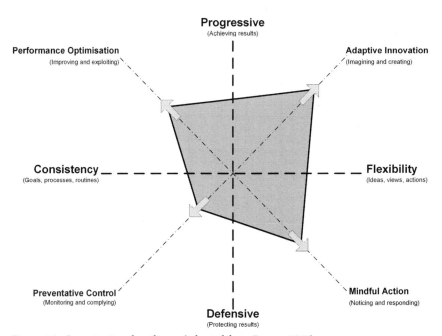

Figure 1.2 *Organisational resilience (adapted from Denyer 2017)*

A progressive organisation longing for consistency focusses its attention on Performance Optimisation, relying on aspects of continuously improving its capabilities while focussing on efficiency gains through standardisation: the objective is to eliminate human error through compliance with rules, processes and procedures.

Adaptive Innovation applies to organisations that themselves shape or even disrupt the market in which they are operating. In contrast to Performance Optimisation, it is less focussed on continuously improving the status quo and more on setting a (radical) new standard through innovation.

Mindful Action puts situated human cognition centre stage – in opposition to Performance Optimisation – as experience, expertise and teamwork are seen as answering the need to anticipate and adapt to threats.

Preventative Control aims to maintain capabilities over time to protect the organisation from threats. The emphasis is on the standardisation of rules, processes and procedures. This mode of resilience may well be the most common approach to resilience in business as it appears to be the most stable, most efficient and, supposedly, simplest form of resilience.

The challenge in being resilient on 'all fronts', to be progressive and defensive, to be flexible and consistent, lies in the tension between the opposing poles. It is really a question of what to focus on, making trade-offs in regard to the opposite pole. The practical dilemma is that consistency-seeking organisations tend to eliminate situated human cognition as a possible source of error, yet flexibility relies on fostering that same cognition to develop new solutions. At times, an 'autopilot', rule-based way of working suffices to counter the effects of complexity, but in the face of uncertainty, mindfulness must be allowed to flourish. It is understandable that a rapid transition from consistency-to flexibility-based management, and vice versa, is challenging as managers tend habitually to pursue their chosen way of thinking and working until external circumstances force them to change. It is well established that managers find it demanding to be simultaneously compliant with rules, processes and routines while deviating from them in order to permit creative solutions to take effect. The literature offers solutions to these two problems which require fundamentally different approaches, setting up a tension which is not easily reconcilable. In a nuclear power plant, for example, where resilience is of the utmost importance, this problem is close to insurmountable:

> We cycled endlessly through the problem of insuring rapid, unquestioning response to orders from on high (or orders in the procedures manual), and at the same time allowing discretion to operators. Regarding discretion, the operators would have the latitude to make unique diagnosis of the problem and disregard the manual, and be free of orders from remote authorities who did not have hands-on daily experience with the system. We could recognize the need for both; we could not find a way to have both.
>
> (Perrow 1999, 335)

THE NEED FOR RESILIENCE IN 1940

From the outset, the campaign in the west in 1940 was more demanding for the Germans than it was for the French and their Allies. The positions along the river Meuse at the southern edge of the Ardennes were not as strongly fortified as those sections further to the east. However, the Ardennes, both the rivers Meuse and Semois, and the heights overlooking the area around Sedan posed an additional obstacle for the Germans. In this line, two potent French armies were deployed: the French Second Army under General Charles Huntzinger and the French Ninth Army under General André Georges Corap. The aim of these two armies was to establish a defence line in depth and repulse any German attempt to cross the rivers Semois and Meuse. In addition, the purpose of the Ninth was to serve as a hinge for the more eastern armies to move into Belgium to cover the Dyle river and reinforce the military forces of the Low Countries to make a stand at the city of Breda.

The Germans had to carry out a range of amphibious crossings, such as over the Albert Canal and the rivers Semois and Meuse. Amphibious crossings take time, and they require a foothold on the other bank of the river before mobile bridges and pontoon bridges can be assembled.

CHAPTER ONE: THE NEED FOR RESILIENCE

The standard technique for crossing a river is to saturate the enemy overlooking the riverbank with firepower. Under cover of smoke, assault troops – in rubber dinghies – cross the river. The enemy needs to be dislodged before any attempt to establish a ferry system or the construction of a pontoon bridge can commence. Having overcome any opposition in close proximity to the initial crossing, the assault troops press farther inland to widen the bridgehead and prepare for any counteroffensive. Meanwhile, a protective shield of anti-aircraft batteries is established to counter air assaults on the still-vulnerable bridgehead. Once heavier equipment can be brought across, tanks and other armoured vehicles can support the assault troops to break out of the bridgehead. This complex, bottlenecked undertaking of an amphibious crossing of a river provides the defending side with ample opportunity to disrupt any crossing or the establishment of a bridgehead.

Another obstacle faced by the Germans was fortification along the Dyle river in Belgium, together with the fortresses of the Maginot Line. In the 1930s, France started building a massive line of fortifications from the Swiss border to Luxembourg. An extension – although less fortified – was built up to the Channel Coast after 1934. The main purposes of the Maginot Line were to protect the industrial areas of Alsace and Lorraine by holding up an enemy until reinforcements could be brought forward to bolster a defence and to support any offensive operation.

A fortress of the Maginot Line (BArch)

11

Belgium similarly built another array of forts along its border with Germany. The mightiest fort was Fort d'Ében-Émael. Attempting to capture this fort by conventional means was out of the question. Hence, the envisaged airborne landing on the supposedly impregnable Fort d'Ében-Émael was a first in military history, and those weapons used to disable the fortress's main armaments were untried. An attacking force, though, needed to spot the weak point of a concrete bunker. These weak points were openings such as doors, air vents or apertures. Spotting them in the heat of battle and under constant fire was no easy undertaking. Approaching these vulnerable areas with the help of suppressing fire required the detection of 'blind spots', which might well be covered by mutually supporting bunkers or openings in the same defending structure. Once a defence had been breached, the attacking parties had to quickly overcome internal defence mechanisms as many of the border fortresses had autonomous defensive sections.

The Allies relied on a largely tightly coupled form of defence, although with some mobile forces. They could count on pre-planned engagements with the Germans. The unknown variables were where and when a breakthrough in their lines would be attempted and how quickly that gap could be plugged. Their rather static defence had the advantage that they would encounter the enemy in a terrain they had prepared for. As a consequence, any approach or attempt to break through a fortified position would be countered by massive, preregistered firepower from artillery and small arms fire from (fortress-)infantry. In order to succeed, any attack on a fortified position would have to be carried out with a force that outnumbered that of the defenders by an estimated three times the number of infantry, six times the amount of artillery and twelve times the quantity of ammunition.

The French and their Allies, from a defensive perspective, would face a more certain environment than the Germans (see Figure 1.3). Relying on a largely immovable defensive shield, they could preload their response and concentrate their preregistered firepower as a method of subduing an attacker:

> The effects of fire are both physical and psychological. They create zones of death where the troops undergo massive and shattering losses which render them incapable of actions. Either the material is destroyed or the units are fragmented.
>
> (Adapted from 1936 French Army regulations, quoted in Kiesling 1996, 137)

However, their largely fixed, immovable line of defence was one that was tightly coupled. Most armaments of the Maginot Line faced east. Once a line of fortified defence was broken, the entire fixed line would become redundant.

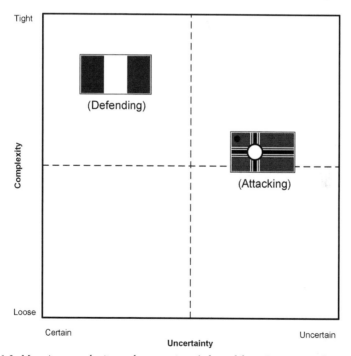

Figure 1.3 *Mapping complexity and uncertainty (adapted from Perrow 1999)*

The looming campaign against France would place greater demands on the Germans to 'surprise' the enemy (see the following textbox). The Germans would need to adapt quickly to a changing situation, be highly creative in developing novel solutions and be agile in exercising those responses, all for the single aim of bewildering the enemy.

VON CLAUSEWITZ AND DE JOMINI: THE SURPRISE

There follows another endeavour which must consequently be just as general in its nature. This is surprising the enemy and it lies more or less at the foundation of all undertakings, for without it, gaining the decisive advantage is not conceivable.

(Adapted from Von Clausewitz 2011, 86)

Now there is one observation that goes to the heart of the matter. A surprise can only be effected successfully by the party which is in command of the situation; that is the party which dictates events. If we surprise the adversary with an ill-conceived measure, then instead of reaping good results, we may have to bear a heavy blow; in any case our adversary need not trouble himself much about our surprise, because our mistake enables him to avert any evil consequences. As the offensive, by definition, entails much more positive action than the defensive, so the element of surprise is certainly more likely to lie with the assailant, but this is by no means invariably the case, as we shall see hereafter. Surprises delivered by the offensive may therefore be countered by defensive surprises, and ultimately the advantage will lie with whoever has planned most effectively.

(Adapted from Von Clausewitz 2011, 88)

I will not speak here of the small-scale surprises which are the chief features in wars of partisan or light troops, for which the light

> Russian and Turkish cavalry are so well adapted. I will confine myself to an examination of surprise in the context of whole armies.
>
> Before the invention of firearms, surprises were more easily effected than at present for the reports of artillery and musketry firing are heard at so great a distance that it is now next to impossible to surprise an army, unless the first duties of field service have been forgotten, there are no outposts to give the alarm and the enemy is able to penetrate the midst of the army before his presence becomes known. The Seven Years' War offers a memorable example in the surprise at Hochkirch.[2] That shows that a surprise does not simply consist in falling upon troops that are sleeping or keeping a poor look out but that it may result from the combination of a sudden attack upon, and surrounding of, one extremity of the army. In fact, to surprise an army it is not necessary to take it so entirely unawares that the troops will not even have emerged from their tents; it is sufficient to attack it in force at the point intended before preparations can be made to meet the attack.
>
> (Adapted from De Jomini 2008, 165)

From an Allied perspective, it was necessary 'merely' to 'stand their ground' for a defensive system to absorb any attack until countermeasures could be made to go on the offensive against a weakened enemy (see Figure 1.4).

It is no surprise that, as the French relied on a predominantly citizen army, they lacked the capability to be progressive and, in particular, to be flexible. However, French farmers, businessmen and many others from different professions could be moulded into a capable fighting force by focussing on consistency, making people compliant to rules, processes and procedures.

From the attacker's perspective (see Figure 1.5), Germany would face a great many more fluid situations, fleeting opportunities and chaotic conditions. With such great uncertainty, they would need to be more progressively flexible in their attack and defensively progressive in

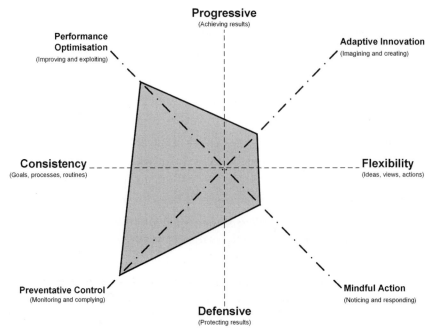

Figure 1.4 *Allied resilience portfolio*

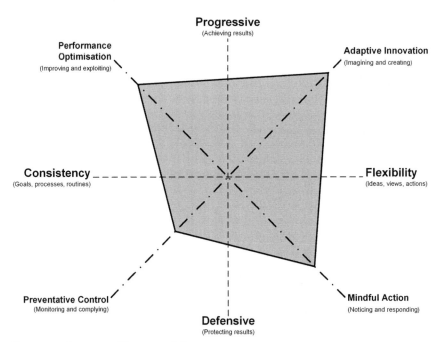

Figure 1.5 *German resilience portfolio*

adapting to any counter manoeuvres by the Allies. They would have to develop a greater repository of methods with regards to where, when and how to attack. Such flexibility would have to be exercised with speed as a prolonged stand-off could not be sustained.

Two distinctively different approaches of resilient organising opposed each other in May/June 1940. These approaches manifested themselves as a result of the historical lessons of the First World War (WWI) as well as the need to be defensive or to be progressive. The need for German progressiveness was rooted in the need to 'surprise' the Allies as a traditional attack was likely to lead to a stand-off the Germans knew they could not sustain. The Allies prepared to defend themselves with a rigid defensive approach that allowed only so many scenarios.

DE JOMINI: GRAND TACTICS AND BATTLES

DEFENSIVE BATTLES

1. To have communications to the front so as to make it easier to fall upon the enemy at a favourable moment than it is for him to approach the line of battle.
2. To give the artillery maximum impact in defence.
3. To have ground suitable for concealing troop movements between the wings so that they can be massed at any desired point.
4. To have a good view of the enemy's movements.
5. To have an unobstructed line of retreat.
6. To have all flanks well protected, either by natural or by artificial obstacles, so as to render impossible an attack upon the extremities and to oblige the enemy to attack the centre or at least some point at the front.

(Adapted from De Jomini 2008, 137)

OFFENSIVE BATTLES

1. An offensive order of battle should have as its object forcing the enemy from his position by all reasonable means.
2. The art of war favours manoeuvres that are aimed at overwhelming only one wing or the centre and one wing at the same time. An enemy can also be dislodged by manoeuvres to outflank and turn his position.
3. These manoeuvres have a much greater chance of success if they can be concealed from the enemy until the very moment of assault.
4. Attacking the centre and both wings at the same time, without having vastly superior forces, is entirely contrary to the rules of the art of war, unless one of the attacks can be made very vigorously without excessively weakening the line at other points.
5. The sole purpose of an oblique order[3] is to unite at least half the force of the army in an overwhelming attack upon one wing, while the remainder retreats to the rear, out of danger of attack, arranged either as an echelon or in a single oblique line.
6. Every formation – convex, concave, perpendicular or otherwise – may be varied by having lines of uniform strength throughout or by massing troops at one point.
7. As the object of the defence is to defeat the plans of the attacking party, the arrangement of a defensive order should be such as to make it as difficult as possible to approach a position, keeping in hand a strong reserve that is well concealed and ready to fall at the decisive moment upon a point where the enemy least expects to meet it.
8. It is difficult to state with precision what is the best method for forcing a hostile army to abandon its position. A perfect order of battle would unite the double advantages of the use of weaponry and the moral effect produced by an onslaught. A skilful mixture of deployed lines and columns,

acting alternately as circumstances require, is always a good combination. In the practical use of this system many variations will arise from differences in the coup d'œil of commanders, the morale of officers and soldiers, and their familiarity with manoeuvres and use of weaponry of all kinds from varying localities.

9. It is essential in an offensive battle to drive the enemy from his position and to cut him up as much as possible. The best means of accomplishing this is to use as much material force as can be accumulated against him. It sometimes happens, however, that the direct application of main force is of doubtful value; better results may follow from manoeuvres to outflank and turn whichever wing is nearest the enemy's line of retreat. When threatened thus, he may retire, whereas he would fight back strongly, and successfully, if attacked by main force.

10. The combination of these two methods – the frontal attack by the main force and the turning manoeuvre – renders victory more certain than the use of either separately, but too extensive a movement must always, and in every case, be avoided, even when dealing with an inferior enemy.

11. The manner of driving an enemy from his position by main force is as follows: throw his troops into confusion with heavy and well-directed artillery fire; increase confusion with vigorous cavalry charges; and follow up the advantages gained by pushing forward a mass of infantry, well covered to the front by skirmishers and flanked by cavalry.

12. From all this it's possible to arrive at the following truth: that the most difficult as well as the most certain of all the means the assailant may use to gain victory consists in strongly supporting the first line with troops of the second line, and these with the reserve, and in proper employment of masses of cavalry, and of batteries, to assist in striking the decisive blow at the second line of the enemy; for that

> tackles the greatest of all the problems in these battles. At the turning points of battles, theory becomes an uncertain guide; at such points it is not up to addressing the crisis and can never compare in value with a natural talent for war nor be a sufficient substitute for that intuitive coup d'œil that experience in battle confers on a general of tried bravery and coolness.
>
> (Adapted from De Jomini 2008, 161)

ORDER OF BATTLE

On May 10th 1940, two powerful armies clashed with each other, each with a fundamentally different doctrine of warfare that originated in the lessons of WWI. For the French, it was a question of not losing while avoiding casualties in the millions. For the Germans, it was a question of winning quickly as it could not sustain any prolonged stand-off.

The campaign in the west can be divided into three fronts (see Map 1.1): Northern, Central and Southern (see Timeline and Order of Battle).

In the north, *Heeresgruppe* (Army Group) B, under the leadership of Von Bock, planned to drive through the Netherlands and Belgium, the same route the German armed forces took in 1914. They would be faced by the French 7th Army (Giraud), the British Expeditionary Force (BEF) led by Lord Gort and the French 1st Army (Blanchard).

The centre of attack consisted of Army Group A under Von Rundstedt. However, of importance was the creation of a dedicated unit that included elite regiments, such as the *Grossdeutschland* regiment and large parts of the motorised Panzer corps – *Panzergruppe* (Panzer Group) *Kleist*. This unit was destined to 'spearhead' a breakthrough in the 'centre' of the attack. On the

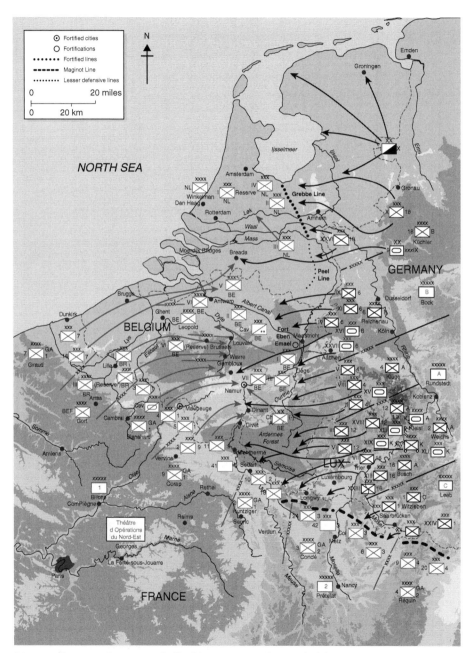

Map 1.1 *Opposing German and Allied forces, May 10th 1940 (Dildy 2014, 4)*

French side, Corap's Ninth and Huntzinger's Second armies posed a formidable barrier.

The majority of the French fortresses were located in the Southern Sector to be defended by the French 2nd and 3rd Army Group. They were opposed by Army Group C (Leeb), with only infantry divisions at their disposal and no panzer corps.

On May 10th 1940, six German armies attacked the Low Countries (Holland, Belgium, Luxembourg). A mere three days later, they crossed the river Meuse at the picturesque French town of Sedan, with similar crossings not much later at Dinant and Monthermé. The crossing of the Meuse river may sound trivial, but after the Germans overcame the fortifications – part of the extended Maginot Line – on the western bank of this river, *Panzergruppe* Kleist succeeded in breaking through the French lines, overcoming the biggest obstacle in their pursuit of entering the largely undefended countryside and thus falling on the back of the French forces. Nevertheless, the following days were certainly very challenging for the Germans. Battles at Stonne, Bulson and Arras were only some of the bloody encounters between the Germans and the French and their allies, including the BEF, and not all went the German way.

The French campaign climaxed with the evacuation of most of the Allied forces at Calais, Boulogne and Dunkerque from May 27th to June 4th 1940. Even then, the fighting did not stop. Further attempts by the French to stop the German advance took place. These were indeed heroic yet ultimately futile.

On June 14th, the Germans entered Paris, and the scenes of desperation and helplessness drove home a sense of utter defeat and humiliation for the Parisian population. Six days thereafter, the French delegation was summoned to a historic site in the Compiègne Forest, the same railway carriage where, in 1918, the armistice with Germany had sealed the end of WWI. The French delegation – among them General Huntzinger, who had failed to prevent the Germans from crossing the Meuse – were given the terms of armistice. At 08:50 on Saturday, June 22nd, an armistice was signed, only one month and twelve days after the Germans initiated their invasion.

The outcome was a crushing defeat for the Allies. A few months later, on October 21st 1940, Sir Winston Churchill broadcast a message to the defeated French nation:

> Frenchmen! For more than 30 years in peace and war I have marched with you. I am marching still along the same road. Tonight, I speak to you at your firesides, wherever you may be, or whatever your fortunes are: I repeat the prayer upon the louis d'or, "Dieu protege la France."
>
> Here at home in England, under the fire of the Bosche we do not forget the ties and links that unite us to France.
>
> Here in London, which Herr Hitler says he will reduce to ashes, and which his aeroplanes are now bombarding, our people are bearing up unflinchingly. Our Air Force has more than held its own. We are waiting for the long promised invasion. So are the fishes.
>
> Frenchmen – rearm your spirits before it is too late. Remember how Napoleon said before one of his battles: These same Prussians who are so boastful today were three to one at Jena, and six to one at Montmirail.
>
> Never will I believe that the soul of France is dead! Never will I believe that her place amongst the greatest nations of the world has been lost forever.
>
> Remember that we shall never stop, never weary, and never give in. We seek to beat the life and soul out of Hitler and Hitlerism. That alone – that all the time – that to the end. Those French who are in the French Empire, and those who are in the so-called unoccupied France, may see their way from time to time to useful action, I will not go into details, hostile ears are listening.
>
> Good night then: Sleep to gather strength for the morning. For the morning will come. Brightly it will shine on the brave and true,

kindly upon all who suffer for the cause, glorious upon the tombs of heroes. Thus will shine the dawn.

Vive la France!

Long live also the forward march of the common people in all lands towards their just and true inheritance, and towards the broader and fuller age.

COMMON EXPLANATIONS

Over the years, a plethora of explanations of this staggering outcome have emerged. A range of official inquiries were followed by journalist accounts that often, in their pursuit of a 'simple' answer, laid the blame on the French High Command and/or the brilliance of those enigmatic German generals, such as Guderian and Rommel. The key figures who saw the end of WWII published their memoirs, and yet reasons for defeat were 'delegated' down the hierarchy, and explanations for success tended to be glorified, objectified and personalised. Soon, dogmas emerged that provided seemingly easy answers for any future wars. Simplifications included the mythical collapse of French morale or the superiority of German armaments. Of course, there is some truth in those explanations, yet, on their own, they cannot explain this campaign. Let's revise some of these assertions.

BLITZKRIEG

Among the possible explanations for the German victory was the concept of *Blitzkrieg*[4] (lightning war), a military concept for exploiting speed and surprise to disorganise the enemy and enable the attacker to use locally concentrated firepower to create a 'snowball' effect to collapse entire fronts. When Operation Yellow was conceived, traditionalists in the German High Command indeed realised that a war against France needed to be won 'fast' as a drawn-out war of attrition could not be sustained by German industry. Hence, although speed and agility were of the essence, on many occasions, senior officers pleaded for traditional infantry movement and fire. Those with this new vision were opportunists, such as Guderian, misunderstood by their superiors:

> Guderian's doctrine about tank warfare was neither fully understood nor fully approved by his commanders, and Rommel's idiosyncratic doctrine was at odds with it. Still German generals, even German colonels and majors, certainly felt freer to try new approaches and tactics than did their counterparts in the French army or the British Expeditionary Force (BEF).
>
> (May 2009, 449)

While it was later to become an undisputed recipe for success – until a string of defeats rattled that belief – the campaign in 1940 was really an ad hoc military solution, driven by the need to launch an attack in favourable weather and shaped by the existing circumstances: *The breakthrough at Sedan, however, was an experiment for which there were no models* (Frieser 2005, 174).

ARMOURED WARFARE

The *Deutsches Heer* (land component of the German army) in 1940 is often portrayed as an armoured monster, burying any French resistance

A common picture in France (BArch)

under its tracks. Actually, it was not dissimilar to the army of WWI, a force dependent on horses. Only 7 per cent of the German armed forces were motorised; out of 135 divisions engaged, 10 German divisions were fully armoured; the majority relied on foot and horses.

SUPERIOR NUMBERS

The military disposition of both armies slightly favoured the French. The Allies could rely on a total of 136 divisions – 94 divisions, including 13 fortress divisions, an additional 22 Belgian and 9 British infantry divisions, 1 Army tank brigade and 10 Dutch divisions. Hitler could muster 135 divisions, including 10 armoured divisions. In quality, the divisions varied on both sides. The Allies were in possession of around 3,000 tanks that outgunned their German counterparts (2,700 tanks) numerically and provided greater protection. France also excelled in the provision of artillery pieces by a ratio of 3:2. Only in the air were the Allied forces outclassed by the German Air Force *(Luftwaffe)*.

INFANTRY

Numerically, in terms of mere numbers and quantities of divisions, men and materials, the Allied Forces had a slight advantage over their German counterparts. On both sides, many divisions were composed of 'mobilised' conscripts, consisting of soldiers in their 30s and 40s. Their standard of training was dependent on their wave of mobilisation as a reservist force. On average, most had only a couple of weeks of training. Nevertheless – apart from the Dutch army, which were predominantly reservists – professional, well-equipped forces were established on all sides. On the Belgian side, the *Chasseurs Ardennais* were an elite, motorised unit. Most French light and heavy motorised units were formidably trained and equipped.

The Germans could muster some elite infantry units, among them the *Grossdeutschland* regiment. However, a major factor swung the pendulum in favour of the Germans. Overall, roughly 40 per cent of the German forces consisted of reservists, while the comparable figure for the French army was roughly 80 per cent, double the number.

Front-line infantry were equipped with a range of artillery. Most common among the French troops was the quick-firing 75 mm field gun, an updated design from WWI. The Germans fielded fewer but more powerful guns, such as the 10.5 cm *Leichte Feldhaubitze* (light artillery howitzer) or the infamous high-velocity 88 mm multipurpose *Flak (Flugabwehrkanone)*, which was used as an artillery, anti-aircraft and anti-tank gun.

The 88 mm gun became one of the most recognised and most feared guns in WWII. Its high velocity projectile – 840 m/s – could penetrate any known Allied tank design. In 1940, there were only relatively few 'eighty eights' deployed; in this image in the role of attacking Maginot Line fortifications (BArch)

In an anti-tank role, the backbone of the French army was the 47 mm *Atelier de Puteaux* (APX) anti-tank gun, with the Hotchkiss 25 mm *semi-automatique modèle 1934*, each able to penetrate the front armour of any German battle tank at the time. In contrast, the Germans most commonly fielded the 37 mm anti-tank gun, which proved inadequate to overpower French bunkers or most of the medium and heavy tanks deployed by the Allies.

A 37 mm in position in the French countryside. This was a commonly deployed anti-tank gun, which turned out to be inadequate to knock out most French medium and heavy tanks (BArch)

MORALE

The morale of the French army, especially in the initial stages of the Meuse crossing and despite the later rout, can also not be held accountable for the ultimate collapse of the front near Sedan. Multiple accounts (Doughty 1976; May 2009) underline the tenacity and courage with which the French, British and Belgian (in particular the Belgian *Chasseurs Ardennais*) defenders opposed the German invaders.

In the north, two French armoured divisions slowed down two entire panzer divisions between May 12th and May 14th, inflicting substantial losses on their German foes. The French only retreated after their flanks were exposed due to the fall of Fort d'Ében-Émael.

Despite such tactical victories, there are also numerous accounts of retreat and units' being routed by the Germans. On some of these occasions, individual units moved back from their dedicated positions as they were ordered to do so or as they deemed their situation to be unsustainable. On others, units were overwhelmed by the German onslaught, and remnants of the French units fell back in disarray.

CHAPTER ONE: THE NEED FOR RESILIENCE

BEING LET DOWN

It is often said that the BEF let their French allies down and that the retreat and consequential evacuation of the British (and Allied) forces was too hasty, representing a betrayal of the French. Paul Baudouin, the Undersecretary of State and Secretary of the War Cabinet in Paul Reynaud's administration, wrote,

> Friday, May 24th, 1940:
>
> At 10:30 General Weygand came into the Prime Minister's room, and found Marshal Pétain already there. I remained throughout this meeting, which lasted until a quarter to one.
>
> On entering, the General whispered to me, "The situation is very serious, for the English are falling back on the ports instead of attacking to the south." He told the Prime Minister that according to a telegram from the French liaison office with the King of the Belgians, actually the only means of communication between the British Army and General Blanchard, the English had abandoned Arras without being compelled by the Germans to do so, and appeared to be retreating in the direction of the ports. This was contrary to the formal instructions given by General Weygand to the British army according to the plans shown on Wednesday the 22nd to the British Prime Minister and approved by him.
>
> General Weygand declared that this strategy on the part of the British Army did not surprise him, for on the previous evening he had been struck by General Ironside's tone over the telephone. "I would willingly have boxed his ears", said General Weygand, and then went on, "It is impossible to command an army which remains dependent on London in the matter of military operations. All this is the more regrettable in that yesterday and during the night Besson's army group, coming from the south, reached the Somme, while Colonel de Gaulle's armour is at Boves, ready to issue forth to assist the southern army to move north."
>
> (Baudouin 1948, 43)

This perception of treachery was reinforced by Britain's war against the French Vichy forces. The animosity between these two parties found its climax in the bombardment of the French fleet at the Algerian port of Mers-el-Kébir in July 1940, which resulted in the destruction of large parts of the French fleet and the death of 1,297 French sailors. Indeed, throughout the campaign, the Allied efforts to battle the Germans were characterised by a lack of coordination. This was largely due to mistrust, egotism and overconfidence on all sides. It is natural to think that each ally was driven by the need to save their own skin. Given the number of counter-attacks, the occasions on which the Dutch, Belgians, British and French tried to stop the German advance were indeed heroic, but they were most often ill conceived, too little and too late.

TECHNICAL SPECIFICATIONS OF THE TANK

The tank – introduced in late WWI as a battle-decisive weapon system – took centre stage in WWII. In May 1940, the Germans depended primarily on four main battle tanks: the Panzerkampfwagen (PzKpfW) II Ausf. A, the PzKpfW III Ausf. E/F, the PzKpfW IV Ausf. D, and the Czech-built PzKpfw 35(t) and 38(t). Starting with the PzKpfW II, it had 14 mm sloped armour at the front. It was equipped with a 20 mm autocannon and a top speed of 40 km/h. The PzKpfW II and IIIs were augmented by the Czech-designed PzKpfw 35(t) and 38(t) light tanks, with 25 mm of front armour, 37 mm cannon and a maximum speed of 34 km/h.

The PzKpfW III – a medium tank – had an upgraded rolled front of 30 mm armour. The early versions of Ausf. (Mark) E/F used a short 37 mm anti-tank cannon (*Panzerabwehrkanone*, Pak). Later versions were equipped with a 50 and 75 mm cannon. Top speed was also 40 (later increasing to 55) km/h.

The PzKpfW IV was protected by 30 mm of armour at the front and an improved speed of 38 km/h. The 75 mm short-barrelled mounted tank gun was mainly designed to fire high-explosive shells to combat enemy infantry.

PzKpfW IV in the French countryside (BArch)

A knocked out Char B1. German panzer crews quickly figured out the main weaknesses of the tanks. Their firing rate was relatively low and inaccurate. Hence, this allowed the German panzers to get close and aim at their air intakes (Kutsch)

> On the Allied side, the French were supplied with the Renault R35 infantry tank and the Hotchkiss H35. Armour thickness amounted to 30 mm, and each was armed with a 37 mm gun. Their big brothers were the massive 31.5t Char B1 and the Somua S35. The Char B1 had 60 mm front and 55 mm side armour, twice the thickness of the armour of the main German battle tank. Despite its slow speed of 25 km/h, it had a 75 mm gun mounted in the hull as well as a 47 mm high-velocity cannon installed in the turret.
>
> Another of the typical 'land-ships' (slow but heavily armoured) was the Somua S35, with 47 mm of sloped armour and a 25 km/h top speed. Its 47 mm turret-mounted gun outclassed the PzKpfW II and III.
>
> The British infantry tank Matilda Mark II is also noteworthy. Heavily armoured with 78 mm at the front, it could withstand the shells of any German anti-tank gun, apart from the 88 mm Flak. It also had a powerful main armament, a 40 mm '2 pounder'. Despite its weight of 25t it reached a top speed of 26 km/h.

QUALITY OF TANK FORCES

The French tanks were superior to their German counterparts in protection and firepower (see textbox). Most German tanks and anti-tank guns – apart from the high-velocity 88 mm *Flak 18/36* – could not penetrate the front armour of a B1, S35 or Matilda Mark II. However, the Allied tanks had a significant drawback. The French tanks had insufficient radios, and hence communication had to be established via flag signals. In addition, the commander of a 3-man crew in an S35, for example, needed also to act as loader and gunner. Hence, commanders in Allied tanks were often busy operating their own vehicles, resulting in a lack of coordination between vehicles and units.

QUALITY OF AIR FORCES

From a pure performance perspective, the Germans provided greater tactical ground support, with the Junkers 88A *Schnellbomber* (fast bomber), the Dornier 17Z and the Junkers 87 *Sturzkampfflugzeug* – *Stuka* (dive bomber). The French could only muster a few obsolete LeO 451 day bombers or some Bregeut 693 assault aircraft. The Allies were equipped with the American-built Curtiss Hawk, and, although these were undergunned, they were robust and fast. Hawker Hurricanes and Fairey Battles complemented the Allied arsenal.

A British Hawker Hurricane. Its performance equalled that of the early version of the ME109 or BF110 (Kutsch)

A French Bloch MB 152. Its performance also matched that of the most common German fighter (Kutsch)

The Germans quickly established air supremacy over the skies of France and the Low Countries, less because of superior numbers or quality of their air force but rather due to the way in which fighter and ground attack planes were deployed. They wrought havoc on the Allied Forces in the open field. Brigadier Sir John Smyth of the BEF recounted,

> Movement by day on the roads was becoming ever more open to air attack as the German air superiority grew. One had to keep a sharp lookout for enemy aircraft the whole time, and, when they were spotted, there was always a difficult decision as to whether to continue driving on or to halt and take to the ditch. Although the latter procedure meant delay, which was what the German aircraft were striving to impose, I saw some dreadful shambles caused by continued movement. In one case a lorry full of men was hit and several other lorries piled up on top of it. It was difficult to lay down any hard and fast procedure for all eventualities, as it might then have been possible for the Germans to paralyse movement by day completely, simply by threatening the roads with quite a small number of aircraft.

(Smith 1957, 62)

However, German air supremacy was considerably less impactful against a well-fortified, camouflaged and entrenched enemy.

COMPETING CONCEPTS OF RESILIENCE

> The German *Wehrmacht*[5] of 1940, as compared with the opposing armed forces of France, Britain, Belgium, and the Netherlands, was more akin to a middleweight boxer going up against a heavyweight.

(May 2009, IX)

And yet, from the outset, the Germans showed greater resilience in breaking through the French front line and triggering the collapse of what was known as one of the most powerful armies in the world. This book aims to review these events from the perspective of Organisational Resilience, broken down into different levels and disciplines of management.

In contemporary military science, a synthesising expression of how military forces conduct campaigns, major operations, battles and engagements is doctrine (see Figure 1.6):

> Doctrine is defined as 'fundamental principles by which military forces guide their actions in support of objectives. It is authoritative, but requires judgement in application'. The principal purpose of doctrine is to provide Alliance Armed Forces with a framework of guidance for the conduct of operations. It is about how those operations should be directed, mounted, commanded, conducted, sustained and recovered. It captures that which is enduring in best practice whilst incorporating contemporary insights and how these principles are applied today and the immediate future. It is dynamic and constantly reviewed for relevance. It describes how Alliance Armed Forces operate but not about [sic] why they do what they do, which is the realm of policy.
>
> (North Atlantic Treaty Organization and NATO Standardization Agency (NSA) 2010)

In broad terms, a doctrine does not include policy decisions, but it does include strategic decisions that are naturally informed by policy. Strategic management involves planning, coordination and general direction of military operations to meet overall political and military objectives. Tactics comprise the short-term decisions about troop movements and the deployment of weapons on the field of battle that implement the strategy. Von Clausewitz argued, *Tactics is the art of using troops in battle; strategy is the art of using battles to win the war.* The intermediate level, operational, the conversion of strategy into tactics, deals with the formation of units.[6]

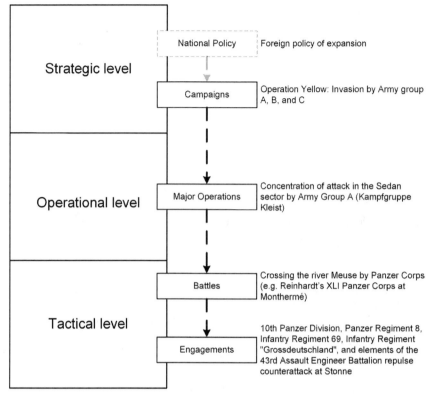

Figure 1.6 *Breakdown of management levels in contemporary military science*

In line with the military definition of strategic, operational and tactical levels of war, this book will explore aspects of Organisational Resilience in the following order:

CHAPTER 2: STRATEGIC RESILIENCE

Chapter 2 looks at the time pre-May 10th 1940 and explores how the campaign in the west was planned by both the Allies and Germany. It addresses the importance of linear versus adaptive thinking. An additional mini-case study – to clarify and often to counter an obvious answer – will relate to the Battle of Kursk in July 1943.

CHAPTER 3: OPERATIONAL RESILIENCE

The crossing of the Meuse at Sedan from May 12th to 15th – a pivotal moment in the entire campaign – will be the focus of Chapter 3.

I will look at these events from the perspective of concentration versus dispersion of resources. In addition, insights into the Battle of the Bulge, which was fought from December 16th to January 25th 1945, will inform the concept of operational resilience.

CHAPTER 4: TACTICAL RESILIENCE

The capture of Fort d'Ében-Émael during May 10th to 12th provides the context in Chapter 4 for elaboration on the distinguishing features of centralisation versus decentralisation. Additional understanding of these concepts will be provided through reference to the Battle of the Philippine Sea on June 19th to 20th 1944.

CHAPTER 5: LEADERSHIP

The city of Stonne – overlooking Sedan and the river Meuse – was the location of the counter-attacks by the French on May 14th. The events that led to the German breakout from the bridgehead along the Meuse will serve as the context for examining the aspect of leadership in Chapter 5. Events during the Battle of Hürtgen Forest between September 12th and December 16th 1944 will contribute to this discourse.

CHAPTER 6: LOGISTICS

Chapter 6 will evaluate the opposing concepts of logistical dependence versus independence, looking at the events from May 18th to 20th, also known as the 'race to the Channel'. Additional insights will be provided by referring to the Africa Campaign in 1941.

CHAPTER 7: ROADS TO RESILIENCE

Chapter 7 will bring all these different insights together and reflect on how organisational resilience can be established in an organisational context as well as what pitfalls may await you on the road to being organisationally resilient.

Each chapter of the book starts with an overview of the unfolding events. It is intended to provide a detailed account of the evolving situation on the ground. The timeline is augmented by an account of a major strategic, operational or tactical objective and how both sides responded in trying to achieve this objective. The context in which both parties operated will set the scene for a breakdown of their 'ways of working' into distinctive managerial components. Their advantages will be evaluated and their application put in perspective, addressing how 'well' they applied their intended approach. Given the complexity of the situation, this is rarely a simple determination. Evaluation in the historical context of 1940 is subsequently translated into reflecting on the 'So What?' question. In other words, what does it all mean for a manager? How can I use these different ways of working in my particular context, and how do I make sense of the options?

LIMITATIONS OF THE BOOK

The events of 1940 are unique and extreme in their nature. Hence, there are limitations in terms of how these historical events can be translated into the modern business environment. It is important to note some key comparisons between what happened then and what we do in the civilian world of today as there are a range of contextual differences that make overall comparison more challenging:

COMPULSORY ENLISTMENT

One specific aspect of a military campaign is that in many cases, not enough volunteers are willing to put their necks on the line. Hence, people can be drafted. If you are able to fight, you have to fight. Often, severe penalties are imposed for evading a draft.

In a business environment, the idea of compulsory conscription for the purpose of 'filling the ranks' is replaced by voluntary commitment to join. The conditions for joining are based on a mutual recognition and exchange of incentives, such as monetary rewards. Should the employees find that the organisation is not to their liking, they are free to leave and join another (even a competitor) relatively easy.

OBEDIENCE

In addition to the issue of compulsory enlistment, military organisations also fall back on principles of obedience. Submissive compliance in putting oneself in danger and participating in acts of war are uncommon in most business organisations though. However, compliance is a driving factor in a commercial environment too, even if it is 'only' compliance to rules, procedures, processes and routines. The difference is the extent of submission expected from military institutions as warfare necessarily requires extreme acts in situations that are simply not experienced in the civilian world.

IDEOLOGY

The compulsory aspect of military service may well be amplified by ideology. It can be a vague, but often strongly held, world view. The impact of a political or social ideology can be great in times of war, when ideologies are often (ab)used as a pretext for committing a society to going to war. Propaganda can influence emotions strongly in such times of crisis. In a business environment, the purpose of organisations is based less on political ideology, to be shared or protected by individuals belonging to the organisation, and is more about the definition of a social ideology, constrained by the boundaries of the organisation, adopting a far more inward-looking perspective. Large organisations have their own cultures, but so do departments and teams, and staff can be attracted to such a 'way of working' or, conversely, can choose to leave and join another firm whose culture they find more attractive.

Despite these contextual disparities, military history has often been used by researchers to contribute to management thought and practice. For example, scholars such as Mintzberg (2003) and Ansoff (1965) used the abundance of factual data from the battlefields during WWI and WWII and more recent conflicts, such as the Vietnam War, to develop leadership and strategic thinking. Building on that tradition, this book looks at the fateful events in 1940 and offers a critical discussion of key managerial aspects – aspects that many managers struggle with in modern times.

ARMAGEDDON

Wars have been an intrinsic part of the history of mankind. As much as we progress in creating life and making our place on Earth ever more comfortable – although not necessarily happier – we have excelled in killing ever more people over an increasingly shorter period of time.

During the six weeks of the campaign, the German casualty rate was 156,400 (killed 27,000; wounded 111,000; missing 18,400). In contrast, the French were estimated to have suffered 2,090,000 casualties (killed 90,000; wounded 200,000; missing/prisoners 1,800,000). Britain endured overall 68,000, Belgium 23,400 and the Netherlands 9,800 killed, wounded or missing.

German Wehrmacht in front of killed soldiers of the British Expeditionary Force (BEF) (Kutsch)

Many of those who were not physically wounded were psychologically affected by the mayhem of battle and the horror of modern warfare. And the battle for France in 1940 was only the beginning. The following years saw technology and human ingenuity elevate the process of killing to an unprecedented scale. Most of those who suffered, though, were civilians.

An all too common picture in the Low Countries as well as vast sways of France. A village in France has been turned into rubble by aerial bombardment, artillery and tank fire (BArch)

Of the estimated 50–80 million killed in WWII, 21–26 million were military dead, but twice as many civilians – between 29 and 54 million – succumbed to strategic bombings, genocide, famines and disease.

All these numbers abstract the notion of human suffering, and we need to remind ourselves what war implies:

> A British tank officer glimpsed some tiny figures beside a wood half a mile away, from which a German half-track had just emerged. He fired a few rounds of high explosives from his gun, then followed up with a long burst of Bess machine-gun fire. Trees caught fire. He saw survivors start to move across the tanks, hands held high. "To my horror, they were civilians," wrote William Steel-Brownlie, "followed by a horse and cart on which were piled all kinds of household goods. They were children, a boy and a girl, holding hands and running as

hard as they could over the rough ploughed earth. They came right up to the tank, looked up at me, and the small boy said in English, 'You have killed my father.' There was nothing I could say.

(Hastings 2004, 501)

An aerial picture of the bombing of Rotterdam by the German Luftwaffe. It marks the start of strategic bombing, with an unprecedented 900 civilians killed. The attack on Tokyo on March 9–10 1945 by American bomber forces claimed the lives of 88,000 (BArch)

The savagery, ruthlessness, inhumanity and lack of compassion in WWII were fuelled by a new form of racism, characterised by supremacist connotations. Not only was a form of prejudice, discrimination, or antagonism directed against a race the breeding ground for the Holocaust, but it also found its way onto the battlefield – most notably in the eastern and pacific theatre:

> While I was removing a bayonet and scabbard from a dead Japanese, I noticed a Marine near me. He wasn't in our mortar section but had happened by and wanted to get in on the spoils. He came up to me dragging what I assumed to be a corpse. But the Japanese wasn't dead. He had been wounded severely in the back and couldn't move his arms; otherwise he would have resisted to his last breath.
>
> The Japanese's mouth glowed with huge gold-crowned teeth, and his captor wanted them. He put the point of his kabar on the base of a tooth and hit the handle with the palm of his hand. Because the

Japanese was kicking his feet and thrashing about, the knife point glanced off the tooth and sank deeply into the victim's mouth. The Marine cursed him and with a slash cut his cheeks open to each ear. He put his foot on the sufferer's lower jaw and tried again. Blood poured out of the soldier's mouth. He made a gurgling noise and thrashed wildly. I shouted "Put the man out of his misery." All I got for an answer was a cussing out. Another Marine ran up, put a bullet in the enemy's soldier's brain, and ended his agony. The scavenger grumbled and continued extracting his prizes undisturbed.

(Sledge 2011, 119)

The end of the world scenario – Armageddon – is described in the Book of Revelations and refers to the final war between human governments and God. Worldwide conflagrations with such loss of life invite such language. We can learn from what happens during war, a conflict by land, sea or air, carried on by force of arms between nations or between parties within a nation. This book creates a discourse about what was 'done' without neglecting the contextual conditions that 'made' both parties 'do' what they did. It seeks to investigate what happened from a managerial perspective of organisational resilience – looking objectively and straightforwardly at what led to one of the strangest military defeats in history. In other words,

But if the Allies in May 1940 were, in the most respects, militarily superior, were not badly led and did not suffer from demoralization (not yet, at least), what then accounts for Germany's six-week triumph?

(May 2009, 7)

NOTES

1 At the start of WWII, on September 1st 1939, the Allies consisted of France, Poland and the United Kingdom. Subsequently they were joined by Australia, Canada, New Zealand and South Africa. With the invasion of northern Europe, the Netherlands, Belgium, Greece, and Yugoslavia joined the Allies.

2 The battle of Hochkirch took place on October 14th 1758. Commandered by Marshal Leopold Josef Graf Daun, an Austrian army of 80,000 surprised their enemy of 36,000, led by Frederick the Great.
3 The oblique order is a military tactic whereby an attacking army focusses its forces to attack a single enemy flank. The force commander concentrates the majority of his strength on one flank and uses the remainder to fix the enemy line.
4 The origin of the term *Blitzkrieg* (lightning war) is obscure; it has not been identified in a German military handbook or used as an official terminology in military circles. The success of the Polish and French Campaign led the British Press to popularise it as *Blitzkrieg* (used in the German translation). In a speech in November 1941, Adolf Hitler said: "*I have never used the word Blitzkrieg, because it is a very silly word*" (Frieser 2005, 5).
5 The *Wehrmacht* was composed of the *Heer* (Army), the *Kriegsmarine* (Navy) and the *Luftwaffe* (Air Force).
6 In management literature, the order of levels tends to be as follows: Strategy, Tactics, Operations. I follow the order of contemporary military science.

REFERENCES

Ansoff, H. I. 1965. *Corporate Strategy*. New York: McGraw-Hill.
Antoine de Saint-Exupéry, Lewis Galantiere. 1942. *Flight to Arras*. New York: Harcourt, Brace & World.
BArch. "Bild 101I-127–0391-21." Koblenz: Bundesarchiv.
——— "Bild 101I-769-0231-11." Koblenz: Bundesarchiv.
——— "Bild 121-0363." Koblenz: Bundesarchiv.
——— "Bild 141-1114." Koblenz: Bundesarchiv.
——— "Bild 146-1981-070-15." Koblenz: Bundesarchiv.
——— "Bild 146-1984-068-10A." Koblenz: Bundesarchiv.
——— "Bild 146-1995-059-07." Koblenz: Bundesarchiv.
Baudouin, P. 1948. *The Private Diaries of Paul Baudouin*. London: Eyre & Spottiswoode.
Burnard, K. and R. Bhamra. 2011. "Organisational Resilience: Development of a Conceptual Framework for Organisational Responses." *International Journal of Production Research* 49 (18): 5581–99.

Carpenter, S., B. Walker, J. Marty Anderies and N. Abel. 2001. "From Metaphor to Measurement: Resilience of What to What?" *Ecosystems* 4 (8): 765–81.

De Jomini, A. H. 2008. *The Art of War*. Kingston, ON: Legacy Books Press.

Denyer, D. 2017. "Organizational Resilience: A Summary of Academic Evidence, Business Insights and New Thinking." BSI and Cranfield School of Management.

Dildy, D. 2014. *Fall Gelb 1940 (1): Panzer Breakthrough in the West*. Oxford: Osprey Publishing.

Doughty, R. A. 1976. "The French Antitank Doctrine: The Antidote That Failed." *Military Review* May: 40–42.

Frieser, K.-H. 2005. *The Blitzkrieg Legend: The 1940 Campaign in the West*. Annapolis, MD: Naval Institute Press.

Gunderson, L. H. 2000. "Ecological Resilience—in Theory and Application." *Annual Review of Ecology and Systematics* 31: 425–39.

Hamel, G. and L. Välikangas. 2003. "The Quest for Resilience." *Harvard Business Review* 81 (9): 52–63.

Hastings, M. 2004. *Armageddon: The Battle for Germany 1944–45*. London: Macmillan.

Holling, C. S. 1973. "Resilience and Stability of Ecological Systems." *Annual Review of Ecology and Systematics* 4: 1–23.

Hollnagel, E. 2006. "Resilience – the Challenge of the Unstable." In *Resilience Engineering: Concepts and Precepts*, edited by E. Hollnagel, D. D. Woods, and N. Leveson. Aldershot: Ashgate.

Home, J. F. and J. E. Orr. 1997. "Assessing Behaviors That Create Resilient Organizations." *Employment Relations Today* 24 (4): 29–39.

Jackson, J. 2003. *The Fall of France*. New York: Oxford University Press.

Kennedy, G. and K. Neilson. 2002. *Military Education: Past, Present, and Future*. Westport, CT: Praeger.

Kiesling, E. C. 1996. *Arming against Hitler: France & The Limits of Military Planning*. Lawrence, Kansas: Press of Kansas.

Kutsch, L. "Frankreichfeldzug." Private Collection.

May, E. 2009. *Strange Victory: Hitler's Conquest of France*. London: I.B. Tauris & Co.

Mintzberg, H., J. Lampel and S. Ghoshal. 2003. *The Strategy Process: Concepts, Contexts and Cases*. Upper Saddle River, NJ: Prentice-Hall.

North Atlantic Treaty Organization, and NATO Standardization Agency (NSA). 2010. "Allied Joint Doctrine AJP-01(D)."

Pagonis, W. G. 2003. "Building Personal and Organizational Resilience." Edited by. *Harvard Business Review*. Boston, MA: Harvard Business Press.

Paton, D., L. Smith and J. Violanti. 2000. "Disaster Response: Risk, Vulnerability and Resilience." *Disaster Prevention and Management* 9 (3): 173–80.

Perrow, C. 1999. *Normal Accidents: Living with High-Risk Technologies*. Princeton, NJ: Princeton University Press.

Sledge, E. B. 2011. *With the Old Breed*. Great Britain: Ebury Press.

Smith, J. 1957. *Before the Dawn*. London: Cassell & Company.

Turner, B. A. 1976. "The Organizational and Interorganizational Development of Disasters." *Administrative Science Quarterly* 21 (3): 318–97.

Tzu, S. 2008. *The Art of War*. London: Penguin Books.

Von Clausewitz, C. 2011. *On War*. United States: Madison Park.

Warner, K. 2011. "Environmental Change and Migration: Methodological Considerations from Ground-Breaking Global Survey." *Population & Environment* 33 (1): 3–27.

Weick, K. and K. Sutcliffe. 2001. *Managing the Unexpected: Assuring High Performance in an Age of Complexity*. San Francisco, CA: Jossey Bass.

———. 2006. "Mindfulness and the Quality of Organizational Attention." *Organization Science* 17 (4): 514–24.

———. 2015. *Managing the Unexpected: Sustained Performance in a Complex World*. 3rd ed. Hoboken, NJ: Wiley.

Woods, D. D. 2006. "Essential Characteristics of Resilience." In *Resilience Engineering: Concepts and Precepts*, edited by E. Hollnagel, D. D. Woods and N. Leveson. Aldershot: Ashgate.

CHAPTER TWO
Strategic resilience

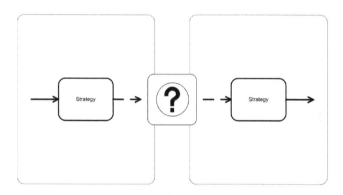

*The Skilful Strategist
Defeats the Enemy
Without doing battle,
Captures the city
Without laying siege
Overthrows the enemy state
Without protracted war.*

(Tzu 2008, 14)

CONTENTS

The story: pre-May 10th 1940	48
La Bataille Conduit *versus* Bewegungskrieg	53
The challenge: 'surprising' an enemy	54
Deciding factors: imagination, sensitivity, adaptability	59
Von Clausewitz and De Jomini: strategy	62
Translation and explanation: linear versus adaptive strategy	64
Towards organisational resilience: the fallacy of determinism	67
Battle of Kursk	70
Outlook	77
Notes	79
References	79

This chapter looks at the art of strategic management as a means of driving organisational resilience. Strategic management is concerned with the organisation as a whole. At its heart, it defines the organisation's overall direction, considering the threats and opportunities that come from within the organisation and from the external environment:

- Strategic decisions are long term
- They set out the mission and vision of the organisation
- They are related to the highest level of planning in an organisation.

THE STORY: PRE-MAY 10TH 1940

THE LEGACY OF VICTORY

The First World War (WWI) armistice came into effect at 11:00 on November 11th 1918 in a private railway carriage at Compiègne – owned by Marshal Foch – the same carriage that 22 years later was the scene of the French surrender. The defeat of the German Empire in 1918 came at a terrible price, especially for the French. Out of about 8,400,000 mobilised soldiers, 44 per cent of the entire male population, 1,500,000 were killed, and 4,200,000 were wounded.

One of the costliest battles of WWI occurred at Verdun from February 21st to December 18th 1916. The city of Verdun and its surrounding forts – most notably Fort de Douaumont – had a symbolic but also strategic importance. Its national importance was attributable to close proximity to the old Gallic-Teutonic frontiers, which had been contested between the French and Germans for centuries. Its strategic value was based on its location on the river Meuse, yet modern technology made these interlocking forts partially redundant. When the Germans crossed into Belgium in 1914, the massive forts at Liège were literally bypassed, delaying the German invasion by no more than five days. One of the 12 forts that were located in the surroundings of Liège – Fort de Loncin – was obliterated by large-calibre German shells, some of them launched by the German howitzer 'Big Bertha'.

As a consequence, Fort de Douaumont and other Verdun forts, being judged ineffective, had been partly stripped of their armaments and left virtually undefended since 1915. On February 25th 1916, Fort de Douaumont was captured in a daring raid by a small German party comprising only 19 officers and 79 men.

Once occupied, the French national obsession with Verdun played into German hands as they rightly assumed that the French would release their reserves and throw them at the Verdun front, while German infantry could defend its positions – to 'bleed France white'. This attrition took a terrible toll on both sides. The French suffered around 160,000 dead or missing, and the Germans suffered approximately 100,000.

The Battle for Verdun in 1916 reinforced the desire of the French people to never again allow an invasion by their traditional foe. Any battle should be fought on the border or if possible in adjacent countries as the rich agricultural and industrial areas of northern France needed to be protected in all circumstances. The plan was for a sustained campaign to wear down any future aggression by Germany.

Similarly, French soldiers should never again be sent to a 'meat-grinder' of 'open battle' – soldiers leaving the relative safety of their trenches and fortifications to recapture 'sacred' French soil. The conclusions drawn were that a defensive stance must offer more adequate protection to the defenders and that any offensive measures needed to start beyond the borders of France.

As a result, these lessons of WWI led to the construction of massive fortifications along the French border with Switzerland, Germany and Luxembourg – the Maginot Line (see Map 2.1).

This line of defence included massive armoured enclosures, such as infantry casemates and fortresses, equipped with a range of machine guns, anti-tank guns and artillery-turrets, accommodating up to 1,000 infantry soldiers, specialised fortress soldiers and engineers. The immediate exterior was fortified with a range of anti-tank barriers and anti-personnel obstacles (e.g. mines, barbed wire).

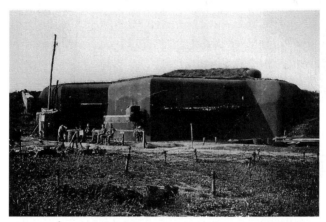

An infantry casemate.[1] This picture was taken after hostilities ceased (Kutsch)

Belgian allies enhanced their fortifications by upgrading their forts around Liège – positioned in a corridor the Allies believed the Germans would use for further attacks – and by constructing a range of new modern forts. One of them – Fort d'Ében-Émael, covering the Albert Canal, which the Germans had to cross in order to 'pass through' Belgium – was deemed impregnable.

The French, exhausted by four years of unprecedented slaughter and ongoing internal instability, were tired of militarism. Their desire was

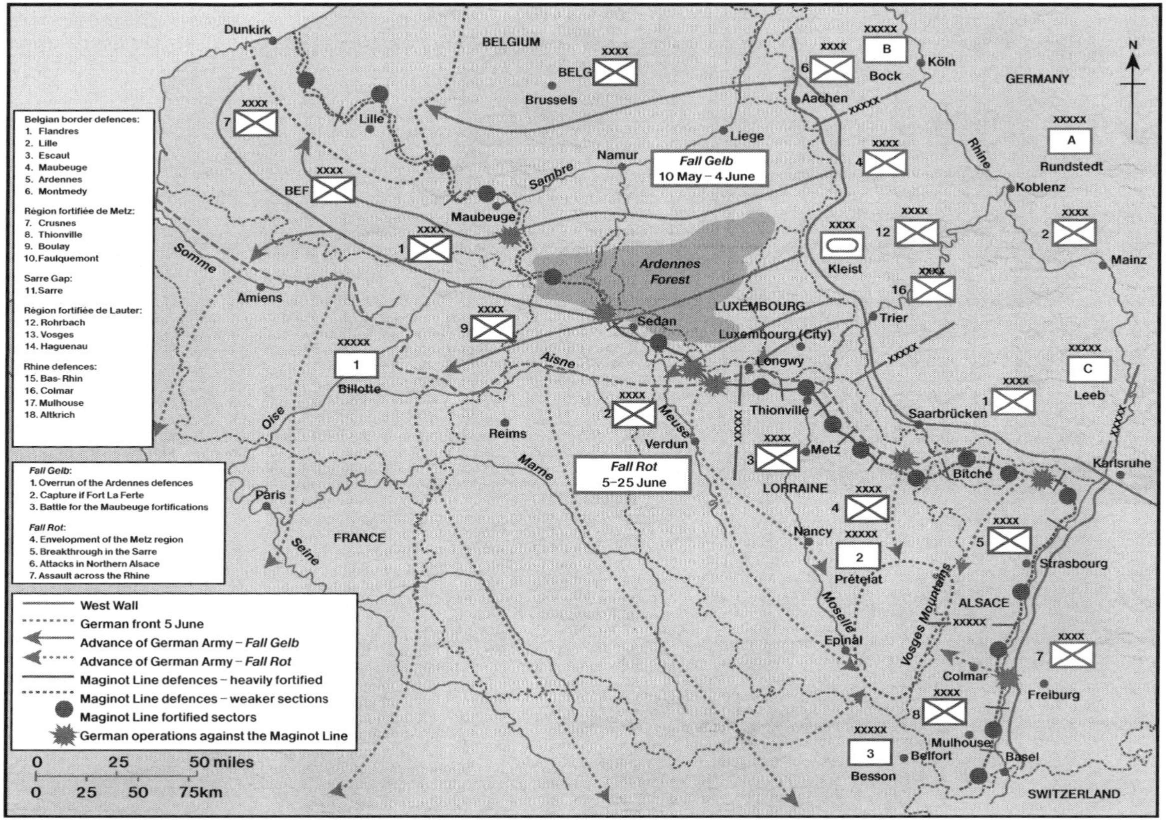

Map 2.1 The Maginot Line, overview of the campaign 10th May–25th June 1940 (Romanych and Rupp 2010, 4)

to build up a protective shield strong enough to repulse any further attempt by Germany. The years up to 1940 saw a strengthening of border fortifications and the build-up of one of the most powerful armies in the world, a juggernaut that was not prepared to lose but had a desire to avoid the en-masse casualties seen in WWI. Nevertheless, the French stance was not entirely statically defensive. Mobile reserves were stationed behind the lines of concrete and armaments primarily for the purpose of plugging breaches and conserving a continuous front, although, if the opportunity arose, they could also be put onto the offensive. Shortly after Adolf Hitler took over power in Germany in 1933, Sir Winston Churchill is said to have remarked: *Thank God for the French army.*

THE MORROW OF DEFEAT

The rearming and expansion of the German army was done in relative secrecy. The treaty of Versailles, signed on June 28th 1919, forced Germany to disarm, to make territorial concessions – among them the Rhineland that was occupied until 1930 and then declared demilitarised – and to pay reparations that brought the German economy to its knees in the following years. Years of anarchy and turmoil reduced the hope of a democracy – the Weimar Republic – to a pipe dream. Extreme political views, on the left as well as on the right, found their audiences. The late 1920s and 1930s saw the rise of the *Nationalsozialistische Deutsche Arbeiterpartei* (National Socialist German Workers' Party, abbreviated NSDAP). As its party leader, Adolf Hitler turned adequate electoral support, augmented by deception, anti-Semitism and anti-Marxism slogans, into absolute governing power.

The military restrictions imposed by the Treaty of Versailles were meant to strip Germany of the capability ever to wage war again. The post-war German armed forces – the *Reichswehr* – were allowed to have no more than 100,000 men, the equivalent of roughly 10 divisions. Given the increasing importance of air power, Germany was forbidden from establishing an air force. Naval strength was reduced to a limited number of battleships, cruisers, destroyers and torpedo boats. Submarines – one of the most potent weapon systems in WWI against the British – were forbidden altogether.

In violation of the Treaty of Versailles (and the Locarno Treaties signed in 1925), the German army entered the Rhineland on March 7th 1936. The aggressiveness of that move by Adolf Hitler followed a range of diplomatic manoeuvres by the Allied powers, but these only reinforced Hitler's view that such violations of international law would remain unpunished. His resolve to impose his fascist view on other countries led to a rapid expansion of Army divisions – from 39 in 1937 to 98 in 1939 for the invasion of Poland.

Whereas the French were bound by the trauma of Verdun and fixated on static warfare by means of fortifications – a recipe that had indeed brought French victory, although at a terrible price – the German defeat in 1918 revived a concept of warfare that had already emerged in the trenches of WWI: *Bewegungskrieg* (war of manoeuvre)[2]. This concept focussed on the speed and flexibility of units' manoeuvrability to make the enemy react to one's intention and not the other way around. In WWI, this kind of warfare was restricted to just those units capable of exercising speed and flexibility – *Stosstruppen* (shock troops). Relatively small infiltration units consisting of specialists (e.g. flamethrower operators) ventured into no man's land and tried to flush out pockets of resistance or assaulted narrow sections of trenches. These tactics, although successful, were too few and applied too late to turn the tide of WWI. In the Second World War (WWII), the *Stosstruppen* were transformed to *Kampfgruppen* (combat formations) as ad hoc combined formations of tanks, infantry and artillery.

LA BATAILLE CONDUIT VERSUS *BEWEGUNGSKRIEG*

This chapter provides a contrasting analysis between two distinctively different military doctrines – *La Bataille Conduit* (Methodical Battle) and *Bewegungskrieg* (Manoeuvre Warfare). Indeed, it shows that both parties, the French and their Allies as well the Germans, focussed their efforts on strategising, on preparing themselves for the next war.

What is different is that the Allies rested on the laurels acquired from winning the last war, whereas the Germans put forward visionary strategies that allowed them to avoid fighting a battle on terms dictated by their enemy.

The French were to conduct their operations in carefully planned steps, pausing after each one to allow the artillery to move forwards. The pace was to be set by the speed of the infantry and the time needed to prepare for the next artillery bombardment (Doughty 1985). The Germans, in contrast, relied on a doctrine of anticipatory military opportunism; they were bold and novel in appreciating the need to avoid a war of attrition, opting instead for their best and only chance of bringing the most powerful army in the world to its knees. They attempted to defeat it by incapacitating its decision-making capacity through shock and disruption: by surprise.

THE CHALLENGE: 'SURPRISING' AN ENEMY

Planning a campaign in the west, the Germans were faced with a range of challenges, among them how to break through the Maginot Line. And yet, pressure was mounting to commence a campaign as the French and British were in the process of reorganising their forces, and the United States of America had been stepping up its deliveries to France. The USSR (Union of Soviet Socialist Republics) was also perceived as offering an imminent threat of a strike against Germany after Poland was divided up between the two countries.

Poland capitulated on September 27th 1939. On October 10th, Hitler produced a memorandum that outlined a campaign against France and ordered the German High Command (OKH – *Oberkommando des Heeres*) to start detailed planning. Only 10 days later, the first plan, code-named 'Deployment Directive Yellow' *(Aufmarschanweisung Gelb)*, was presented to Hitler. This plan strongly resembled the *Schlieffen* plan used in WWI (see Map 2.2):

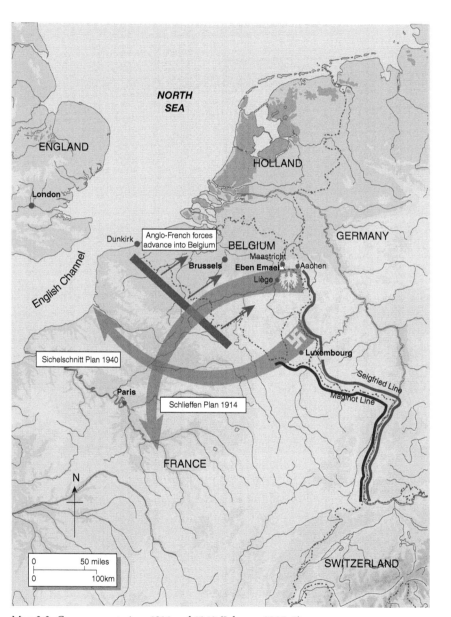

Map 2.2 *German campaigns 1914 and 1940 (Johnson 2005, 7)*

> It was manifestly a bad plan, so conservative and uninspiring that it might well have been thought up by a British or French General Staff of the inter-war years, and through its many imperfections glimmered the half-heartedness of the OKH and the Army commanders.
>
> (Horne 1990, 187)

The following weeks saw a string of revised plans, all thrusting north of the Maginot Line, very much in line with the *Schlieffen* plan. Such a thrust would not have come as a surprise to the Allies. The continuous infighting between the general staff of the OKH – used by Hitler to gauge loyalty to him personally – and the perceived reluctance to commence an attack against a supposedly stronger enemy, led Hitler to berate his general staff on December 28th, although he stopped short of accusing them of cowardice.

The onset of bad weather in December made a winter offensive in 1939 unfeasible, and 1940 began with the 'Phoney War', a period of subdued hostilities between two major European powers in a state of war.

On January 9th 1940, an incident occurred that was to shape the conception of an entire campaign. Helmuth Reinberger, a German major involved in the deployment of airborne troops, was summoned to a meeting in Cologne. At a local airbase in Münster, he was offered a lift to Cologne in a tiny *Messerschmitt* (Me)-108 airplane. As a passenger, they set off in the early hours and made their way westwards. On board, Reinberger carried a small briefcase containing top secret documents outlining the German air plan for invading the Low Countries.

Bad weather was closing in; suddenly the engine cut out for no apparent reason, and they were forced to make an emergency landing. The pilot made a quick assessment of their location, and they realised they had landed in Belgium, near a town called Mechelen. In a frantic hurry, Reinberger tried to burn the documents, with the help of a Belgian peasant who lent him a lighter. Not long after, Belgian troops arrested Reinberger and his pilot, and they were marched to the Belgian *gendarmerie*. Reinberger tried to destroy the remaining papers once more by throwing them into a stove. Nevertheless, quick action by the Belgian captors provided the Belgian High Command with insights into the German plan to repeat the *Schlieffen* strategy, with the main thrust through Holland and Belgium.

The mishap of the German invasion plans falling into Allied hands increased the haste in which new plans were conceived. Gradually, planning driven less by strategy and more by operational necessity was conceived to provide a 'hammer blow' to the Allies from which they could not recover, to punch through the Allied front at the centre of attack and encircle and destroy large parts of the northern Allied forces. Wargaming gave the OKH confidence that an alternative attack through the thickly forested Ardennes, crossing the rivers Semois and Meuse, was a doable undertaking.

By February 24th, a new directive was issued by Hitler, concentrating forces at the French city of Sedan. This plan, often referred to as the *Manstein* Plan – the *Sichelschnitt* ('cut of the sickle') – was backed by Hitler and subsequently operationalised.

The German strategy (see Map 1.2) was to use Army Group B as the 'matador's cloak' to lure the bulk of the French forces into Belgium and away from the main point of attack. Army Group B's purpose was to contain the enemy forces and disallow them to disengage from battle in order to reinforce other areas further south.

Army Group C, with only 18 divisions, was left to defend the *Siegfried* Line (a line of defensive forts and tank defences) and launch diversionary attacks on the Maginot Line without any intention to breach it. Their aim was likewise to tie up French reserves.

The audacity of the plan was the focus of an attack on an area that placed great demands on German ingenuity. The weight of the armoured attack was to be at the upper Meuse in the area of Sedan, at the outer edge of the Maginot Line, which was assumed to be the weakest point in the French front line. It was an area unsuitable for major armoured operation but offered a gateway into the rear of the Maginot Line and of the bulk of the French forces committed to the north. Once across the Meuse, Army Group A, and in particular Panzer Group *Kleist*, with 41,000 vehicles, was to swing westwards, enacting the *Sichelschnitt*, and thrust to the Channel Coast, thereby encircling the French forces and their allies.

Operation Yellow set out to cross the river Meuse, and break through the French lines in the area around Sedan, followed by a drive westwards. These plans did not detail what should have happen afterwards. Guderian, in charge of the XIX Panzer Corps, in addressing this ambiguity, recalled,

> 'Unless I receive orders to the contrary, I intend on the next day to continue my advance westwards. The supreme leadership must decide whether my objective is to be Amiens or Paris. In my opinion the correct course is to drive past Amiens to the English Channel'. Hitler nodded and said nothing more. Only General Busch, who commanded the Sixteenth Army on my left, cried out: 'Well, I do not think you cross the river in the first place!'
>
> (Horne 1990, 212)

In 1936, France was embroiled in political and economic turmoil. Germany reoccupied the Rhineland. The increasing threat of Germany concluded in a mechanisation and conscription programme to match that of Germany in quantity of men and materials. That would allow the Allies to go on the offensive as early as 1941. Gamelin's – the Supreme Commander of French Land forces's – considerations, however, curtailed the offensive ambitions that had been laid out as early as 1919 to prevent another bloodshed on France's 'sacred' soil. Hence, the focus was on two areas. Along the southern border, the Maginot Line provided enough protection to contain any German offensive. In the north, the Allies would have to rely on the Dyle-Breda Plan, where they would place the strong Seventh Army under General Giraud. In collaboration with the British Expeditionary Force (BEF) and General Blanchard's First Army, the bulk of the Allied forces were supposed to move to the river Dyle to absorb the weight of the German attack. General Corap's Ninth Army was to occupy the area along the Meuse just north of Sedan. Below Sedan, occupying the gap between Sedan and the start of the Maginot Line, General Huntzinger was placed with his Second Army. The divisions under his command were of mediocre quality because a German attack through the thickly forested area of the Ardennes was regarded by the French High Command as unlikely, and if such an attack from that direction did occur, the French believed they would have sufficient time to reinforce.

The 'Mechelen' Incident reinforced the resolve of the Allies to meet their enemy in the north, with their best armoured and mechanised divisions. The 'Breda Variant' manifested the commitment of most of the Allies' crack forces to the north, leaving the centre of around a hundred miles behind the 'impenetrable' Ardennes forest largely undefended with a mere four light cavalry divisions and 10 infantry divisions.

On May 10th 1940, the strategies of both countries were put to the test. On May 15th – five days after the beginning of the campaign in the west, the Germans established three bridgeheads over the Meuse. They broke through the French defences and repulsed major counter-attacks by the French. They raced north, encircling those Allied forces that had pushed into Belgium and Holland to contain the expected main German assault. The battles that followed only prolonged the French struggle to contain the German advance; at no point did they manage to stop it.

DECIDING FACTORS: IMAGINATION, SENSITIVITY, ADAPTABILITY

The French High Command rigidly stuck to its plans and its expectations of how these plans would work out. They expected the Germans to attack in the north, through the Low Countries, and so they prepared themselves for the fulfilment of this expectation, constrained by their own capabilities and blind to the capabilities of their enemy.

IMAGINATION

The Germans displayed an extraordinary wealth of novel ideas on how combat operations should be conducted. These were not just documented as theoretical thought pieces, such as *Achtung Panzer* (Guderian 1999), originally published in 1937. Visionary ideas were tested in field exercises and war games, and further validated in those early campaigns of WWII, such as in the invasion of Poland on September 1st 1939 as well as in the campaign against Denmark and Norway on April 9th 1940, a mere four weeks prior to the invasion of France.

The insights gained from these successes and failures – Norway was successfully invaded but at a terrible cost to the German Navy – were heeded, despite ongoing conservatism among German generalship. In order to surprise an enemy, the envelope had to be pushed beyond what one knew from past experience. Visionaries took the upper hand.

If there is a criticism of the strategic planning of the Germans, it is that their vision mainly referred to the operational necessity of breaking through the French lines in the Centre and then, through encirclement, demoralising the French. Once that aim was accomplished, lack of vision beyond the capitulation of France left a vacuum. At the eve of Operation Yellow's commencement, no vision, let alone any plan, was in place to defeat another enemy: Great Britain.

In contrast to opportunistic thinking, the French strategy was characterised by myopic, outdated expectations. The campaign in the west in 1940 was preceded by a range of engagements that could have provided the French with an idea of what the German forces were capable of. Despite these valuable insights, the common belief that 'It cannot happen to us' prevailed. This perception revealed overconfidence in their own plans which were believed to be so detailed and complete that they would cover all eventualities. Readiness to counter any eventuality other than an attack in the north severely limited their strategic flexibility as prevailing overconfidence was rarely challenged. Concerns about their defences, in particular in the area around Sedan, were ignored. Exercises or war games probing these defences and the readiness of the Allied forces either did not take place, or their outcomes were discounted as not applicable to a 'real-life' scenario. In a memorandum written by Colonel Charles de Gaulle, General Keller (Inspector General of Tanks) pointed out,

> Even supposing that the present fortified line were breached or outflanked, it does not appear that our opponents will find a combination of circumstances as favourable as *Blitzkrieg* was in Poland. One can see, then, that in future operations the primary role of the tank will be the same as in the past: to assist the infantry in reaching successive objectives.
>
> (Horne 1990, 179)

CHAPTER TWO: STRATEGIC RESILIENCE

SENSITIVITY

The Germans did plan. Nevertheless, the credo of German commanders was Helmuth von Moltke the Elder's (1800–1891) *no plan survives contact with the enemy*. It was a necessity for German commanders to lead from the front, to remain tactically sensitive to an unpredictable, ever-changing situation. Such sensitivity at a tactical level, and its translation into operations and strategy was assisted by the use of wireless communications (see Chapter 4).

In contrast, French generalship received many situation reports about the unfolding campaign. Communications from the front line arrived frequently, but they were often outdated and ambiguous (see Chapter 4). Fuelled by overconfidence, reports that indicated a deteriorating situation near Sedan were flatly ignored, until the pleas of front-line officers made them 'wake up' to reality; that the front had been broken.

ADAPTABILITY

On some occasions, Allied logistics (see Chapter 5) prevented a timely deployment of forces. At the time when Allied reserves were deployed and on the move, the Germans had already occupied the area in contention, gaining a defensive advantage. On others, French columns of men and material on the move were surprised and subdued by lightly armoured German reconnaissance forces.

The German forces showed greater adaptability, facilitated by tactical sensitivity (see Chapter 4) and logistical independence (see Chapter 6). A common pattern emerged in this campaign: one of quick action in line with tactical and operational necessities, but still in line with strategic foresight. In essence, German planning allowed and encouraged forms of improvisation, an extreme form of adaptability. Its purpose was to create and maintain uncertainty and ambiguity for the enemy to such an extent that he was incapable of adapting to circumstances.

VON CLAUSEWITZ AND DE JOMINI: STRATEGY

1. Hypothetical combats should be judged just as if they were real, on the basis of their results.

    If a detachment is sent away to cut off the retreat of a fleeing enemy, and the enemy therefore surrenders without further resistance, it is the threat of combat offered by the pursuing detachment that has forced this decision on him.

    If a part of our army occupies an undefended enemy province and thus deprives the enemy of very considerable means of keeping up the strength of his Army, the threat of the battle that would be necessary if the enemy attempted to recover the lost province is a deterrent that enables us to keep it.

    In both cases, therefore, the mere possibility of a battle has produced results, and so should be classed as if it were a real event. Suppose that in these cases the enemy opposed our troops with superior strength, and thus forced our armies to give up their object without combat – then certainly our plan has failed, but that does not mean the resistance we offered at (either of) those points has been without effect, because it drew the enemy's forces to that point. And if it becomes the case that our whole undertaking has done us harm, it cannot be said that these positions, these possible battles, had no consequences; in such a situation, their effects are similar to those of a lost battle.

    So we see that the destruction of the enemy's military forces, the overthrow of the enemy's power, is only to be achieved through the effect of a battle, whether or not it actually takes place or is merely offered and not accepted.

2. Twofold object of the combat

    But these effects are of two kinds, direct and indirect. They are the latter kind if other things intervene and become the object of combat – things which are not in themselves the destruction of the enemy's force, but lead up to it, certainly by a circuitous road, but with so much the greater effect. The possession of provinces, towns, fortresses, roads, bridges, magazines, etc. may be the immediate object of a battle but never the ultimate one. Things of this description can never be looked upon otherwise than as a means of gaining greater superiority, so as at last to offer battle to the enemy in such a way that it will be impossible for him to accept it. Therefore all these things can only be regarded as intermediate links, steps as it were, leading up to the effectual principle, but never that principle itself (Adapted from Von Clausewitz 2011, 71).

Strategy embraces the following points:

1. The selection of the theatre of war, and the discussion of the different combinations of which it admits.
2. The determination of the decisive points in these combinations, and the most favourable direction for operations.
3. The selection and establishment of the fixed base and of the zone of operations.
4. The selection of the objective point, whether offensive or defensive.
5. The strategic fronts, lines of defence, and fronts of operations.
6. The choice of lines of operations leading to the objective point or strategic front.
7. For a given operation, the best strategic line, and the different manoeuvres necessary to embrace all cases.
8. The eventual bases of operations and the strategic reserves.

9. The marching of armies, considered as manoeuvres.
10. The relation between the position of depots and the marches of the army.
11. Fortresses regarded as strategic means, as a refuge for an army, as an obstacle to its progress: the sieges to be made and to be covered.
12. Points for entrenched camps.
13. The diversions to be made, and the large detachments necessary (Adapted from De Jomini 2008, 46).

TRANSLATION AND EXPLANATION: LINEAR VERSUS ADAPTIVE STRATEGY

Over the years, a plethora of models on strategy have emerged. In principal, two basic models may be distinguished: Linear and Adaptive strategy (Chaffee 1985). A linear strategy resembles the Methodical Battle, applied by the French; it is a methodical approach to achieving long-term organisational goals. Managers identify these goals, plan in detail and formulate and implement strategy.

Adaptive strategy can be viewed as a managerial expression of the manoeuvre warfare favoured by Germany; it is less focussed on long-term goals but instead seeks the means to achieve a fit between an organisation's capabilities and the environment it operates in. This suggests greater attention to risks and opportunities; the outcome is a product of the fit between the organisation and its environment, and ultimately depends on the efficacy of that strategic fit.

The major differences between these views on strategy are shown in Table 2.1.

Table 2.1 Key Differences between Linear and Adaptive Strategy

Linear Strategy	Adaptive Strategy
Environment	
In organisations adopting a linear strategy, top managers define long-terms goals and assess how organisational capabilities support these long-term goals. If necessary, organisational capabilities and resources need to be expanded or enhanced to ensure goal achievement. Top managers are 'inward looking'; the external environment is seen as a 'nuisance' that does not necessarily affect their planning.	Adopting an adaptive strategy takes the external environment (such as competitors) into consideration. An adaptive strategy implies an 'outward looking' organisation. Top managers constantly assess the external environment, in order to align their internal capabilities and resources with environmental opportunities and risks.
Means and ends	
The focus of managerial attention is on 'ends', the long-term orientation of an organisation, over a period of five years or more. Long-term goals may include specific improvements in the organisation's competitive position, technology, leadership, profitability, return on investment, employee relations and productivity, and corporate image.	Pursuing an adaptive strategy, the emphasis is predominantly on the 'means' of an organisation to adapt to a changing environment; to allow organisational capabilities and resources to match a changing external environment. Such means may include intangible assets such as business process know-how, customer and business relationships, reputations, organisational culture and leadership values.
Responsiveness	
The forward-looking nature of a linear strategy assumes that environmental conditions will remain stable and thus predictable or that any change in the environment will not significantly constrain organisational capabilities and resources in accomplishing the set long-term goals.	The organisation is not insulated from its environment. Proactive and reactive responsiveness to the environment is paramount and engages not only with major but also with subtle changes and trends.

One of the distinguishing features of a linear strategy is its dissociation from the wider environment. In essence, a linear strategy is inward-looking, defining a long-term outlook that 'shapes' the wider environment. It is for other competitors to adapt their own organisational strategies. In contrast, an Adaptive strategy aims not only to align with an external environment but also to be ahead of the adaptive challenges it will pose.

Following a linear or adaptive strategy involves distinctive benefits, as shown in Table 2.2.

Table 2.2 Advantages of Linear and Adaptive Strategy

Linear Strategy	*Adaptive Strategy*
Enables greater internal foresight within the organisation	Promotes greater sensitivity to the environment
Efficient in providing and maintaining capabilities and resources	Effective in adapting to a changing environment
Establishes stable robustness	Establishes adaptiveness, and robustness

A linear strategy has the benefit of providing foresight in environments that remain relatively stable and thus predictable. The organisational resources and capabilities necessary to accomplish the set long-term goal can be defined early on and procured efficiently. These resources do not have to be dynamic in nature as changes to the goal are not envisaged. This makes planning straightforward. Plans are defined by top management, broken down into tasks and channelled down the hierarchy of an organisation. Progress towards goal accomplishment is transparent and easily measured. As changes in the environment are discouraged or not expected, a linear strategy produces robustness in the sense that the organisational goal's viability and the means to achieve it are not susceptible to possible changes in the environment.

Contrary to a linear strategy, an adaptive strategy is not insulated from the environment in which it is enacted. It provides greater sensitivity to changes in the environment and allows changes to be made after initial planning. Hence, a change in stakeholders' expectations, often only visible in the form of trends and patterns in needs and wants, can be accommodated and satisfied. But such sensitivity and the resulting adaptability require dynamic resources and capabilities that allow an organisation to implement an adaptive strategy; such as

- the ability of employees to learn quickly and build new strategic assets;
- the integration of these new strategic assets, including capability, technology and customer feedback, into company processes;
- the transformation or reuse of existing assets which have depreciated (Teece 2007; Teece et al., 1997).

Ultimately, competitiveness is established by the organisation's adaptiveness as it constantly addresses environmental adaptive pressures and builds up adaptive challenges for key competitors.

TOWARDS ORGANISATIONAL RESILIENCE: THE FALLACY OF DETERMINISM

A fallacious argument may be deceptive in appearing better than it really is; and this can also happen when adopting a linear strategy in business. A linear strategy appears to be more straightforward; strategic planning is 'easier', more efficient, at least in the short term. A fixed strategic plan can provide a 'clear', well-defined road map to achieve a specific long-term goal, and can thus be broken down into its components in order to drive the more detailed planning of people, structure and procedures within an organisation.

Nevertheless, the Achilles heel of a linear strategy is uncertainty in the form of incomplete knowledge about the future state of an environment and its impact on the organisation. What if an unpredicted future makes the fixed, well-defined long-term goal redundant? Let's use the example of Kodak. In January 2012, Kodak, an American technology company that concentrated on imaging products and had invented the handheld camera, filed for bankruptcy. What was once considered a hub of technological wizardry suddenly became an institution with little hope of surviving much longer into the future.

The demise of Kodak, like nothing else, highlights the ongoing need for top-level managers to cope with the effects of uncertainty. The use of photographic film was pioneered by George Eastman, who started manufacturing paper film in 1885 before switching to celluloid in 1889. His first camera, which he called the 'Kodak', was first offered for sale in 1888. It was a very simple box camera with a fixed-focus lens and single shutter speed which, along with its relatively low price, appealed to the average consumer. The first camera using digital electronics to capture and store images had been developed by 1975. The adoption of digital cameras was slow. In 1999, with the rise of broadband technology to share digital images, the demand for digital stand-alone cameras suddenly exploded, fuelled by the introduction of the iPhone in 2007. The volatility in the environment, amplified by the rise of the smart phone, caught Kodak off guard:

> Kodak's top management never fully grasped how the world around them was changing. They hung on to now obsolete assumptions about who took pictures, why and when.
>
> (Munir 2016)

Recent generations of Kodak manager were too wedded to the past business model to take the radical steps needed to reposition their company as a digital leader.

LIMITATIONS IN FORECASTING

Forecasting is a management process that attempts to make predictions based on past and present events, patterns or trends. The selection of a forecasting method, such as the Delphi method, depends on a range of factors, among them the availability of historical data or the time horizon to which predictions are needed. And there lies the problem: the availability and accuracy of historical data. The past has much to tell us about how we might manage future events, but it is rarely a template for the future. What is certain is that the future will be different from the past. The longer the planning horizon, the worse is the past's accuracy in predicting future outcomes. Long-term planning is a leap of faith, assuming that the world will not change at all or will only change as predicted. In the case of Kodak, the introduction of an iPhone was a one-time event, unlike any in the past, that changed consumer attitudes in a very short period of time.

LIMITATIONS IN CONTROL

Given that, in the long term, organisations have considerable difficulty in predicting the future, there will be events that, even if predicted, remain uncontrollable. A linear strategy should mean that an organisation is sufficiently robust to withstand changes in the environment. Kodak believed that its current strategy would weather the change in technology and consumer attitudes. Their optimistic bias towards analog photography prevailed for too long; when Kodak eventually realised that their organisation was in a downward spiral, it was already too late.

In principle, a linear strategy may well drive – as we see in a range of organisations – an illusion of certainty and controllability, working towards a pseudo-future, reinforcing assumptions such as 'Uncertainty will not happen to me!' and/or 'Uncertainty, if it happens, will not affect me' (see following textbox).

BATTLE OF KURSK

The winter of 1942/43 saw the defeat of the 6th Army at Stalingrad. With it, the German army lost considerable resources in men and materials. It was also the first time since the start of WWII that an entire German field army surrendered. The following months saw continuous fighting. The *Wehrmacht* conducted a series of withdrawals to solidify the frontline, under constant pressure from the forces of the Soviet Union. In March 1943, the Germans successfully counter-attacked a Soviet offensive that had threatened to destroy Army Group South. It not only stopped the Russians in their offensive but inflicted substantial losses. Both sides pondered what to do next.

Generalfeldmarschall (Field Marshall) Erich von Manstein, the mastermind behind the successful campaign against France and its Allies in 1940, proposed – in the light of the exposure of his position with depleted men and material – taking a defensive stance, launching only sporadic counter-attacks into the flanks of Soviet attacking forces, until his forces were replenished to launch a major offensive. Hitler rejected this approach – only a substantial victory, as in 1940/41, would restore the *Wehrmacht's* prestige after Stalingrad.

Von Manstein proposed further plans to doubly envelop Soviet forces, directed at the city of Kursk, a vital road and rail junction. This would allow the Germans to repeat the encircling manoeuvres that had been so successful in the first years of the campaign in the east. On March 13th, Hitler issued Operational Order No. 6, codenamed Citadel (*Zitadelle*).

The launch of Operation *Zitadelle* experienced serious delays as Hitler impatiently waited for the production of new types of tanks that, in his mind, would miraculously turn the tide and provide a decisive success in the east. In May 1943, the *Afrika Korps*

(Panzerarmee Afrika under General Ernst Rommel) surrendered. Fortunes in the Battle in the Atlantic also turned. In May 1943, the Germans lost 34 U-Boats, 25 per cent of total operational strength. Hitler needed a decisive victory to keep his Axis[3] partner Italy on board and the German people committed to the war effort.

By then, the German forces were being gradually equipped with powerful weaponry; among them the 54t Tiger I and the 68.5t Tiger II tanks each equipped with the dreaded high-velocity 88 mm gun. The medium Panther, ultimately destined to be the most formidable medium tank of WWII – also arrived in greater numbers. However, most of these were heavily over-engineered and underpowered – the engine power had not kept up with the weight – and broke down before or during the first days of the Kursk offensive.

Logistical shortcomings further delayed the German offensive. Stockpiles of fuel and ammunition were rushed to the front. In addition to 2,451 tanks, the Germans amassed 777,000 soldiers, 7,417 artillery pieces and around 2,000 aircraft in the area, a third of all their available military strength. The launch date for Operation Zitadelle was finally set for July 5th 1943. General Friedrich von Mellenthin argued, *No offensive was ever prepared as carefully as this one* (Fawcett 2010).

Surprise had been at the centre of German success in the past. However, thanks to their own intelligence and that coming from Bletchley codebreakers, the Russians surmised early on that the Germans would attempt a major offensive in this area. In March 1943, four months prior to the offensive, Soviet intelligence indicated major German troop concentrations around Orel and Kharkov, the two staging areas for the planned pincer movement.

The Russians started preparing for a defence in depth across a 150 km-wide front north of Belgorod, heavily relying on minefields and interlocking fire. Trenches and anti-tank ditches were dug with the help of 300,000 conscripted civilians. 400,000 mines were laid: 2,400 anti-tank and 2,800 anti-personnel devices were placed in every mile in the path of the planned German assault. Whereas the line of defence in France in 1940 had amounted to 25 km, the Red Army's depth of defence extended to approximately 300 km.

On July 5th 1943, the Germans embarked on their last major offensive in the east. Although rapidly gaining air superiority, the advance on the ground was bogged down. Many of the newly arrived tanks – Panthers, Tiger I and IIs – broke down. Others were disabled by anti-tank fire and anti-tank mines. These did not often lead to tanks being destroyed, but most were write-offs as they could not be recovered, or they did not have spare parts as these were delivered in woefully insufficient quantities.

The Germans advanced, but by no means at the speed of 1940. The Red Army had learned its lessons from the enormous defeats in 1941/42, and gradually retreated once its position became untenable. In doing this, they kept the Germans engaged in a war of attrition, allowing their own front to be drawn back but not broken.

On July 12th, the Germans ran into an armoured counter-attack at the city of Prokhorovka to be known as arguably the biggest tank battle in military history. It was a tactical victory for the Germans, but ultimately it dawned on the German High Command OKW (*Oberkommando der Wehrmacht*) that gains were far below expectations. During the 12 days of *Zitadelle*, they suffered losses of 9 per cent of operational strength (33,708 casualties, including 6,643 dead). On July 15th, Operation *Zitadelle* came to an end with losses of German men and material that the German army could ill-afford. In WWII, it was the last occasion on which Germany launched a major offensive in the east.

Operation *Zitadelle* was the antithesis of an adaptive strategy; it contained no element of surprise. The Red Army had learned, in a near catastrophic manner in 1941/42, how the Germans operated. The Germans, however, could not envisage that applying an adaptive strategy might, over time, cease to be infallibly successful, regardless of how the external environment had changed. Their insistent belief that they still faced the Red Army of 1941/42 was their downfall.

An adaptive strategy needs to remain adaptive by continuously developing dynamic capabilities. Operation *Zitadelle* was the opposite, characterised by linear thinking that was entirely uncharacteristic of the previous German way of thinking. Resources were indeed strengthened and improved over time (e.g. more advanced equipment and tanks). Nevertheless, the way in which they were deployed lacked imagination, allowance for contingencies and thus surprise.

SCENARIO PLANNING INSTEAD OF FORECASTING

I seem to be arguing that we should abandon forecasts altogether. That would be foolish. Without any foresight, an organisation would be virtually blind in engaging with the future, with no sense of direction and alignment. Nevertheless, in order to adapt to changes in the environment, many organisations may choose to *replace straight forecasting with more sophisticated "scenario" building, and simple deterministic planning with more complex "contingency" planning* (Mintzberg 1994, 248).

While scenario planning has its origins in military strategy studies, it was transformed into a business tool by, among others, Wack (1985) and Schoemaker (1995). In contrast to risk management that drives the anticipation of individual risks, scenario planning caters to multiple future realities and encourages thinking to the extremes of what is possible and plausible. The aim of scenario planning is the definition of a group of possible and plausible (not necessarily probable) futures tha should constructively challenge each other. In comparison with traditional risk management, this approach does not aim to focus attention on quantifying a single future; rather, it provides multiple, more abstract projections of alternative futures.

Scenario planning is a powerful tool if applied in a 'safe,' non-threatening environment. The culture of an organisation needs to be 'open-minded' for the effects of scenario planning to take effect. It requires:

- receptiveness to multiple, sometimes divergent, perspectives;
- openness to having one's views questioned and challenged;
- the use of a leader or facilitator who can manage the process of scenario planning in a controlled but non-threatening manner;
- willingness to provide resources to deal with important scenarios that may occur;
- acknowledgement that scenarios are uncertain in their predictive power and that the 'truth' will not be forthcoming through this technique.

There is much written about Scenario Planning, so we will provide just a brief overview here of the key stages to work through:

Identify the drivers in your environment

Some future trends can be forecast with reasonable accuracy: for example demographics and population growth. Others, though, are far more unclear. These can include, for example, the future oil price (a major issue in determining investment choices in the petroleum industry), anticipated or unknown changes in the regulatory or political environment (upcoming elections create uncertainty and often business investment is delayed until the outcome is known), regional geopolitical uncertainty, future interest rates or the impact of technological innovation.

Work out a response for each of these scenarios

In line with critical drivers of uncertainty, develop a range of 'what if' scenarios. For example, if sales are low, we could respond by increasing advertising, considering a pricing change or even a rapid redesign if customer feedback indicates that some aspect should be modified. If sales are high, might we perhaps even need to consider expanded factory capacity? A competitor product introduces different challenges. How close is their alternative, and how does its performance and price compare? This can lead to a wide range of response options. So, even with just two variables, we can end up with some very complicated alternatives. How do we go about dealing with these?

Identify the data that will help make sensible decisions

The rapid availability of sales data, product reviews and initial customer feedback will be helpful in understanding the market response to the launch. Similarly, ensure that your team is monitoring market information regarding competitors.

Initial brainstorming to identify responses to each scenario is valuable and allows team members to contribute ideas and opinions. This is not a one-off event, though. Scenarios can be refined and options generated as more data become available. It is therefore a 'living' process as clarity is generated. It can sometimes be useful to have a 'war room' in which data are collated and shared visually and where discussions can be had regarding not only the 'what-if' questions but also taking account of the new and unfolding situation at regular intervals (adapted from Kutsch, Hall, and Turner 2015, 56).

CONTINGENCY PLANNING INSTEAD OF DETERMINISTIC PLANNING

Thinking in multiple scenarios is a first stepping stone towards moving away from a linear strategy and adopting a mindset of adaptation. Scenario planning goes hand in hand with contingency planning – with the creation of alternative plans in order to accommodate different scenarios. Contingency planning requires the following:

Sensitivity

It is important to remain 'close' to the environment, to understand even subtle changes (e.g. consumer trends). Define trigger points that allow you to question your current strategy as well as switching to an alternative plan.

Buy-in

Switching to an alternative plan for adapting to a changing environment is often associated with disruption. Readying a workforce for potential transitions in ways of working is important. This has two main aspects. First, organisational resources and capabilities need to be dynamic. They need to be versatile, capable of serving more than one function. Second, people need to be committed to establishing and maintaining the use of dynamic capabilities and resources. They need to be incentivised, not to maintain the status quo, but to adopt an alternative plan quickly.

Scepticism

People need to look beyond the adoption of an alternative plan. They need to monitor whether a Plan B might actually reduce those dynamic capabilities and resources that an organisation depends on if it is to adapt to a changing environment.

OUTLOOK

From a French perspective, the fallacy of predeterminism came true, with monumental consequences. It is not that the French did not engage with scenario planning or war games; nor did they fail to prepare for contingencies, for a Plan B. They did plan for a range of scenarios, including one where the Germans tried to cross the river Meuse. However, these scenarios were deemed unlikely, close to being impossible, despite contrary evidence from preceding campaigns, such as the Polish campaign. In full view of the world, the Germans displayed their capabilities to deal with rugged or forested terrain, their ability to cross rivers and punch through enemy fortification lines. Regardless, the French remained confident that this evidence of the state of modern warfare did not apply to them. From their perspective, the world had stood still since WWI. Their linear strategy – expecting another war of attrition, expecting to gradually wear down an enemy – was based on a straightforward long-term goal. It allowed simple planning, efficient and 'foolproof', for a French population that needed reassurance. Since the cessation of WWI hostilities, the French and their Allies had planned for numerous scenarios and prepared for contingencies. But their lack of readiness to envisage any scenario other than a German push through the Low Countries sealed the fate of France.

Organisations may similarly give in to the temptation to follow a linear strategy, being fixated on a long-term goal and oblivious of changes in the environment that can erode an organisation's robustness in withstanding those very changes. A linear strategy provides certainty and is generally more efficient, but only in the short-term. By the time environmental changes have exceeded the organisation's degree of robustness, it may already be too late to bounce back, to be resilient enough to survive. This is what happened in the case of Kodak.

Reflection

To what extent does your work unit adhere to a Linear or Adaptive Strategy? For each item, select one box only that best reflects your conclusion.

	Neutral	
We spend a lot of effort defining our long-term goals, and they are 'set in stone'	○ ○ ○ ○ ○	We define long-term goals but they remain 'flexible'
We forecast a single, most-likely future	○ ○ ○ ○ ○	We anticipate multiple futures
We plan in detail for years ahead	○ ○ ○ ○ ○	We make assumptions about the long term-future, but our planning is based on weeks and months, not years

	Neutral	
We build up organisational robustness	○ ○ ○ ○ ○	We focus on organisational adaptiveness
Our resources and capabilities, necessary to achieve our long-term goals, are rigid	○ ○ ○ ○ ○	Our resources and capabilities are dynamic in nature
We plan for the expected	○ ○ ○ ○ ○	We plan for the unexpected

Scoring: If your answers tend to the left, you are pursuing a more traditional Linear Strategy approach. If your answers are more on the right, your organisation has adopted a more Adaptive Strategy.

NOTES

1 A combat block in which the principal armament fires through embrasures in the block's walls. Casemates are classified as either artillery casemates or infantry casemates depending on their primary armament. Interval casemates are stand-alone, self-contained infantry casemates defending the line of anti-tank obstacles and barbed-wire entanglements.
2 I am not using the word *Blitzkrieg* (Lightning warfare) as it was a concept that emerged and was widely used in the later years of WWII.
3 In 1943, Axis powers included Germany, Italy, and Japan as well as Bulgaria, Hungary, Romania, and Yugoslavia. The Axis powers were led by Nazi Germany.

REFERENCES

Chaffee, E. E. 1985. "Three Models of Strategy." *Academy of Management Review* 10 (1): 89–98.

De Jomini, A. H. 2008. *The Art of War*. Kingston, ON: Legacy Books Press.

Doughty, R. A. 1985. *The Seeds of Disaster: The Development of French Army Doctrine 1919–1939*. Mechanicsburg, PA: Stackpole Books.

Fawcett, B. 2010. *100 Mistakes That Changed History*. New York: Penguin.

Guderian, H. 1999. *Achtung Panzer!* London: Cassell.

Horne, A. 1990. *To Lose a Battle: France 1940*. London: Penguin Books.

Johnson, H. 2005. *Fort Eben Emael: The Key to Hitler's Victory in the West*. Oxford: Osprey Publishing.

Kutsch, E., M. Hall, and E. Turner. 2015. *Project Resilience: The Art of Noticing, Interpreting, Preparing, Containing and Recovering*. Farnham: Gower.

Kutsch, L. "Frankreichfeldzug." Private Collection.

Mintzberg, H. 1994. *The Rise and Fall of Strategic Planning: Reconceiving Roles for Planning, Plans, Planners*. New York: Free Press.

Munir, K. 2016. "The Demise of Kodak: Five Reasons." *Wall Street Journal*. http://blogs.wsj.com/source/2012/02/26/the-demise-of-kodak-five-reasons/, accessed December 17th 2017.

Romanych, M., and M. Rupp. 2010. *Maginot Line 1940: Battles on the French Frontier*. Oxford: Osprey Publishing.

Schoemaker, P. 1995. "Scenario Planning: A Tool for Strategic Thinking." *Sloan Management Review* 36 (2): 25–40.

Teece, D. J. 2007. "Explicating Dynamic Capabilities: The Nature and Microfoundations of (Sustainable) Enterprise Performance." *Strategic Management Journal* 28: 1319–50.

Teece, D. J., G. Pisano, and A. Shuen. 1997. "Dynamic Capabilities and Strategic Management." *Strategic Management Journal* 18 (7): 509–33.

Tzu, S. 2008. *The Art of War*. London: Penguin Books.

Von Clausewitz, C. 2011. *On War*. New York: Madison Park.

Wack, P. 1985. "Scenarios: Unchartered Waters Ahead." *Harvard Business Review* 63 (5): 73–89.

CHAPTER THREE
Operational resilience

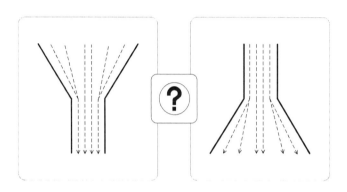

*I am concentrated
Into one;
He is divided
Into ten.
I am
Ten
To his one;
Many
Against
His few.*

(Tzu 2008, 33)

CONTENTS

The story: May 10th–May 12th 1940	82
Schwerpunkt *versus* La Colmatage	85
De Jomini: assembly of forces in space	86
Von Clausewitz: assembly of forces in space	88
The challenge: crossing a river	88
Deciding factors: redundancy, determination, agility	94
Centre of gravity determination	95
Translation and explanation: dispersion versus concentration	98
Towards organisational resilience: the fallacy of protecting everything at minimal cost	102
Battle of the Bulge	107
Outlook	112
Notes	115
References	115

This chapter looks at the operational level of organisational resilience. Operational decisions tend to be carried out by middle managers.

- They follow on from strategic decisions and aim to meet the objectives stated in any strategic decision
- These are medium-period-based decisions.

THE STORY: MAY 10TH–MAY 12TH 1940

At 03:00 on May 10th the German government issued a 'Memorandum', informing the Dutch and Belgian governments of the imminent arrival of the *Wehrmacht*. At 05:35, the Germans crossed the Dutch, Belgian and Luxembourg border in force.

In the south – apart from a few forward units – four French armies remain static in their lines of fortifications. In the north, As planned, the bulk of the French and British forces moved towards the Dyle-Breda Line to link up with Dutch and Belgian armies behind a protective curtain of Belgian forts.

Paul Baudouin remarked,

CHAPTER THREE: OPERATIONAL RESILIENCE

> Since four o'clock this morning I have been kept informed by telephone of the way the German attack is developing. At 07:30 I was with the Prime Minister at 5 Place du Palais Bourbon, and while he finished dressing he read me the appeals for help from Holland and Belgium, giving me such details as were in his possession. He went on, "Gamelin is saved. Now he has the battle he waited for, and for which he never ceased to prepare and hope. I know our troops have advanced, and Giraud's army is to enter Holland".
>
> (Baudouin 1948, 28)

In the north, Giraud's 7th Army tried to support the beleaguered Dutch forces but with little success. It soon became clear that the main thrust was through the area of Liège. On May 11th, the massive fort – Fort d'Ében-Émael – protecting the Albert Canal surrendered. General Georges addressed the British Air Force in France the same day:

> In view of the seizure by German detachments of the bridges over the Albert Canal south-east of Maastricht, I demand instant intervention by the British and French Air Forces to slow down the progress of the German columns which might use the crossing points in order to effect a breach in the Belgian line. This operation must be kept going as long as the threat continues.
>
> (Benoist-Méchin 1956, 78)

The Belgian effort to destroy captured bridges over the Albert Canal was in vain though. Their bombers were met by fierce anti-aircraft fire, and most were shot down during their first approach or damaged beyond repair. Requests for massive Allied air-attacks on those crossings were made, but only a few dozen planes were mustered. The Germans started ferrying substantial forces across the Albert Canal at Vroenhoven, largely unopposed. The Belgian front was broken in the north, the Dutch were cornered against the sea, the French 7th Army was retreating. The 1st French Army was thrown into the gap to take the brunt of the attack.

In the centre, Van Kleist's armoured group threw back the forward deployed 5th Light Cavalry Division and the 1st French Cavalry Brigade.

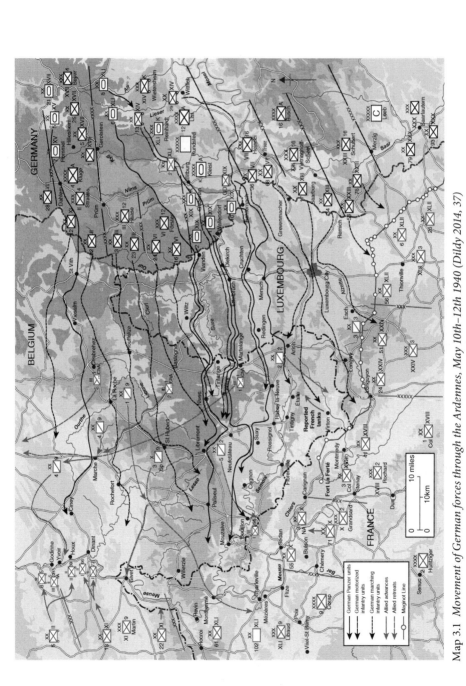

Map 3.1 Movement of German forces through the Ardennes, May 10th–12th 1940 (Dildy 2014, 37)

They proceeded towards the river Semois and crossed it, facing desperate, piecemeal resistance by *Belgian Chasseurs Ardennais* and French forces.

The weeks and months leading up to the German invasion had been used by the French Second and Ninth army to reinforce their defences while training their forces. During the Phoney War, the depth of defences around Sedan was increased from 2.5 to 5 km, with the construction of a second defensive line 15 km behind the principal line of defence:

> In all the depth of the position on the principal line, as well as the stopping line or between these lines, the defence will be organised into circular fighting positions or centres of resistance, capable of defending themselves when isolated, even if bypassed by enemy infantry or tanks. As a consequence, the fighting positions or centres of resistance will be interwoven with obstacles of terrain, woods, villages, etc.
>
> (Adapted from IIe Armée, 14th January 1940)

Great effort was expended by both the Second and Ninth army on improving their defences along the river Meuse, at times at the cost of preparing the units needed to utilise these defences. Most bridges had been demolished or prepared with explosive charges in anticipation of a German attack. Allied reconnaissance flights had indicated that a massive column of vehicles congested all those roads towards the Meuse, south of Namur. The German land forces lined up alongside the Meuse between Monthermé and Sedan, and their seven armoured divisions prepared to hurl themselves across it, just at the junction between Corap's Ninth and Huntziger's Second Army (see Map 3.1)

SCHWERPUNKT VERSUS *LA COLMATAGE*

In executing an operation, the Germans relied on the principle of *Schwerpunkt* (centre of gravity (COG)) which implies that maximum effort should be 'concentrated' on where the enemy is believed to be weakest. An attack would start with a frontal attack to tie down enemy forces and prevent them from diverting forces to the actual area of the *Schwerpunkt*, narrow sectors of attack. In WWI, particularly in the east, the Germans achieved considerable successes with the use of intensively concentrated effort, piercing the enemy's line and thus accomplishing the main objective of creating disruption in the rear of an enemy army. Elite-units would create a breach in the enemy's front line by which mobile forces could break through and quickly move to the rear of the enemy. The reserves that followed would widen the breach and engage in flanking (*Flankenangriff*), enveloping (*Umfassungsangriff*) and encircling (*Einkreisung*) the enemy in order to widen the breach and prevent an effective counter-attack. As a result, while mobile units drove deeper into enemy territory, any forms of enemy countermeasure from the flanks and rear of the *Schwerpunkt* were subdued. The *Schwerpunkt* principle builds on having the best units driving a wedge into the enemy's front line, the support of reserves to preserve the breach and the freedom of front-line officers to use their judgement as to where the COG concentration of efforts should be.

DE JOMINI: ASSEMBLY OF FORCES IN SPACE

The proposal is that there is one great principle underlying all the operations of war, a principle which must be followed. It is summed up in the following maxims:

1. Use strategic movements to throw the mass of your army, in successive waves, at the decisive points in the theatre of war, and at the communications of the enemy, as far as possible without compromising your own.
2. Manoeuvre so that you engage subdivisions of the hostile army with the bulk of your own forces.

> 3. On the battlefield, throw the mass of your forces at the decisive point or at that portion of the enemy line which you most need to overthrow.
> 4. Make sure that these masses are not only thrown at the decisive point but that they will engage the enemy with optimum timing and energy (Adapted from De Jomini 2008, 47).

In contrast, the French, as well as their Allies, banked on the tactical measure of having a 'continuous' defence in depth providing massive firepower. Several lines of resistance were established that might not stop an attacking force but would slow it down. Time would be gained to repair the gap in the main line of resistance – based on the principle of *colmater* (plugging a hole) – and, if that were not possible, to allow forces to fall back to a succession of prepared defences in the rear of the main line of defence.

Whereas *Schwerpunkt* requires mobility in attack, *La Colmatage* is directed at massing resources, partially immobile, along a continuous fortified front. Ultimately, any attempts to plug the breaches at Dinant (and Houx), Monthermé and Sedan were half-hearted as most of the available mobile forces were not ready to be dispatched or were used in a 'drip-feed' manner, in stark contrast to what *Schwerpunkt* implies.

Only later in the campaign did the French switch to a 'hedgehog' tactic of defence. Instead of maintaining a continuous front, they established strongpoints – usually fortified towns and villages – to allow the Germans to bypass them, striking their flanks, and cutting off their supply columns, to 'strangle' the forward-most units. This principle was part of the Weygand line and was implemented to disrupt Operation Red (see Chapter 7).

> ## VON CLAUSEWITZ: ASSEMBLY OF FORCES IN SPACE
>
> The best strategy is to always be very strong, first generally then at the decisive point. Therefore, apart from the energy which creates an Army, a work which is not always done by the general, there is no more imperative and no simpler law of strategy than to keep the forces concentrated. No portions should be separated from the main body unless called away by some urgent necessity. On this maxim we stand firm and look upon it as a guide to be depended upon. What the reasonable grounds are on which to allow a detachment of forces, we shall learn by degrees. Then we shall also see that the principle cannot have the same general effects in every war; these are different according to means and ends.
>
> It seems incredible, and yet it has happened a hundred times, that troops have been divided and separated merely through a mysterious convention without any clear perception of the reasons.
>
> If concentration of the whole force is acknowledged as the norm, and every division and separation of it as an exception which must be justified, not only will that folly be completely avoided, but also many a groundless argument for separating troops will be avoided (Adapted from Von Clausewitz 2011, 91).

THE CHALLENGE: CROSSING A RIVER

Crossing the Meuse river posed a formidable challenge for the Germans. The east bank of the river was fortified, and the surrounding area was dotted with thick forest and high ground that allowed defenders to train their artillery. However, once the river was crossed, the defenders' main line of defence pierced, the Germans could run amok across the open and undefended French countryside.

CHAPTER THREE: OPERATIONAL RESILIENCE

An aerial photograph of Sedan. The area is littered with bomb and artillery craters (BArch)

At the centre of the attack, Reinhardt's XLI Panzer Corps approached the Meuse at the French town of Monthermé on May 12th 1940. Odds on their crossing the river were stacked against them. The majority of their supplies had not arrived yet, and most of the Luftwaffe's effort was concentrated on Sedan. They faced well-prepared French positions manned by regulars of the 102nd Fortress division. The Germans needed to cross the river in full sight of the French defenders, who had entrenched themselves in the town of Monthermé as well as in the overlooking heights since the beginning of the war.

In the early hours of May 13th, 6th Panzer, under the leadership of General Kempf, cleared the areas on the east bank of the Meuse. Under the protecting fire of some Panzer IIIs and IVs, the first wave of assault troops had prepared themselves to enter the fast-flowing stream when the French opened fire.

Infantry crossing the river Meuse (BArch)

French machine-gun fire from well-camouflaged positions destroyed the rubber dinghies with its occupants in a matter of minutes. The remaining infantry took cover, but casualties mounted under the incessant fire of machine guns and artillery. Gradually, some bunkers on the left bank were identified and tank fire poured into their viewing ports until they were silenced.

A few flimsy dinghies, the main means of crossing the Meuse, were carried away and entangled in the remains of a demolished bridge. Frantically, more dinghies and wooden planks were rushed forward to improvise a footbridge. The remnants of a rifle battalion made it across until midnight. They dug in to establish a pitifully small bridgehead. Owing to the unrelenting fire from the heights overlooking Monthermé, there was little chance to get heavier equipment across the Meuse by the next morning.

Further north, sheer luck played into the hands of the Germans. On the afternoon of the 12th, a forward unit of General Rommel's 7th Panzer (as part of Hoth's XV Panzer Corps) took a foothold on the west bank of the Meuse at Houx, to the north of Dinant. To their utter surprise they discovered an ancient weir that connected to a very small island midstream. Under the cover of nightfall, they attempted to cross. The French guns remained silent, oblivious to the idea that, two days after

CHAPTER THREE: OPERATIONAL RESILIENCE

beginning the campaign, German units might cross the Meuse in the very spot they were trying to defend.

Nevertheless, an attempt to cross the river was planned for Dinant at 03:00 on May 13th. Likewise, at Monthermé, assault engineers were bound to make a dash across the river under the cover of smoke:

> But we had no smoke unit. So I now gave orders for a number of houses in the valley to be set alight in order to supply the smoke we lacked.
>
> Minute by minute the enemy fire grew more unpleasant. From upriver a damaged rubber boat came drifting down to us with a badly wounded man clinging to it, shouting and screaming for help – the poor fellow was near to drowning. But there was no help for him here, the enemy fire was too heavy.
>
> (Horne 1990, 325)

Those infantry elements that had made it across the river were pinned down by well-concealed French bunkers. Rommel rushed to his headquarters to demand greater fire support from the artillery and tanks. Help finally arrived in the form of Panzer IVs from the 25th Panzer Regiment. Cruising along the east bank, they poured fire into the French defences. Under cover of this tank fire, engineers established a cable ferry that brought the first armoured vehicles across the Meuse. Rommel rallied his battered troops to solidify their gains on the west bank and start setting up a pontoon bridge that allowed more equipment to reach the other side of the Meuse. His situation remained precarious though.

On the west bank, the Belgian *Chasseurs Ardennais* – who had retreated across the Meuse the day before – and the French 66th Regiment stood their ground to contain the German bridgehead. Nevertheless, fatigued and running out of ammunition, they were in dire need of a relieving force that could drive the Germans back across the Meuse. But a powerful counter-attack never materialised. Most French divisional commanders of mobile armoured units were situated up to 15 km behind the front line. Communications were broken due to German artillery fire and aerial bombardment. It took considerable time for divisional headquarters to become fully aware of the unfolding situation. Counter-attacks were postponed for no apparent reason. While the German bridgehead was precariously vulnerable, the French response in this section amounted to an improvised counter-attack by an armoured squadron unsupported by infantry or artillery. They were quickly destroyed.

The crossings of the Meuse at Dinant and Monthermé were mere sideshows, if one considers the amount of air and ground support that Guderian's XIX Panzer Corps had at its disposal at the picturesque city of Sedan. Roughly 1,500 aircrafts – more than the combined British and French air strength – were brought down on a narrow stretch. At 07:00, incessant waves of Dornier 17 and Junkers Ju87 '*Stukas*' concentrated their bombing runs on the less well-camouflaged artillery positions. The cacophony of bomb blasts was intensified when German artillery opened up, and *Flak* (22 mm, 37 mm and 88 mm) guns targeted the French positions at close range:

> The engineers bring up their assault boats, but they cannot reach the river. Despite our covering fire the enemy can watch all movements out of his bunkers and hits back at us. Assault guns roll up, but even their shells can do nothing against the concrete and iron. Valuable time is lost, until finally a heavy 88 mm Flak silences the enemy.
>
> (Horne, 1990, 352)

One by one, French bunkers were knocked out or blinded by the massive smoke screen generated by the ongoing bombardment. French forward artillery observers found it very difficult to relay targets to their artillery, not least because communications had been smashed.

At around 15:00, the bombardment of the west-bank defences was shifted towards the rear to allow assault engineers to embark on a 60-yard crossing with rubber dinghies. The first waves had relatively few casualties crossing the river, but as soon as they stepped on the west bank of the Meuse, they were pinned down by machine-gun and sporadic but well-registered artillery fire. Some individual detachment leaders – such as Feldwebel Rubarth or Lieutenant Colonel Balck – took the initiative to take out those fighting positions that had prevented establishing a cable ferry or pontoon bridge. Equipped with explosive charges, they rushed from one strongpoint to the next, pushing inwards.

Anxious times followed. No heavy equipment – anti-tank guns, artillery or tanks – had made it across yet. While the west bank of the Meuse was being cleared, the Germans rushed forward bridge-building material.

Pontoon bridge crossing the river Meuse (BArch)

A recurring picture emerged on the French side. It was understood that counter-attacks had to be launched to detach the Germans from the west bank of the Meuse and to prevent any armoured support crossing. Powerful units, such as the 3rd Armoured and the 3rd Motorised Division were placed under Huntzinger's control. They should have routed any German infantry that had made it across the Meuse by now. But not one unit moved forward in this section; Grandsard (X Corps) argued that there was

> too great a facility to interpret an order than to execute it as received; too great a facility to modify under the pretext of initiative, when confronted by unchecked information.

> (Horne 1990, 365)

The wait to 'plug' the emerging gaps at Sedan, Dinant and Monthermé could not have come at a higher price for the French. On May 12th/13th, the first panzers crossed the river Meuse at Sedan; shortly after, others followed suit.

DECIDING FACTORS: REDUNDANCY, DETERMINATION, AGILITY

The French and their Allies established a largely rigid defence to be 'plugged' if in danger of being pierced. However, the Germans punched through the front line, around Sedan, just three days after they commenced their offensive. The French front line was not robust enough in the first place to stop the concentration of German effort. Second, the French were too slow to move their mobile resources to the section of the front line in question. Most of their crack divisions had already been committed to the north, where the Allies expected the Germans to focus their *Schwerpunkt*.

REDUNDANCY

The Germans made efficient use of their limited men and material. They concentrated their best divisions on the core outcome trajectory: the operational goal to cross the river Meuse and drive through the French front line, letting loose their armoured divisions in the rear of the main Allied force. A breadth of expertise and resources was focussed on succeeding in an incredibly difficult undertaking: an amphibious crossing. This endeavour was carried out with redundancy contingencies in place. Not just one but four panzer corps were tasked to cross the river Meuse in three different sectors (XV Panzer Corps Hoth, Kleist's Panzer Group with XLI Panzer Corps Reinhardt, XIX Panzer Corps Guderian and XIV Motorised Corps Wietersheim). The priority was to generate the greatest impact; being efficient in doing so was a subordinate concern.

From a French perspective, a continuous front line, up to a depth of 15 km, had been established, with some sections more fortified than others. Nevertheless, large sections of those resources were rigid, bound to become redundant and thus ineffective, once the front line had been broken at other places. The Maginot Line was predominantly manned by fortress division, not trained for open ground warfare. Weaponry installed in casemates could not be reinstalled quickly for use at other hot spots. Large swathes of the French forces were destined to become redundant if the Germans focussed their attack on a relatively narrow stretch. So when the Germans launched distraction attacks against the Maginot Line, though they pinned down a considerable number of divisions, the fortresses' protection and massive firepower became unfocussed and thus useless.

DETERMINATION

The Germans were opportunistic, imaginative and purposeful in focussing their COG at the most vulnerable point in the French defence: the area around Sedan. Such determination was, however, risky as this area also presented the greatest environmental obstacles, whether in the thickly forested staging area of the Ardennes or in the need to make multiple amphibious crossings of the rivers Semois and Meuse.

The French determination of the German COG was largely defined by focussing on the 'obvious' (see Chapter 2), and anchored expectations that the main attack would be executed in the north. In this respect, determining the COG was of critical importance (see following textbox).

CENTRE OF GRAVITY DETERMINATION

Identifying COGs[1] is one of the most significant decisions that a commander can make. The right selection will focus the campaign plan on what is decisive in delivering the end state, whereas the wrong choice will lead to effort being wasted on chasing a goal that does not necessarily lead to campaign success. The choice should be clearly justifiable with evidence to show why alternatives have been rejected. Intuition will rarely suffice. The process of identifying COGs will also expose more detail on the operating environment as the commander and staff focus their energies on considering their own and their adversaries' sources of strength.

Once COGs have been identified, analysis seeks to expose their vulnerabilities; those of the friendly force will be protected, and those of the adversaries attacked. In this way COGs represent an adversarial relationship. COG analysis will define the operational progression as objectives or decisive conditions are identified and sequenced in different courses of action. Analysis must also be done from a perspective other than one's own. One's own perspective is the obvious one, but widening the pool of analysts to encompass competitors' perspectives ('red teaming') may provide valuable alternative viewpoints. (For more information on red teaming, see DCDC's Red Teaming Guide.[2])

There may be different COGs at different levels but, if so, they should all be nested. At the strategic level, a COG is often an abstraction, like the cohesion of an alliance. At the tactical level, it is usually a capability or strength that can be affected through defined action over specified timescales. Identifying an operational-level COG depends on the context, circumstances and anticipated military activity. Even where there is no obvious single COG, a commander may still find the concept useful to ensure that he remains focussed on what is militarily critical to the desired outcome. COGs may change during the course of a campaign. Commanders must also be open to the possibility that the wrong COG may have been selected during planning. COGs should therefore be reviewed throughout a campaign as understanding evolves of the relationship between cause and effect within a conflict.

CENTRE OF GRAVITY IN THE SOUTH ATLANTIC

Argentinian forces invaded the Falkland Islands on April 2nd 1982. Britain responded rapidly by despatching a task force to retake the Islands. The Argentinian Armed Forces had 220 jet aircraft. The British Task Force had 34, all Harriers. Control of the air was vital to enable amphibious landings and provide the freedom of manoeuvre for surface forces. Initial planning showed that even after a successful reoccupation of the Islands, the Royal Navy would have to retain two aircraft carriers in the South Atlantic for several weeks, and probably longer. The only hard-surface runway in the Falklands, at Stanley, was not long enough to operate fast jet aircraft and could not easily be extended. The Royal Navy had two aircraft carriers: HMS HERMES and HMS INVINCIBLE. HMS ILLUSTRIOUS had been launched but was not yet operational. The deduction was simple: for control of the air, the Task Force could not afford to lose a carrier. That premise shaped the naval campaign. The Falklands lie 300 miles east of Argentina. Placing the two carriers east of the Falklands would keep them out of range of enemy aircraft. That had implications for the availability of air cover; the Harriers had to make relatively long transits to, and from, station. Because relatively few aircraft were available, they could only patrol for short periods. It was planned to build a forward operating base to accommodate 12 Harriers once land operations got underway. However, the loss of much of the stock of perforated steel planking on the ATLANTIC CONVEYOR limited the capacity of that base to only four aircraft. HMS ILLUSTRIOUS joined the Task Force later in the year, but only after the Falkland Islands had been retaken. Using today's planning concepts, two functioning carriers would arguably have been the Task Force COG. The Argentinians knew how important the carriers were, and repeatedly tried to find and sink them (Development Concepts and Doctrine Centre 2013, 2–71 (UK National Element)).

AGILITY

Thinking about whether the Germans were prepared to move the COG quickly enough from one area to another is hypothetical. Their first attempt to break through the front at Sedan succeeded partly because of their tactical abilities (see Chapter 4).

However, such astounding success – the front line was broken within three days of the commencement of the offensive – revealed the limitations of the Allies in moving their COG once they had committed their resources to the northern sector. Allied fixation on the north may explain their reluctance to direct their mobile reserves to Sedan. Their lack of sensitivity at a strategic and tactical level (see Chapters 2 and 4) amplified this fixation. Nevertheless, once a realisation set in that the COG pointed at the area around Sedan, Allied leadership at tactical level (see Chapter 4) was cumbersome and incredibly slow. By the time mobile forces were (re)directed to the endangered front line, the Germans had already established a bridgehead on the west bank of the river Meuse, and after a fierce but brief struggle (see Chapter 5) commanded the high grounds overlooking Sedan; the gateway to a largely undefended countryside.

TRANSLATION AND EXPLANATION: DISPERSION VERSUS CONCENTRATION

In principle, one may distinguish between the principle approach of concentration and the dispersion of resources and capabilities. In regard to the latter, dispersion refers to scattering of resources and capabilities for the purpose of being robust (see Chapter 2) enough to withstand or bounce back from any changes in the external environment. This is a rather passive, defensive stance for an organisation, providing static efficiencies; it is the stance adopted by the French in 1940.

In contrast, the Germans concentrated their resources and capabilities and focussed their attention on the vulnerabilities of their enemy as part of the *Schwerpunkt* principle. In a commercial world, such concentrated activity is best known as 'lean' (Womack and Jones 2003). The premise of lean thinking is to recognise that total time and effort can be focussed in a value-driven manner, reducing the need for 'wasteful' redundancy in an organisation. Lean thinking revolves around four key principles:

VALUE

Value is defined by the customer perspective but created by the producer. Anything that helps to realise the customer perspective is value-adding.

VALUE STREAM

The value stream encapsulates all actions to produce value and realise a value proposition; it identifies value-adding activities in an organisation.

FLOW

Lean is preoccupied with identifying bottlenecks, blockages and obstacles to the value stream. Anything is deemed 'wasteful' that does not directly contribute the value stream.

PULL

Value is only 'pulled' in accordance with customer demand – customers' needs and their required quality and cost. This contrasts with a 'push' system where the available organisational value stream defines and imposes value on the customer (Womack and Jones 2003).

The following table (see Table 3.1) provides a comparison between key properties of these two opposing concepts:

Table 3.1 Key Differences between Dispersion and Concentration

Dispersion	Concentration
Focus of attention	
Operationalising resources and capabilities in an unfocussed, dispersed manner allows the build-up of robustness throughout an organisation, providing continuous, linear defence/offence against environmental conditions. Hence, all organisational functions are developed to be 'strong' and 'effective' in withstanding and bouncing back from changes in the environment.	Concentrating one's resources is directed at critical organisational functions, necessary for the organisation to remain viable, and at focussing organisational effort solely on value. Other functions are not neglected altogether as their working order is supportive, but not essential, to the operation of those functions deemed critical.
Temporality	
In a dispersion approach, the extent of robustness expected from each function remains static, unless predicted environmental changes lead to a bolstering of their 'defences'. Capabilities and resources are incrementally improved; however, their configuration (where and how they are deployed) is relatively stable.	Resources and capabilities remain in a state of reconfiguration. They are deployed in a Pull and Flow manner, leading to different organisational configurations, with different strengths, driven by changing environmental demands.

A key factor in distinguishing between dispersion and concentration is the degree of attention on critical functions in an organisation. From a 'defensive' standpoint (see Figure 1.3), dispersing one's resources and capabilities aims to prevent any risk from destabilising the entire organisation.

From a defensive *Schwerpunkt* perspective (see Figure 3.1), only those functions that are considered critical are bolstered; hence any successful disruption – by a competitor or by environmental volatility – would end up threatening the viability of the entire organisation.

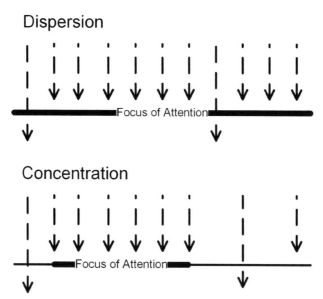

Figure 3.1 *Focus of attention*

Progressively, resources and capabilities could be targeted at the competitor's weakest point. Achieving results could relate to concentrating one's efforts on creating a competitive advantage derived from economies of scale and greater efficiency gains (e.g. by relying on lower labour costs). Alternatively, a differential advantage can be driven by patent-protected products, superior quality and a distinguishable strong brand identity.

Defensively or progressively, both operational ways of working – dispersion or concentration – are associated with distinctive benefits (see Table 3.2).

Table 3.2 Advantages of Dispersion and Concentration

Dispersion	*Concentration*
Static redundancy	Dynamic redundancy
No determination	Greater local focus
Stability	Dynamic
Wide focus	Narrow, localised focus

Where resources and capabilities are unfocussed, they can provide a continuous defence/offence against disruptions from internal and external environments. Static redundancy is established across the first line of defence/offence to back up primary resources and capabilities in case that first line of defence/offence fails. It provides stability for an organisation and a continuous buffer. This approach is beneficial in organisations that are uncertain of where their critical functions reside and thus unsure about their own vulnerabilities.

A concentrated effort is focussed and provides 'just-in-time' redundancy to enable the greatest impact in defensively withstanding unwelcome change or progressively focussing on the vulnerabilities of a competitor. Hence, instead of covering all eventualities – risks and opportunities – it provides a more dynamic COG that, depending on circumstances, may shift and adopt a different type and strength of concentration.

TOWARDS ORGANISATIONAL RESILIENCE: THE FALLACY OF PROTECTING EVERYTHING AT MINIMAL COST

Indiscriminate investment in organisation-wide robustness is a worthwhile goal. However, strengthening the entire organisation to cover all functional vulnerabilities may also reveal which of them are most crucial to the functioning of the organisation. The spread of resources and capabilities, and their permanent embedding in an organisation, waters down the robustness of critical functions by default. Once these critical functions cease to operate properly, they are likely to start a chain reaction, threatening the operation of other related work units.

Such watering down is often driven by the need to save costs across the organisation, without acknowledging where vulnerabilities lie. An example of this is the information technology (IT) meltdown of British Airways (BA) on May 27th 2017. Supposedly, the entirety of BA's data centre switched off or was switched off by the actions of a single technician. On the first day alone, 1,000 flights from London Heathrow and Gatwick were cancelled, with scenes of chaos at these airports as unsuspecting customers arrived in droves, only to realise that their flights were cancelled. The problems with the airline's IT systems, not just its operations planning but also its customer call centres and website, continued for three days.

Apart from the damage to its reputation, BA can now expect a compensation bill of up to a £150 million. The root cause of the IT crash is still being investigated:

> Willie Walsh, chief executive of IAG, BA's parent company, attributed the problem to a back-up system known as an "uninterruptible power supply"—essentially a big battery connected to the mains power — that is supposed to ensure that IT systems and data centres can continue to function even if there is a power outage.
>
> (Powley and Thomas 2017)

Regardless of whether this incident is down to human error or a mechanical fault, BA has been on a cost-cutting binge to compete with low-cost carriers. On some flights, for example, meals have been axed. Such measures may have little impact on customer satisfaction as the driving factor in the airline industry remains the ticket price. However, critical functions had also been scrutinised to cut costs even further, among them BA's data centres which have been largely outsourced to India.

In a world of digitisation, technology replaces human interaction with a customer. To ensure reliable functioning, the technological interface with the customer (e.g. booking and checking-in via the Internet) is of critical importance for an airline. However those functions are also subject to stripping of expertise and to (social) redundancy in order to reduce operational costs. In 2016, an electrical fault at the American airline Delta grounded more than 1,500 flights. It is not that airlines are unaware of their vulnerabilities. Increased competition does not appear to leave much wriggle room to increase the robustness of critical functions. It is not so much a question of if, but rather of how much redundancy can be stripped away before such vulnerabilities threaten the viability of an organisation.

LIMITATIONS IN DISPERSION

In modern times consumers' expectations have become more 'complex' and thus 'riskier'. The delivery of solutions needs to be close to perfect, and wholly reliable in terms of providing a constant state of satisfaction. For example, mobile networks need to provide a range of services. Being cut off from Internet access, for example, has already generated a range of lawsuits against mobile operators. Customer tolerance of failure is decreasing quickly.

It is no surprise that organisations try to 'manage everything', to switch to a defensive mode, to protect every function that is customer facing and to increase their operational reliability across the entire range of their activity. Everyone in an organisation becomes more preoccupied with managing their own risk, and everyone assumes his or her function is critical to the survival of the organisation.

Such indiscriminate, unfocussed investment, useful as it might seem for addressing any eventuality, tends to be undermined by an indiscriminate, unfocussed pursuit of cost-cutting. Paradoxically, with the absence of failure, organisations such as BA go on a cost-cutting binge, undermining the very functions that operated reliably in the past. Being noncritical or complacent about past achievements, it can become easy to question whether a service or product can be provided equally dependably, but at a lower cost.

As a result, it is folly to think that one can manage everything and provide a linear defence. Increasingly, it is equally nonsensical to bolster functions in an organisation that are not customer facing or that provide little or no direct or indirect value to a customer. Organisations tend to thin out their operational robustness indiscriminately or allow their resources and capabilities to be eroded and depleted (see following textbox), until disaster strikes.

CHAPTER THREE: OPERATIONAL RESILIENCE

LIMITATIONS IN AGILITY

Lack of good sense becomes apparent in the belief that, even after pockets of failure have started to disrupt operations, it will still be possible to divert resources and capabilities to 'plug' *(La colmatage)* the gap and prevent the situation from cascading into a disaster. As has already been said, the increased complexity of modern solutions and operations does not allow much time to contain the problem. As happened in the BA data centre, the problem – supposedly of an external employee switching off the power supply – led to an immediate shutdown of the entire subsystem; it took three days to bring it back to full working order.

In order to move resources and capabilities to where they are needed, defensively and progressively, they need to be dynamic in an operational sense (for the strategic importance of dynamic capabilities, see Chapter 2): they must be able to operate in different contexts, providing a wide range of expertise that can be quickly deployed wherever needed.

Many organisations, though, turn their resources and capabilities into static lines of defence/offence that are defined for a single purpose, 'routinised' to operate in a single context. This has the advantage of deploying expertise efficiently, and in a way that is focussed. However, the resulting rigid focus, although efficient and stable, cannot be moved quickly enough to enable its application in another context. In the case of the IT meltdown at BA, the organisation could only – in a somewhat helpless manner – watch the crisis unfold and hope that their outsourced services would be back to normal as soon as possible. BA's own staff (those not already outsourced) simply did not have expertise in running data centres, nor did they have the authority or time to support those outsourced services which are now critical to the viability of an entire airline. They resembled the French fortress soldiers, hunkering down in rigid fortifications, their expertise in defending a casemate or bunker of little value in the open field. They were bound to watch from the distance, forced to remain inactive as the Germans bypassed them.

LEAN INSTEAD OF MEAN

The concept of Lean is not to be mistaken for a head count or an attempt to address cost-cutting pressures by indiscriminately reducing resources and capabilities. It is indeed a focussed effort to distinguish between costs associated with waste, and with value. Value is, as mentioned before, anything in the value stream of an organisation that helps to realise the customer perspective. Hence, costs that deliver value to customers need to be ring-fenced, maintained and enhanced. Costs that are incurred but do not contribute to the creation of value, are considered to be waste, and need to be scrutinised. These may include wasted inventory due to overproduction, wasted movement or wasted time because of unnecessary approval procedures or replication of procedures or because of bottlenecks and potential error spots.

However, although some costs do not directly add value, they may be critical in supporting (e.g. as back office functions) and enabling customer facing value production. It may seem prudent, in the light of cost cutting pressures, to scrutinise back office functions, such as running a data centre for an airline. But, if coupled with essential value-adding operations, indirect value-adding functions need also to be strengthened and made more robust so that they can bounce back from adversity; or develop their capabilities to provide a competitive advantage.

REFOCUSSING INSTEAD OF RESTRUCTURING

Enhancing the flow of value-adding activities also goes hand in hand with being able to refocus the COG of activities if necessary. The Pull concept refers to refocussing the organisation's attention to what, when and where value needs to be created. All too often, Lean is seen as an excuse to restructure, an exercise in moving resources and capabilities around, with the sole purpose of combining and/or displacing resources and capabilities.

From a Lean perspective though, resources and capabilities need to be reconfigured and restructured to address the Pull factor in the value stream. Likewise in 1940, resources and capabilities were reconfigured to Panzer Group Kleist, in order to have the biggest impact where it was needed. The main purpose was to change the work itself, for a limited period of time, to produce the maximum value progressively, quickly bringing a competitor to its knees. Such Pull does not solely require an organisational ability to dynamically reconfigure resources and capabilities. The COG itself also has to be 'powerful' enough to provide robustness and/or have a disruptive effect on a competitor (see following textbox).

BATTLE OF THE BULGE

On June 6th 1944, the Allies landed in Normandy, France, and opened a third front to be distinguished from the Russian and Italian fronts. It only took two months for the Allies to reach the outskirts of the Third Reich, an impressive feat given the initial delays and losses in the *Bocage* country (the Normandy hedgerows). September 1944 though, saw the disastrous campaign – Operation Market Garden – that failed to capture bridges over the river Rhine at Arnhem (Holland). As a result, the Allies were forced to divert their forces westwards, towards Aachen and Cologne, to open up a corridor to the Ruhr valley, the industrial heart of Germany.

In December 1944, a German offensive in the west – Operation *Wacht am Rhein* – was envisaged. Intended to replicate the *Schwerpunkt* principle as in May 1940, a force of seven panzer and thirteen infantry divisions (with two panzer and seven infantry divisions in reserve) were to push through the American lines south of Liège, cross the river Meuse, and drive towards the deep-water port of Antwerp. The intention was to split the British and Canadian 21st Army Group and the US 9th

Army, and lay the grounds for another Dunkirk like rout of the Allied forces, followed by peace negotiation with the west.

The battering ram consisted of four *Kampfgruppen* (battle groups), outfitted with the most advanced equipment that Germany could muster at that time. Among them were probably the best medium tank of the Second World War (WWII): the PzKpfW V, better known as the Panther, as well as the Tiger II, also christened by the Allies King Tiger, the heaviest production tank, weighing in at 70t. The most powerful battle group was the Kampfgruppe Peiper, led by the notorious *Waffen-SS* officer Colonel Joachim Peiper. Its objective was to get to the Meuse, through a narrow corridor of around 50 km wide, through the thickly wooded terrain of the Ardennes and its single-track roads and hairpin turns; this was unsuitable terrain for tanks that had grown considerably in weight and size since 1940.

'H'-hour was set for December 16th 1944. Operation *Bodenplatte* – the destruction of the Allied air forces on the ground – and *Stoesser* – a parachute drop near Malmédy, achieved little success. The artillery and rocket barrage that preceded the major assault by the four battle groups was equally in effective.

Peiper's advance was quickly reduced to walking pace as mines and dependence on a single road through thickly forested pinewoods took their toll on the forward-most units. By the time they moved off from the town of Büllingen on December 17th – having taken a score of American prisoners – the weather had cleared, and P47 Thunderbolts rained down on slow-moving German columns, unopposed by the German Air Force.

In the afternoon of December 17th, at around 13:30, the German advance columns encountered an American detachment largely consisting of battery maintenance trucks and ambulances. After the first vehicles were destroyed by elements of the 7th SS Panzer Company, the remainder surrendered and at around 14:00, 113 US soldiers were assembled in a field just south of Malmédy. For reasons that remain unknown, German soldiers of the battle group Peiper opened fire and massacred 84 American prisoners of war.[3]

The battle group soon proceeded further to the west, but constant harassing fire from American defenders forced the battle group to stop – delays they could not afford:

> When our advance more or less came to a halt at the crossroads I passed Peiper's order, he was in the SPW [armoured personnel carrier] right behind me, on to Sternbeck. He was to take Ligneuville immediately, to secure the bridge which was strategically important to us and at the western edge of the village he was to wait for further instructions. I also told him that an HQ of considerable rank was possibly in the town. The other units were instructed to advance to Ligneuville without delay. We knew that Spitze with its two tanks and few SPWs was very weak. As we had no other armoured vehicles immediately available, my Panther and behind me Colonel Peiper in his SPW followed Spitze as fast as we could. To start off with I did not notice any fighting and therefore wanted to cross the bridge. On the bend before the bridge I was shot up from behind. My Panther went up in flames. We got out of the tank under machine gun and rifle fire coming from nearby houses.
>
> (Reynolds 1995, 99)

The Americans – thinly spread out in this area – could only retreat, and carry out rearguard actions to slow down the German advance and establish a more substantive defence in the area of Stavelot and Stoumont (Belgium):

> Around 15:00 on 19th December we could hear German tanks ahead of us coming down the road towards our position ... we were dug in on the curve in the road with our tank support and waited. When the Panther tanks came round the curve in sight of us our tanks cut loose at them and ... the shells hit the cobblestone road and ricocheted up under the belly of the tanks where their armour was thin and exploded the tanks. Our young and inexperienced tank crews fired four shells and knocked out three Panther tanks.
>
> (Reynolds 1995, 149)

On December 21st, it dawned on Peiper that his position was precarious. His tanks were running low on fuel, and American fuel storages had either not been captured or had been destroyed. His stock of ammunition did not fare much better. To make matters worse, the pressure along his flanks was increasing, but he could not spare men and material to protect those flanks if he wanted to keep pushing westwards towards the Meuse.

By Friday, December 22nd 1944, Peiper's Kampfgruppe reached the most western tip of the salient – halfway to their planned objective, the river Meuse – at a picturesque village called La Gleize, in the heart of the Ardennes Forest.

Before an attack on a city or village, the Americans tended to 'soften' up their objective with a massive artillery barrage. Over the next few days, the American 30th Division alone spent around 58,000 shells. La Gleize was turned to rubble. Those who took shelter in the church recounted,

> Two GIs [prisoners] and some Germans have built a fire for warmth using furniture as firewood. The whole time debris

is falling from the walls and arches around them ... a shell tears open the wall behind the choir, another demolishes the corner walls above the crypt and undermines the supports of the church tower. The smell of powder burns their throats as they huddle against one another near the choir stall...

(Reynolds 1995, 225)

The attacks on La Gleize by the Americans were initially repulsed due to the clever positioning of tanks and tank destroyers, and yet Peiper's force was surrounded, critically short of fuel and ammunition. During the night to December 24th, Peiper's forces started slipping through the American positions, leaving most of their heavy equipment – among them three Tiger IIs and thirteen PzKpfW Vs (Panthers) – behind.

The eastward march of the exhausted men of the Kampfgruppe Peiper through American lines saw the beginning of the end of the Battle of the Bulge. The battle would continue until January 25th, but the events at La Gleize had sealed the fate of Germany's attempt to turn the tide in the west.

In May 1940, the Germans had pushed through the thickly forested area of the Ardennes to breach the Allied defences around Sedan. They covered 200 km in the first 36 hours alone. In contrast, in December 1944, the Germans only managed to create a 'bulge' that ranged from Hallschlag (Germany) to La Gleize (Belgium), a mere 80 km in eight days. Environmental conditions played a considerable role in slowing the German advance – too few roads, often single-track roads, unsuitable in particular for heavy tanks, exceeding 60ts; the lack of fuel and the absence of the German Luftwaffe providing effective ground support further hampering necessary agility in movement. On many occasions, the Germans could only advance under cover of darkness.

> The Allies performed better than four years earlier. The slow, predictable advance of the Germans offered ample opportunity to establish a moving defence. Initially, rear-guard actions covered the retreat of those front-line units that felt the brunt of the German attack. Nevertheless, in the rear, new lines of defence were established; an opportunity the defenders in 1940 had not been given.
>
> As a result, the German advance lacked the support and thus the 'punch' to disorganise an enemy. Over the years, the *Wehrmacht* suffered terrible losses on all fronts. In December 1944, the *Wehrmacht*, and *Waffen-SS* were shadows of their old selves. In addition, their enemies had enhanced their capabilities. The defenders could bolster their defences to slow down, halt, and ultimately repulse the last German offensive in the west with ease. In this respect, the German COG had too little disruptive effect.
>
> A progressive COG requires imagination, a focus on the weakest point of an enemy. However, it also requires disruptive power to prevent an enemy from deploying defensive capabilities. If the *Schwerpunkt* principle breaks down and the concentration of efforts cannot be resumed or quickly changed to another 'focal point' (Plan B), an enemy can either circumvent his opponent's COG and attack his flanks or just wait until the impact of the COG is absorbed.

OUTLOOK

After WWI, the French, and to some degree their Allies, expanded their military forces, although this was more a matter of quantity than of quality. As a predominantly citizen army, their fighting ability was limited. Men and material were also dispersed along the border to Germany, being tied down in the Maginot Line and to a lesser extent along the Dutch and Belgium border fortifications. During the interwar years and during the eight-month period of the Phoney War, little training and few exercises were carried out to widen their response repertoire. From the Allies' perspective, the COG was, and had to be, in the north. In any case, once hostilities commenced in May 1940 the centre was too thin to even slow down a German advance long enough until reinforcements could bolster defences. Second, the Allied COG could not be moved from the north to the centre and reinforcements failed to materialise on time to prevent the Germans from crossing the Meuse.

The Allies applied an operational way of working that focussed predominantly on dispersion of effort, and a limited, ill-defined use of COG. In essence, their *Schwerpunkt* indeed inflicted serious losses on the Germans, but even in the north, their COG was not powerful enough to halt the German advance. It is all hypothetical, but more power (combining more forces), and more agility (changing the COG from the north to the south) might have been just enough to break through the German front line and threaten the German heartland. Both parties would then have switched to a cat-and-mouse game, progressively exploiting each other's weakness. That, though, required dynamic resources and capabilities. The Allies tied down most of theirs in a defensive stance.

In the commercial world, a dispersion of resources and capabilities seems straightforward – for the protection of an organisation in all eventualities or for the progressive development of a wide-ranging *Schwerpunkt*. However, resources and capabilities are scarce and are subject to permanent cost-cutting pressures (at times through outsourcing). To indiscriminately thin out resources and capabilities can generate the required cost-savings – until a value-adding function breaks. British Airways seemed to believe that a data centre was not its highest priority value-adding function. But once that went into meltdown, the customers aired their voices. It is still to be seen whether this breach in their own front line will lead to permanent damage to the company's reputation.

Reflection

To what extent does your work unit adhere to Dispersion or Concentration of resources and capabilities? For each item, select one box only that best reflects your conclusion.

		Neutral			
We try to prepare ourselves for all eventualities	○	○	○	○	○	We concentrate our efforts on our competitors' vulnerabilities
We indiscriminately look for efficiency gains	○	○	○	○	○	Only non-value adding functions are subject to cost-cutting
We tend to restructure our resources and capabilities for efficiency gains	○	○	○	○	○	We reconfigure our resources and capabilities for pull-gains

		Neutral			
Our resources and capabilities are largely static	○	○	○	○	○	Our resources and capabilities are largely dynamic
Our centre of gravity of operations is unknown and thus uncommitted to	○	○	○	○	○	Our centre of gravity of operations is known and committed to
We do not distinguish between costs associated with waste and with value	○	○	○	○	○	We discriminate between costs associated with waste and with value

Scoring: If your answers tend to the left, you are pursuing a more dispersionary approach. If your answers are more on the right, the concept of concentration (Lean) is paramount in your ways of operating.

NOTES

1 The term *Schwerpunkt* is most often translated into Centre of Gravity (COG). The definition has gone through multiple iterations. Contemporary expressions combine the notion of concentrated effort but directed at critical vulnerabilities of the enemy.
2 www.gov.uk/government/uploads/system/uploads/attachment_data/file/142533/20130301_red_teaming_ed2.pdf.
3 The Malmédy massacre in 1944 was one among many during WWII, but received considerable attention during post-war trials. Seventy members belonging to or associated with Peiper's battle group were tried, and 43 death sentences were pronounced, none of which was actually carried out. All were converted into lengthy prison sentences.

REFERENCES

BArch. "Bild 141-1107." Koblenz: Bundesarchiv.
———. "Bild 146-1971-088-63." Koblenz: Bundesarchiv.
———. "Bild 146-1978-062-24." Koblenz: Bundesarchiv.
Baudouin, P. 1948. *The Private Diaries of Paul Baudouin*. London: Eyre & Spottiswoode.
Benoist-Méchin, J. 1956. *Sixty Days That Shook the World – The Fall of France: 1940*. New York: Putman.
De Jomini, A. H. 2008. *The Art of War*. Kingston, ON: Legacy Books Press.
Development Concepts and Doctrine Centre. 2013. "Allied Joint Doctrine for Operational-Level Planning (+UK National Elements)."
Dildy, D. 2014. *Fall Gelb 1940 (1): Panzer Breakthrough in the West*. Oxford: Osprey Publishing.
Horne, A. 1990. *To Lose a Battle: France 1940*. London: Penguin Books.
IIe Armée. "Ordre Général D'opérations No. 17."
Powley, T. and N. Thomas. 2017. "BA's Computer Meltdown: How Did It Happen?" *Financial Times*. www.ft.com/content/0a37047c-460f-11e7-8d27-59b4dd6296b8?mhq5j=e1

Reynolds, M. 1995. *The Devil's Adjutant: Jochen Peiper, Panzer Leader*. Staplehurst: Spellmount Limited.
Tzu, S. 2008. *The Art of War*. London: Penguin Books.
Von Clausewitz, C. 2011. *On War*. New York: Madison Park.
Womack, J., and D. Jones. 2003. *Lean Thinking: Banish Waste and Create Wealth in Your Corporation*. New York: Free Press.

CHAPTER FOUR
Tactical resilience

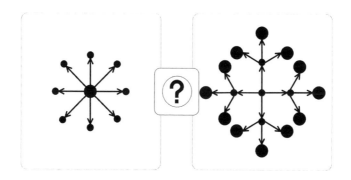

*Discipline troops
Before they are loyal,
And they will be
Refractory
And hard to put to good use.
Let loyal troops
Go undisciplined,
And they will be altogether
Useless
Command them
With civility; Rally them
With martial discipline,
And you will win their
Confidence.*

(Tzu 2008, 61)

CONTENTS

The story: May 10th–May 11th 1940	118
Auftragstaktik *versus* La Bataille Conduit	120
Allied Joint Doctrine – mission command	121
The challenge: capturing Fort d'Ében-Émael	124
Deciding factors: autonomy and sensitivity	130
Von Clausewitz: information in war	134
Translation and explanation: centralisation versus decentralisation	135
Towards organisational resilience: the fallacy of centralisation	138
Communicating intent	143
Battle of Leyte Gulf	144
Doctrinal principles in operations planning	150
Outlook	151
References	154

This chapter looks at the tactical level of organisational resilience. Tactical decisions are executed at lower levels of management:

- These decisions are related to the working of employees in an organisation
- These decisions relate to the day-to-day functioning of the organisation
- They are taken according to strategic and operational circumstances.

THE STORY: MAY 10TH–MAY 11TH 1940

The experience of the First World War (WWI) led the Allies to believe that the concentration of any German attack would occur through a narrow corridor between Maastricht and Liège. This corridor would have provided the Germans with easy access to northern France if it was not for the river Meuse and the Albert Canal (completed in 1939), which posed a natural defensive barrier. This barrier was augmented by a range of forts, defining the *Position Fortifiée de Liège I* – a truly formidable challenge for the Germans to overcome.

At first light on May 10th, the Germans launched a massive air assault against Belgian and Dutch airfields. They met little resistance and destroyed the meagre air forces on the ground. Behind this protective curtain of air cover, airborne troops were dropped on crossings at Rotterdam, Dordrecht and Moerdijk to seize bridges before they could be destroyed by sappers. A dedicated battalion of airborne troops landed in the Maastricht area to seize those bridges over the Meuse and Albert Canal. These gains, however, would be in vain if a key position in the defence around Liège was not taken out of action: Fort d'Ében-Émael.

The Albert Canal. On the left side of the canal, a casemate – Canal Sud (Obj. 38) of Fort d'Ében-Émael is visible (BArch)

Fort d'Ében-Émael (see Map 4.1) is located along the Albert Canal at a strategically important junction where it runs through a deep cutting at the German, Belgian and Dutch borders. It was the most heavily armed fort in the world in the 1940s, with multiple 60 mm, 75 mm and 120 mm guns, providing fire cover up to 17.5 km. Towering over the Albert Canal – 900 m long and 700 m wide – it constituted a network of overground machine-gun and artillery casemates and blockhouses, massive anti-tank ditches, and infantry defences. The fort provided a 360-degree defence and worked jointly with the surrounding forts (*Position Fortifiée de Liège* I: Fort d'Aubin-Neufchâteau, Fort de Battice and Fort de Tancrémont, Aubin-Neufchâteau and Fort d'Ében-Émael) in ensuring supporting fire. Colonel Albert Torreele, a Belgian Officer, commented upon visiting the fort in 1938:

> An officer of the garrison of the fort led us to many of the outer defences and showed what each was intended for. We went to the walls and looked over the countless rows of barbed wire. He led us to the only door on the surface set deep in concrete. It appeared like the heavy steel door of a bank vault. From here [Cupola Nord] infantry in reserve would issue to repel any enemy fortunate enough to get by the tough ground defences.
>
> He took us deep into the interior and we trudged many miles to the end of the tunnel, visiting the crews and the guns of the emplacements we had seen on the surface. Crews gave us their missions and detailed characteristics of their guns. All was very professional. Later, we assembled in the command post. The commandant gave a detailed account of how he proposed to defend the fort in the event of an attack. I got the impression of tremendous power and first-rate efficiency. I was convinced nothing could happen!
>
> (Dunstan 2005, 32)

AUFTRAGSTAKTIK VERSUS *LA BATAILLE CONDUIT*

Two fundamental tactical concepts clashed in these fateful beginnings of the campaign in the west: *Auftragstaktik* (Mission-Oriented Tactics) and *La Bataille Conduit* (Methodical Battle). *Auftragstaktik* is an evolutionary concept that found its origin in the Prussian (1866) and Franco-Prussian (1870–1871) wars. Commanders of the Prussian army noticed that, given increasing battlefield complexity and uncertainty, they found it challenging trying to exercise control over their forces. The Prussian Army asked themselves how to prepare better for battles and campaigns characterised by the fog of war.

In 1888, new drill regulations stipulated that commanders should provide subordinates with an intent – *what* was to be accomplished and *why* – while equipping them with the autonomy to act – to determine by themselves *how* to do it. This implies that decision-making was less centralised. Subordinate leaders (such as non-commissioned officers), being close to the problem, were encouraged to show initiative in action, which was related to a defined Intent. If commanders were unable to make sound decisions – because they were remote to the situation or perhaps incapacitated – subordinate leaders could continue their mission or even adapt the intent to an evolving situation.

Nevertheless, the concept of mission-oriented tactics did not absolve the commander from control over these empowered subordinate leaders. Commanders commonly placed themselves at the front line, being sensitive to volatility on the ground. They would also intervene if they believed that their subordinate leaders were making clearly incorrect decisions.

ALLIED JOINT DOCTRINE – MISSION COMMAND

A commander's responsibility for mission accomplishment is total, but delegation of authority to subordinates and their responsibility to act in support of the higher commander's intentions are included in the principle of decentralisation. Through mission command, commanders generate the freedom of action for subordinates to act purposefully when unforeseen developments arise and to exploit favourable opportunities. Mission command encourages the use of initiative and promotes timely decision-making. Commanders who delegate authority to subordinate commanders need to state clearly their intentions, freedoms and constraints; designate the objectives to be achieved; and provide them with sufficient forces, resources and authority to accomplish their assigned tasks. Although the emphasis given to a mission command style in the doctrine and practice of different services and nations may differ, commanders and their staffs should employ the principle of mission command. Successful mission command has the following prerequisites:

(a) Commanders and staffs should concern themselves primarily with joint operational matters, taking account of component issues only as necessary.

(b) The subordinate commander must understand fully the operational commander's intentions and what he is required to achieve, and be free to exercise initiatives based on that understanding, within a minimal level of control imposed from the higher level of command.

(c) There should be an active involvement in the doctrine development process by the nations and a common understanding of the operational doctrine governing the employment of forces. The latter is achieved through education, training and exercises.

(d) Trust (total confidence in the integrity, ability and good character of another) is one of the most important ingredients in building strong teams. Trust expands the commander's options and enhances flexibility, agility and the freedom to take initiative when conditions warrant. Trust is based on the mutual confidence that results from the demonstrated competence of each member of the team. The opportunity to observe each member's capabilities in training builds trust and confidence in a Joint Force.

In stating his intent, the Commander provides subordinates with the freedom to operate within the broader context of the mission, rather than within the restrictions of a particular CONOPS [concept of operations] or scheme of manoeuvre. The Commander's intent provides subordinates with the flexibility to adapt their actions to achieve success. By focusing on the end-state rather than sequential events, it allows commanders to operate with increased speed and confidence in decision-making. This allows subordinate forces, and hence the whole force, to operate faster, and with greater agility, than the adversary, which keeps him off-balance and unable to respond coherently. This end-state focus supports the initiative of Commanders at all levels by freeing them to focus on the desired results, even when the CONOPS should be adapted to changing events, when communications are disrupted, or additional guidance or directives are lacking. The Commander's intent also provides subordinates with the platform to develop a vision of their end-state, as it supports that of the force as a whole.

Without unity of effort and the necessary trust to plan and execute a joint and multinational campaign or major operation, there can be little chance of success. Shared operational understanding of the problem and environment couples with a mutual understanding of strengths and weaknesses, provides the foundation of cooperation and trust, which is vital in the planning and successful execution of joint and multinational operations. This should stem from the highest levels. Mutual understanding also rests on a common application of joint doctrine. Familiarity with the procedures of each service and nation is best achieved through joint and multinational training. A common approach should be inherent in thought and practice; joint and multinational training should be undertaken whenever possible, but it is particularly important, should time be available, prior to any operation. The greater the degree of standardization (in terms of both equipment and doctrine), the better the prospects are for fruitful cooperation, mutual understanding, and ultimately, for success.

(North Atlantic Treaty Organization and NATO Standardization Agency (NSA) 2010, 6–3)

Whereas mission-oriented tactics are more of an art of command, methodical battle is a more traditional – more widespread pre-1940 – 'scientific' approach to complexity and uncertainty. It represents a centralised attempt to make precise and unambiguous decisions in a virtually 'perfect' linear environment. In principle, detailed plans are conceived, and subordinate ranks receive detailed orders, defining the *what* as well the *how*. Initiative to adapt the *how* because the *why* has changed is considered a source of error and thus discouraged; it is seen as a way of potentially undermining a well-developed plan.

THE CHALLENGE: CAPTURING FORT D'ÉBEN-ÉMAEL

A frontal assault by armour and infantry on the bridges across the Meuse and the Albert Canal, and on the forts covering these bridges, was likely to lead to a prolonged stand-off that the Germans knew they could not win. Deployment of airborne troops was therefore envisaged, delivering a surprise factor expected to paralyse the defender long enough to enable reinforcements to be brought in to exploit breaches in the Meuse front.

In October 1939, Kurt Student received the orders to prepare an airborne raid on Fort d'Ében-Émael and the Meuse/Albert Canal bridges. At his disposal were parts of an airborne regiment – *1. Fallschirmjäger-Kompanie des Fallschirmjäger-Regiments 1, Fallschirmjäger Pionierzug* – as well as supporting units from the *Luftwaffe*.

The paratroopers were not supposed to parachute into their operating area but to be landed on top of the fort, with the help of gliders. Their extensive training, under the supervision of Hauptmann Koch, included the use of hollow charges (*Hohlladung*) these were explosive charges with a cavity which focussed the blast into a small area suitable for penetrating armoured casemates. The physical

CHAPTER FOUR: TACTICAL RESILIENCE

training for this undertaking was unrelenting, and even glider pilots, hand selected, were trained in assaulting casemates and bunkers of various types.

The German assault force was split into units, each with its own objective. The *Sturmgruppe Granit* (assault group Granite) was allocated the capture of Fort d'Ében-Émael, with *Sturmgruppe Beton* (Concrete), *Eisen* (Iron) and *Stahl* (Steel) given the objective of taking intact the bridges at Vroenhoeven, Kanne and Veldwezelt. *Sturmgruppe Granit* was led by Oberleutnant Witzig and was composed of two officers and 84 men – a tiny force taking on the most powerful fort in the world.

The Belgian garrison of Fort d'Ében-Émael could call upon 985 men under the leadership of Major Jottrand. Their fragmentation under different units led to an extraordinary complexity in decision-making. For example, the crew of Maastricht 1 and 2 (see Map 4.1) belonged to the *18e Régiment d'Infantrie de Ligne*, yet Visé 1 was manned by *2e Grenadiers Régiment* and Visé 2 by *Secteur Meuse-Aval*.

Being summoned to do duty in a fort was not seen as a high point of anybody's career. Most defensive preparation for an assault on Fort d'Ében-Émael involved guard duty or rather mundane tasks, such as the cleaning of anti-tank ditches or clearing fields of fire. There was little effort to deliver inter-unit training or to rehearse the ability of the fort to counter an attack from the east, let alone one from the air.

At 03:30 on May 10th 1940, a fleet of *Junkers* JU52 towing gliders started from separate airfields and tried to rendezvous within the borders of Germany. To form a tight formation was by no means an easy task:

> Sometime later our aircraft and gliders rendezvoused with the 11 gliders of the Iron section which had taken off from the Cologne-Butzweilerhof airfield. And it was then that an unforeseen and wholly unanticipated accident threatened the hitherto smooth running organisation of the operation. Manoeuvring into a compact air formation the machine pulling the glider with *Oberleutnant* Witzig aboard flew across the path of one of the other aircraft, and Witzig's pilot had to bank sharply to avoid his tow rope getting

entangled with that of the second glider. Unfortunately, the extra stress occasioned by this evasive manoeuvre resulted in the tow rope snapping and Witzig's glider was no longer under tow. Turning back, the pilot was just able to get his glider back across the Rhine before landing. But the assault section had lost its commander.

(Kuhn 1978, 33)

The assault on Fort d'Ében-Émael commenced without their nominated leader Witzig, crossing the border to Belgium.

At around 06:45, the first gliders were released, and in downward circles they made their way to the top of the fort. The Belgian defenders noticed the towing aircrafts but were unperturbed as they were making their way back to Germany. Not much later, though, they were puzzled about some sort of airplanes that appeared to want to land on top of them. Some defenders present on the top of Fort d'Ében-Émael opened fire. Their obsolete weaponry did pin down the landed attackers for a brief time; however most mobile anti-aircraft weapons positioned on the surface of the fort remained silent or were put out of action quickly.

The alarm in the fort was raised, although it was the wrong one. The alarm indicated an assault from the surrounding countryside. Precious minutes were lost when crew members rushed to their observation cupolas and the fighting positions that covered the top of the fort. They noticed in awe more people disembarking from gliders and saw them running towards their fortified position with 'strange' boxes. However, most casemates did not fire a single shot. Some crews had not occupied their positions yet; others had not received orders to open fire.

In quick succession, the Germans placed these boxes – shaped charges – on specific weak points of the firing positions posing a threat to the landed forces. Coupole Nord and Mi-Sud and Mi-Nord were knocked out. At Maastricht 1, Oberjäger Arendt placed a 12.5 kg shaped charge into the embrasure of the left-hand 75mm gun. The explosion of this smaller hollow charge – the larger is 50 kg – blew the gun, with its gun carriage, into the casemate. Hand grenades and small arms fire followed, and Maastricht 1 was also out of action.

CHAPTER FOUR: TACTICAL RESILIENCE

The effect of a hollow charge on Mi-Nord and Eben 2 (Obj 19) (BArch)

Between 07:30 and 08:00 – at a time when most observation cupolas and fighting casemates had already been knocked out – the Belgian defenders ordered the surrounding forts to shell the surface of Fort d'Ében-Émael. Heavy artillery rained down fire. Nevertheless, at that stage most Germans had taken shelter in already breached casemates. In its new improvised headquarters in Mi-Nord, *Oberfeldwebel* (Sergeant) Wenzel – *Oberleutnant* (Lieutenant) Witzig had not reached the fort yet – took over command and radioed back, *"Target reached. Everything in order"* (McNab 2013, 51).

But not everything was 'in order'. The outer periphery of the fort remained in Belgian hands, and Coupola 120 – with its double-barrelled 120 mm guns – had not yet been silenced because it had been allocated to a German unit that had not made it to the fort. Its commander – Maréchal de logis Cremers – was keenly aware of the Germans milling around his cupola. The initial attempt to knock out his position with demolition charges failed, giving Cremers an opportunity to at least disrupt the German attempts to cross the river Meuse. However, like so many other occupants of Fort d'Ében-Émael, he would not receive an order to open fire until another hollow charge finally destroyed the turning mechanism of the most potent long-range weapon (range of 17.5 km) of Fort d'Ében-Émael.

Jottrand started launching a range of counter-attacks, though they were minor in size and unprepared. His personnel were mostly artillery staff, lacking the required infantry training. Reinforcements from the surrounding garrisons arrived, but they were woefully unfamiliar with the environment. Meanwhile, Luftwaffe attacks on the periphery of the fort contributed to the chaos inside and took their toll on morale. A serious counter-attack to sweep the Germans from the surface of the fort never materialised.

At 08:30, Wenzel's time to be in command of the operation came to an end:

> It was around 08:30 when a lone glider flew over the fort and landed not very far away from the northern rampart. In it was *Oberleutnant* Witzig and Trupp 11, who had been forced to land in a meadow beside the Rhine when the tow rope broke shortly after take-off. Witzig was quickly briefed by Oberfeldwebel Wenzel and he assumed command of the assault group.
>
> (Dunstan 2005, 56)

The German troops at Fort d'Ében-Émael were in dire need of reinforcements. These could only come from the east, where the airborne troop Eisen failed to prevent the vital bridge at Kanne from being blown up by Belgian sappers. The other two bridges, at Veldwezelt and Vroenhoeven, were contested viciously, but the initial airborne raid led to most of the bunkers covering the bridges being destroyed. The Belgians launched several counter-attacks to try to recapture the bridges from the Germans, but, with the help of the *Luftwaffe*, these attacks could be repulsed. Two bridges remained intact. Reinforcements began heading towards the beleaguered paratroopers at Fort d'Ében-Émael.

The night was tense for both attackers and defenders. The Germans forces had not slept since 02:00 the previous night, and, despite some supply drops, they were running out of ammunition. They kept up the pressure on the fort, pushing into the interior, blowing their way through steel doors and sandbag barriers. Nevertheless, stiff resistance by the Belgian defenders did not allow them to proceed into the heart of the fort.

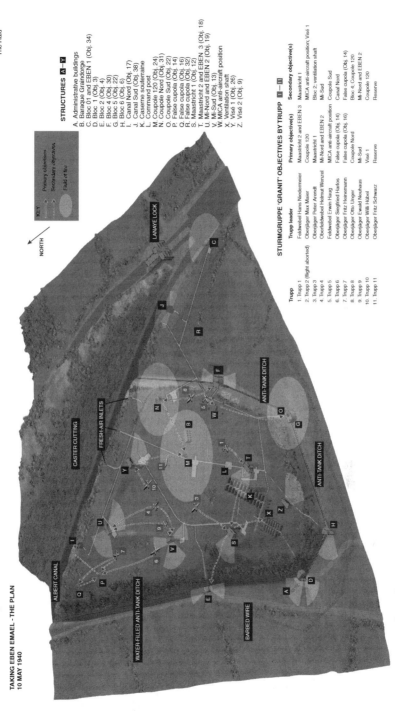

Map 4.1 *Taking Eben-Emael – The Plan* (McNab 2013, 45–6)

The morning of May 11th saw some sporadic fire from the fort, mostly from the still intact Coupole Sud and Canal Nord. Having no electricity, running low on ammunition, being virtually surrounded by newly arrived German reinforcements and with little hope of launching a coordinated major counter-attack, a Belgian bugler sounded the call of surrender at 12:15 on May 11th. The fall of Belgium's most powerful fortification opened a breach in the northern front for the Germans.

DECIDING FACTORS: AUTONOMY AND SENSITIVITY

What made the difference in outcome in capturing a massive fort at a tactical level? The Germans were swift in partially 'blinding' the fort, despite being stripped of their nominated leader for some time during the first day of the assault. The French occupants were sluggish in interpreting the danger they faced. An assault from the air by gliders was not something they expected.

A Wehrmacht soldier in front of the captured Fort d'Ében-Émael. In the background one can see Bloc 6 (Obj. 6) (BArch)

CHAPTER FOUR: TACTICAL RESILIENCE

AUTONOMY

From the outset, German leaders of each of the assault groups were given considerable leeway to act. If this leeway could not be enacted by leaders, for whatever reason, subordinates stepped into the breach and assumed authority. In the case of the capture of Fort d'Ében-Émael, the nominated commander of the operation – Oberleutnant Witzig – did not arrive on the scene until most of the defences were silenced. However, his subordinate leaders took the initiative in continuing the operation and subduing the fort's defences. Subordinates quickly showed initiative, decisiveness and persistence in accomplishing their given intent.

This degree of autonomy was exercised by many commanders in the field. For example, General Heinz Guderian later reflected,

> During the French campaign, I never received any further orders as to what I was to do once the bridgehead over the Meuse was captured. All of my decisions, until I reached the Atlantic seaboard at Abbeville, were taken by me alone.

(Guderian 2000, 251)

From a French perspective, decision power did not migrate – fast enough – to those leaders who were most aware of the situation. Commanders of the fighting positions at Fort d'Ében-Émael were not allowed to assume authority unless they received an order, despite their understanding that their fort was being attacked. These orders would not have come from Major Jottrand, but from their own unit commander. These obscure levels of authority, combined with the lack of sensitivity and initiative at the front line, produced a peculiar scenario. Coupola 120, the most powerful artillery position, was left unmolested by the Germans for a considerable time. The commander was keenly aware of the intentions of the German assault; yet never received an order to open fire from a higher authority. The gun was finally disabled by German shaped charges.

It is no surprise that in the first crucial days of the campaign, action on the French side was slow. The sluggishness in responding to the rapidly changing environment was amplified by the lack of means to communicate. Wired relay of information broke down quickly due to the incessant artillery fire of the Germans. As a result, pigeons were used. Once information was received at headquarters, more precious time was used by staff to get the information to the appropriate general, often using a runner. Real-time communication was virtually out of the question. By the time information reached its intended recipient, it was already outdated.

The business of real-time communication was less of an issue on the German side as most key decision makers were already close to the front line and thus were able rapidly to establish what was going on in their sectors.

SENSITIVITY

The greater the distance communication has to travel, the more links in the communication chain it has to travel through, the greater is the chance that communications are misplaced or misinterpreted.

German commanders in many cases operated close to the front line. At the top of Fort d'Ében-Émael, they were able to rely on non-verbal cues as they were observing the unfolding operation first hand. Constant updates from subordinates were matched in real time by the impressions the commander was able to ascertain through direct personal observation. Relaying verbal communication was facilitated by the fact that the area of operation was relatively small, so that fighting forces operated in close proximity with each other. Even the artillery fire called in from other surrounding forts did not considerably reduce sensitivity to the unfolding situation. Notwithstanding, the lack of attention given to the still functioning Coupola 120 also underlined the reality of the 'fog of war'.

The tactical sensitivity displayed in the capture of Fort d'Ében-Émael was displayed on numerous occasions, such as in the crossing of the river Meuse further south. Officers such as Guderian (XIX Panzer

CHAPTER FOUR: TACTICAL RESILIENCE

Corps, Sedan) and Rommel (7th Panzer, Dinant) 'led from the front', rushing between their headquarters and the developing events. Rommel, for example, tried to be always in the 'picture' of developing events by crossing the Meuse with one of the first wave of assault teams. His scepticism about initial success turned into curiosity to know what was going on and only to share such oversight with his chief of staff if it became necessary.

From a German perspective, ambiguity was less of an issue, given the closeness of key decision makers to the unfolding events. Nevertheless, the Germans managed quickly to relay intelligence beyond their regimental or divisional boundaries. This was not done to enable others to make decisions from afar, but to ensure that the higher echelons could monitor the situation at hand and to give them updates so that they, as key decision makers, could retain oversight.

The Belgian decision makers at Fort d'Ében-Émael were remote to the ongoing events on top of the fort. Hence, Major Jottrand relied on those personnel manning the observation cupolas who provided him with status reports indicating what was happening and whether his orders had any effect in battling the German paratroopers. He relied very much on verbal cues, unable to 'see for himself'. The resulting confusion was amplified by the wrong signal indicating an attack occurring from the outer perimeter of the fort rather than from above.

Without such crucial sensitivity, and amplified by the complexity of authority, Major Jottrand was acting upon ambiguous, and in most cases already outdated, information. From the outset, he was partially 'blind', relying on indefinite or unclear meaning in verbal cues; and he was 'shackled', constrained from requesting autonomy from a variety of higher level authorities. His fort was at the mercy of the Germans.

The lack of sensitivity was not only limited to the occupants of fortresses. Throughout the struggle in May/June 1940, key decisions were mostly based on ambiguous, out-of-date information. For example, on May 13th, at the time when the Germans had already successfully crossed the river Meuse and were close to breaking through the French defences, Colonel Henry

Lacaille, chief of staff of the French Second Army, reported to headquarters, Allied Forces, North-Eastern front: *"There has been a rather serious hitch at Sedan"* (May 2009, 391). An understatement with serious consequences.

Reserves were committed prematurely, on the basis of ambiguous intelligence, to the theatre in the north of the French Front, and much of the battle for France was fought in something of an information vacuum. Transmitted information lacked details and meaning. French Generals truly believed that the situation at the front was under control given the ambiguous messages they received; messages that – by default – obscured the true picture.

VON CLAUSEWITZ: INFORMATION IN WAR

A great part of the information in War is contradictory, a still greater part is false, and by far the greatest part is of a doubtful character. What is required of an officer is a certain power of discrimination, which only knowledge of men and things and good judgement can confer. The law of probability must be his guide. This is not a trifling difficulty even in respect of the first plans, which can be formed in the chamber outside the real sphere of war, but it is enormously increased when, in the thick of war itself, one report follows hard upon the heels of another; it is fortunate if these reports, in contradicting each other, show a certain balance of probability and thus themselves call for scrutiny. It is much worse for the inexperienced when accident does not render him this service, but one report supports another, confirms it, magnifies it, finishes off the picture with fresh touches of colour, until necessity in urgent haste forces from us a resolution which will soon be discovered to be folly, all those reports having been lies, exaggerations and errors.

(Adapted from Von Clausewitz 2011, 31)

CHAPTER FOUR: TACTICAL RESILIENCE

TRANSLATION AND EXPLANATION: CENTRALISATION VERSUS DECENTRALISATION

The military concepts of Mission-Oriented Tactics (or Mission Command) and Methodical Battle have found their way into the realm of management, although often referred to under a different name: centralisation and decentralisation. At the core of these concepts is the location of decision-making power.

Centralisation implies that authority is accumulated at the higher, strategic echelons of an organisation (see Table 4.1). Decisions are made 'at the top' and then communicated down to subordinates, who are compliant to their execution. Decentralisation is the opposite. Authority is devolved to the tactical level of an organisation, to regions or to subordinates.

Both approaches to centralisation and decentralisation may thrive in their own right, providing distinctive benefits as shown in Table 4.2.

The benefits of centralised ways of working are efficiency in the form of economies of scale. Strategies are broken down into repeatable rules, processes and routines. Such consistency and transparency in operational/tactical ways of working offer cost-effective standardisation. Those who are compliant to these standards 'only' require minimum skills and knowledge to carry out tasks in a standardised manner. Hence, depending on the availability of these skills and knowledge, these resources can be replaced without requiring substantial time and cost to shed one resource and set up another.

The concept of decentralisation promises greater speed and adaptiveness at a local level. In addition, top managers are relieved from day-to-day decision-making, so they can focus on strategising. Such local resilience comes at a price, though. Top Managers and 'front-line' employees must invest in establishing the conditions in

Table 4.1 Key Differences between Centralisation and Decentralisation

Centralisation	Decentralisation
Hierarchy	
The principle of centralisation is that key decisions should be taken at the top of the organisational hierarchy. Senior managers, having the greatest knowledge of the environment and the 'big picture', are best-placed to decide on key issues of long-term strategy, planning and resourcing. Control is from the top, and the mechanisms for that control comes through the organisational systems and processes.	Decentralisation is where decision-making is devolved further down the organisational hierarchy. It is assumed that at the 'front line', people are most sensitive to what is going on. Hence, decision power migrates to where a strategy is enacted, to a tactical level. In contrast to a centralised way of working, decentralisation implies more of a bottom-to-top flow of ideas and decision-making. It does not mean that higher echelons of management are not influential. They define a strategy but allow it to be put into practice by front-line employees.
Autonomy	
The freedom to act and implement a policy or plan is defined and constrained by frameworks of rules and procedures. Those frameworks define boundaries of decision-making power. In addition to these boundaries, plans are conceived and broken down into instructions and delegated to lower echelons of the organisation. In case subordinates are unable to carry out these instructions, issues are escalated up the hierarchy. Plans – outlining what tasks have to be carried out and how to accomplish them – can only be changed by those higher up. Any change to strategy will be converted into new instructions for subordinates to carry out. This does not mean that staff at the 'front line' are not skilled professionals, though. They need to be experienced enough to carry out the task at hand.	Decentralisation is not an invitation for front-line employees to form their own organisational strategy. Plans are conceived at the top. The difference is in the execution of those plans. The superior tells his or her subordinates what to accomplish, but not how to accomplish it. In military terms, lower-level ranks are being provided with an intent, a vision of the intended outcome, with less of a detailed breakdown of the specific tasks to carry out. Being compliant implies conformity to the intent, not to individual tasks that may not fit the fluidity of the evolving situation.

Initiative

The ability to assess and initiate independently is generally discouraged in a centralised environment. The focus is very much on keeping to the plan or instructions from above. Performance is mainly determined by the degree of compliance to rules and procedures, and to those commands or instructions received from higher up in the hierarchy. In extreme cases, staff are not explicitly required to assess the problems they are facing. An example of this would be in the early days of Henry Ford's production line, where 'optimised' jobs were designed, and staff merely had to perform their assigned roles. Nowadays, it is fair to say that 'automaton' jobs – those that can be automated – either have been or soon will be. The role of initiative, then, is one of degree. In a centralised organisation there is less scope for initiative at the lower levels, but there will likely be scope for 'in the moment' decision-making at an operational level.

In a decentralised organisation, front-line staff members are encouraged to be decisive. Inactions and omissions are discouraged, and a will to realise the intent is fostered. A barrier to being decisive is often the perception that errors in judgement are to be avoided at all costs. However, unsuccessful localised decision-making should be seen as less of a setback than no action at all, and ideally as an opportunity to try again. In this respect, superiors are reluctant to 'take over' immediately. Likewise, subordinates do not give way to the temptation to escalate a problem away from them and pass the problem 'upwards'. Initiative means that localised decision-makers should be able to try again, until the intent is realised. This does require a culture in which sensible ideas that are genuinely tried in good faith, but which don't work, aren't punished. If it is unsafe to suggest alternatives, or failure to deliver on a risky idea is perceived as career-limiting, then the natural incentive is to remain quiet.

Sensitivity

Both the 'what' to accomplish and the 'how' to accomplish it are defined in detail by the higher echelons in an organisation, and then broken down for subordinates to carry out. Centralisation tends to lead to a more vertical style of communication. Senior management and/or head office primarily issue instructions, and those lower down the hierarchy implement them and report back regularly. Should a major overall operational change be required (such as a new IT system or the provision of an additional product or service), this can generally be implemented more smoothly from above. Power residing at the top should also prevent one part of the business deciding to go its own way on important issues, and retaining budgetary control is a powerful mechanism for ensuring this.

Closeness to the customer is valuable as this gives greater insight into their needs, but teams need to be authorised and empowered with decision-making authority to do what is required. Decentralisation therefore implies a wider variety of tasks or processes. Thus locally accountable staff may implement their ideas to ensure better performance, rather than passing queries up their chain of command for someone else to fix who may not actually have the detailed knowledge.

Table 4.2 Advantages of Centralisation and Decentralisation

Benefits of Centralisation	Benefits of Decentralisation
Single point of contact	Greater local speed and flexibility
Easier to coordinate	Relieving top managers from day-to-day operational/tactical decision-making
Use of less skilled subordinates	Reduction in bureaucracy
Easier implementation of standard practices	Empowerment leads to greater job satisfaction
Avoidance of duplication of roles	

which decentralisation will flourish. People 'close' to problems are equipped with skills and capabilities to deal with uncertainty and complexity in a mindful manner; to be creative and agile, although within the boundaries of an intent.

TOWARDS ORGANISATIONAL RESILIENCE: THE FALLACY OF CENTRALISATION

Centralisation appears to be a simple, clear-cut approach to producing organisational resilience. 'Front-line' employees receive 'orders', that contain detailed instructions about 'what', 'why' and 'how'. Being compliant to these 'orders' is paramount. Situated thinking in the form of creativity is discouraged. Disobedience is followed by some form of punishment. Nevertheless, in a famous economics essay of 1958, Leonard Reid argued that no single person on earth had all the knowledge even to make something as straightforward as a pencil. This seemingly simple artefact – just some wood, graphite, printed labelling, lacquer and a metal end to hold an eraser – is actually the work of many specialists who do not share each other's expertise. There is no central coordinator who

CHAPTER FOUR: TACTICAL RESILIENCE

brings these into existence. Reid's insight was profound. The notion of 'centralisation or not' seems inadequate, and we need to think a little deeper.

In September 2015, Volkswagen AG, by then the biggest car manufacturer in the world, got embroiled in an emission scandal. Up to 11 million cars worldwide had been equipped with an illegal software, a 'defeat device' that misrepresented lower nitrogen oxide (NOx) emissions in order to satisfy testing agencies in the United States and Europe. The hidden damage from these VW vehicles could equate to all of the UK's yearly NOx emissions from all power stations, vehicles, industry and agriculture. The organisational damage was equally astounding. The overall bill to Volkswagen to cover fixes to the affected cars, and to cover penalties and potential customer compensation could amount to $25 billion.

In 1993, Ferdinand Piëch became the chairman of Volkswagen. At that time, Volkswagen was close to bankruptcy, and Piëch was central to the turnaround. In the following years, he up-marketed the Volkswagen and Audi brands with great success. By acquiring such brands as Lamborghini, Rolls-Royce and Bentley, he turned Volkswagen into a global player.

Despite these successes, Piëch was also known for his autocratic style of leadership and his need to micro-manage the operations of Volkswagen. His centralised way of decision-making, informed by a group of advisors, created a climate of 'fear'. Those who did not meet his aggressive sales targets would have to leave the organisation. The supervisory function in the organisation, primarily through the supervisory board but also through investors and shareholders, had no significant independent voice. In short, what Piëch said was not to be questioned or simply could not be questioned.

A centralised approach, although seemingly more straightforward faces two limitations that could well lead to the demise of Volkswagen.

LIMITATIONS IN INFALLIBILITY

In centralised decision-making, leadership takes place at the top of the hierarchy and lies exclusively with senior managers. They need to establish a clear vision and share that vision with those who are supposed to follow through operating a form of compliance. Strategising and operationalising are centred around these individuals. Followers are to be 'obedient' to senior managers' decisions, and little autonomy is provided to lower level echelons to question rules, processes and procedures. 'Front-line' situated human cognition – in the form of creativity – is discouraged as a source of error.

The demands on these senior managers, equipped with authority, are exceptional. Senior Managers need to be close to infallible as their followers cannot critique their decisions or exercise any autonomy that would enable them to deviate from what is being prescribed. Such geniuses are rare and few in management, and when they exist (e.g. Steve Jobs) their successes may turn them into insensitive strategisers, indulging in and pressurised by their expected infallibility, careering headlong into dogmatism and disaster. There is only so much we can expect from those rare individuals. What we cannot expect is that they are always 'right' in the what, why and how.

LIMITATIONS OF ACCOUNTABILITY

Accountability is defined as the obligation of individuals to account for their own actions and accept responsibility for the outcome of those actions. In centralising working, this implies compliance: obeying an order, rule or request. There lies the problem. The willingness of a follower to spend time and energy on actions is dependent on a belief – the what and the why – defined by a leader. Hence, belief in the message or the messenger is paramount. If one does not have faith in the order, rule or request, or in the messenger who conveys such rule, order or request, commitment to act in the best interest of the organisation is easily undermined.

This erosion of commitment is also fuelled by a degree of disempowerment and lack of direct influence on one's individual objective. For the former, receiving an order, rule or request tends to be perceived as a deprivation of power and interest. The latter refers to the 'blame' attributed to the one that provides order, rule and request that turns out to be 'wrong'. As a consequence, centralisation – by default – undermines commitment to carry out an order, rule or request for the greater good of the organisation.

INTENT INSTEAD OF TASKS

Under a decentralised way of working, people are helped to acquire the skills and capabilities to work independently, show initiative and improvise if necessary. This does not mean that autonomous working is encouraged without any form of alignment. In general, the concept of intent is defined as a mechanism that provides purposeful direction which people are committed to. In other words, an intent does not only consist of the 'What to do' but also provides meaning in the sense of 'Why' and boundaries for 'How'.

Klein (1999, 225) describes seven types of information deemed crucial to convey an intent:

The purpose of the task (the higher-level goals)
It provides the 'bigger picture', conveying an understanding of a broad vision of aspirations and goals.

The objective of the task (an image of the desired outcome)
The objective of the task is conveyed through a representation or image of the end-state, and what *the successfully completed request will look like.* (Klein 1999, 226)

The sequence of steps in the plan
This step in defining an intent produces – in general terms – a plan that outlines a sequence for how to reach the desired objective. This should not be mistaken for a detailed work breakdown structure that needs to be rigidly obeyed. It is a plan that provides general direction and alignment.

The rationale for the plan
The reasoning behind the plan makes people understand why the sequence of steps in the plan has been suggested. Given that they have autonomy to deviate from the suggested plan, this step enhances understanding about how to implement it and when it might be appropriate to deviate from the suggested How.

The key decisions that may have to be made
Deviations from a suggested plan include the key decision to change direction and alignment. Key decisions and priorities are part of conveying an intent, providing people with the readiness to enact key decisions to match a changing situation.

Antigoals (unwanted outcomes)
Antigoals are undesired objectives. They define what 'must' not or 'should' not go wrong. Antigoals represent an opposite pole to the desired outcome, and hence boundaries are defined for the outcome that is desired and the outcome that is to be avoided.

Constraints and other considerations
The final step in defining and conveying intent is the definition of what aspects of the environment constrain the accomplishment of an objective – what to 'watch out for'. It may also include limitations on the degree of autonomy or limitations on the resources necessary to exercise such autonomy.

COMMUNICATING INTENT

Communicating intent can be surprisingly difficult to achieve, particularly when language and cultural barriers get in the way. Montgomery used simple speech patterns and phrases when speaking to his soldiers, pitched at a level where reasonably complex ideas could be articulated, but using a simple vocabulary that would normally be associated with a 14 year old. He was rarely misunderstood. Care should be taken in a multinational environment. Metaphors that add much colour to the English language rarely translate well. Moreover, a large proportion of communication is nonverbal, using gestures and body language. Therefore, face-to-face communication is often the most effective means. Even where a common language is used, understanding is conditioned by factors that cannot be vocalised, including:

- expectations (based on personal style and the depth of experience of working with someone);
- military expectations (based on doctrine, training and ethos, which do not always translate well across departmental boundaries); and
- cultural expectations (based on societal values, which are deeply rooted and hard to overcome).

In the multinational environment, use clear language, speech and text.

(Development Concepts and Doctrine Centre 2013, 3–41)

The concept of an intent is crucial in both military and social science. In reality, this practice requires senior managers to 'let go' of authority and their own personal objectives; a challenge that led to a near-disaster in the Pacific arena in 1944.

BATTLE OF LEYTE GULF

In early 1944, the Japanese had gradually been driven back from their Pacific bases on the Solomon and Marshall Islands. However, the Americans' amphibious landings on these atolls came at a price. At Tarawa (the Gilbert Islands), in a battle fought from November 20th to 23rd 1943, the Americans for the first time faced serious opposition from a well dug-in enemy. US troops killed in action amounted to 895, whereas the entire garrison of 6,500 Japanese defenders was wiped out. Yet Tarawa was only a stepping stone in a long line of 'island-hopping' operations.

At the end of 1944, after a series of naval engagements, the Japanese were on their last legs. Their outer ring of defence was broken, their carrier- and land-based air force reduced to a rag-tag selection of inexperienced pilots. However, their surface fleet – consisting of destroyers, cruisers and battleships, among them two super battleships – still posed an enormous threat to the American landings in the Philippines that threatened to cut off Japan's main supply routes altogether.

General MacArthur planned to invade the island of Leyte in the central Philippines (see Map 4.2). The landings, to be commenced on November 17th, were supported by the amphibious and surface forces of the 7th Fleet, commanded by Vice Admiral Thomas C. Kinkaid. The 3rd US Fleet, with its newest Iowa-class battleships and Essex-class carriers, provided mobile support to counter any threat from the Japanese navy. In charge of this fleet was Admiral William F. Halsey (Jr). The overall objectives were to succeed in the invasion of Leyte, and also to destroy any remaining Japanese surface forces that might enter into Leyte Gulf.

Of great significance was the extent to which these commanders received and established their autonomy. Kinkaid reported to

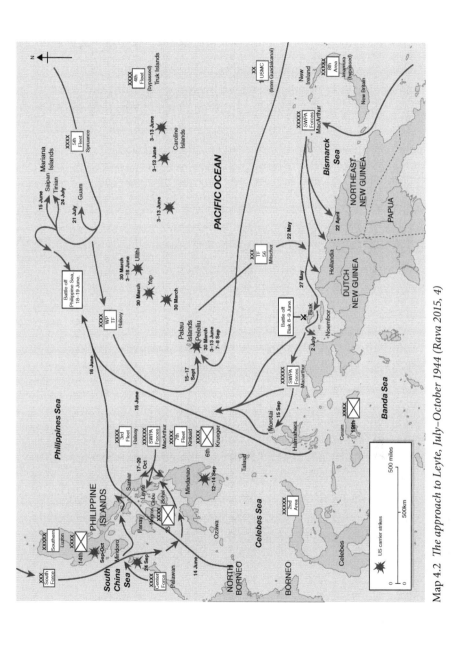

Map 4.2 The approach to Leyte, July–October 1944 (Rava 2015, 4)

MacArthur, whereas Halsey answered to the Commander in Chief, Pacific Ocean Areas, Chester Nimitz – a complex hierarchical structure that later led to delays and ambiguity in communication.

The Japanese were out for a decisive battle, staking their remaining forces on dealing a final blow to the US Navy. Steaming down the South China Sea, they would venture into Leyte Gulf. They would take out the protective forces covering the invasion, and then bear down on the relatively unprotected landing operation. Their plan included a complex three-pronged attack to enter Leyte Gulf. From the north, Ozawa's depleted carrier fleet – with very few planes and largely untrained pilots – would lure away any American carrier force or battleship group that may jeopardise the successful entry into Leyte Gulf. In the south, Admiral Nishimura's and Admiral Shima's surface fleet, consisting of battleships Fusō and Yamashiro as well as four cruisers and 11 destroyers, steamed through the Surigao Strait. The 'Centre Force', which was to sail through the San Bernadino Strait, was commanded by Vice Admiral Takeo Kurita, comprising the 64,000 t super-battleships Yamato and Musashi, as well as the Nagato, Kongō and Haruna, supported by 10 cruisers and 13 destroyers.

On October 17th, the largest fleet of naval vessels ever assembled entered Leyte Gulf. The beaches and rear areas had suffered two days of continuous ship- and plane-based bombardment by Kinkaid's invasion fleet. The opposition to the first waves of landings was light, and a beachhead was widened and secured quickly. MacArthur, following the first assault wave, waded ashore and announced the liberation of the Philippines in his distinctive fashion:

> This is the Voice of Freedom, General MacArthur speaking. People of the Philippines: I have returned. By the grace of Almighty God our forces stand again on Philippine soil – soil

consecrated in the blood of our two peoples. We have come, dedicated and committed to the task of destroying every vestige of enemy control over your daily lives, and of restoring, upon a foundation of indestructible strength, the liberties of your people.

While MacArthur celebrated his return to the Philippines, intelligence indicated an imminent Japanese attack on the landing beaches. Sightings by PT-boats (Patrol Torpedo boat), submarines and spotter planes revealed the intention of the South and Centre Force, although the only force that wanted to be spotted – Ozawa's carriers – remained hidden from the eyes of American intelligence. In order to deal with the southern force, Admiral Oldendorf was tasked to intercept Nishimura's and Shima's obsolete but still potent selection of destroyers, cruisers and battleships. However, Oldendorf had mostly old battleships at his disposal; these had provided fire-support for the Leyte landings and were thus armed with high-explosive munitions unsuitable for combatting heavily armoured ships. Despite this, he set up an ambush in the Surigao Strait, with lines of PT-boats, destroyers, cruisers and battleships. After a fierce but brief night battle, Nishimura's force was annihilated. Shima's destroyer and cruiser group, following 40 miles behind Nishimura, turned around but was constantly harassed by incessant air attacks. Only Kurita's Center Force remained, posing an immediate threat to the landings.

At dawn on October 24th, Halsey launched several waves of fighters, dive- and torpedo bombers in the direction of Kurita's Centre battle group. The Musashi was badly damaged and had to retire. At 15:00, Halsey dispatched a message that instructed four of his six battleships – the New Jersey, Iowa, Washington and Alabama – to block the San Bernadino Strait in anticipation of the arrival of Kurita's remaining Center Force. Soon after, a scout plane radioed back a sighting of heavy fleet carriers in addition to a range of cruisers and destroyers – Ozawa's bait. Halsey, obsessed with eliminating the remaining carriers in the Japanese arsenal, assumed – and expected – that Kurita had retired his forces for good. Fixated on sinking the carriers, he was reluctant to split his force and unilaterally decided to take the entirety of his surface vessels to steam north. He provided ambiguous messages to Kinkaid, who was made to believe that designated parts of his surface fleet – Task Force 34 – would remain in place to block the Surigao Strait. The Leyte landings were now at the mercy of Kurita's Centre Force.

Meanwhile, Kurita re-formed his battered ships and proceeded into the Leyte Gulf. To his surprise, there was no welcome committee for him. Soon after, the first smoke columns appeared on the horizon. In sight were a few destroyers and escort carriers – merchant ships equipped with flattops – that provided fire support for the invasion of Leyte.

Kurita could not believe his luck. His ships moved in range, opening fire with their massive 18 inch guns and closing in further. The Americans watched in awe as coloured splashes (the Japanese used dyes to mark shell splashes) rose around their ships. In desperation, destroyers in the vicinity started charging at the Japanese fleet, launching their torpedoes and releasing smoke screens. Their 5 inch guns had only pitiful impact on Kurita's surface fleet. Not long after – despite the poor gunnery skills of the Japanese force – the first destroyers, most notably the USS Johnston, were sunk. Also, the first US escort carriers began to be targeted; they started to receive a pounding. The situation for the Americans worsened by the minute.

CHAPTER FOUR: TACTICAL RESILIENCE

Halsey, steaming away from Kurita in pursuit of Ozawa's carriers, received a message at 21:20: *The whole world wants to know where is Task Force 34* (Rear Adm. C. A. F. Sprague Report to COMINCH). He had been preoccupied with attacking Ozawa's fleet of largely empty carriers and so had to turn back south, yet he would not reach Leyte Gulf until the next morning.

The heroic ferocity of the American resistance by American destroyers and aircrafts from escort carriers made Kurita believe that he faced a far bigger enemy. Enough was enough. The southern Force had been wiped out, and it was only a matter of time before Ozawa's carrier fleet would also meet its end. Kurita decided to break off the engagement, leaving behind a largely undefended invasion force.

The avoidance of an impending disaster at Leyte Gulf in 1944 was largely due to Kurita's decision to withdraw and desist from pushing further into an unprotected invasion zone, packed with transports and landing crafts. It revealed the issues that can occur when operational intent – a key aspect of *Auftragstaktik* – is undermined by individual pursuit for glory and dislike for each other's rank and status. Such autonomy may well pay off, yet the risk of operating in isolation of each other may also open gaps to be exploited by an enemy with incalculable consequences.

Although disengagement from the 'bigger picture' played a role in Halsey's decision to 'open the door' to Kurita's battle group, the complexity of communications also impeded effective application of the concept of *Auftragstaktik*. In an environment where time is of the essence, relaying communications at Leyte took up to two hours, despite wireless technology. It is no surprise that information was obsolete. And, because of the egocentric behaviour of key decision makers, information was (ab)used to obscure or embellish the pursuit for individual glory.

JUST CULTURE INSTEAD OF BLAME OR LEARNING CULTURE

Conveying and communicating an intent goes hand in hand with providing an appropriate culture in which it can flourish. A Blame culture is one that is driven by individualistic accountability; it entails attributing the root cause of a problem to whichever individual is associated with not having prevented the root cause from cascading into a problem. The outcome is to retrain or to discipline the individual.

The attribution of a problem to an individual tends to be associated an unpleasant emotion of failure, eroding the very essence of an intent; to prepare and ready the collective to the inconvenience of uncertainty and complexity.

The opposite extreme to a Blame culture is a Learning culture. Problems are seen as an opportunity to acquire more knowledge and experience for dealing with future problems. There is encouragement for problems to be shared openly, and employees do not face any repercussions, even if these problems and errors can be associated with them. The downside of such an approach is 'absolution', freeing one from guilt and any form of accountability. On the upside, in the 'heat of the battle', little time is given to defining attribution of blame, so greater attention and space can be given to finding solutions for dealing with the problem at hand.

A hybrid approach to these rather extreme approaches – the Blame or Learning cultures – is a Just culture. Individuals are made accountable for their actions. However, they are disciplined only where they have been grossly negligent, have wilfully violated their obligations or been purposefully destructive.

DOCTRINAL PRINCIPLES IN OPERATIONS PLANNING

(e) Flexibility. Plans should be sufficiently flexible to allow for the unexpected and to allow commanders freedom of action to respond to changing circumstances. This requires an understanding of the superior commanders' intentions, flexibility, rapid decision-making, organisation and good communications. Flexibility also demands physical mobility to allow forces to concentrate quickly at decisive times and places.

(f) Initiative. Commanders should be encouraged to take the initiative without fearing the consequences of failure. At all levels, commanders must be given the freedom to use initiative and should in turn encourage subordinates to use theirs. This requires a training and operational culture that promotes an attitude of risk taking in order to win rather than to prevent defeat.

(g) Maintenance of morale. Commanders should give their command an identity, promote self-esteem, inspire it with a sense of common purpose and unity of effort, and give it achievable aims. High morale depends on good leadership which instils courage, energy, determination and care for the personnel entrusted.

(Development Concepts and Doctrine Centre 2013, 1–4)

OUTLOOK

Centralised decision-making has emerged as an appealing tactic; one that the French and their Allies adopted in both WWI and WWII. The generalship defined detailed plans, which were then broken down into orders. These orders were received by front-line soldiers and, were to be carried out without question, with no need to provide an answer as to 'Why'. The demands on these top military leaders had been great. In essence, the Supreme Commander French Land Forces, and General Georges, C.-in-C. North East Front directed the entire campaign. The lower hierarchical levels (e.g. army generals) were relegated to recipients of orders; creativity in carrying out these orders was discouraged.

This approach seems straightforward, given the fact that the French army was largely a citizen army. Most of their lower ranks just did not have the experience and training to be autonomous and 'intelligent' in their actions. Hence, most of the training of the immobile fortress forces revolved around constructing defences and some around handling their weaponry. They were not meant to adapt to any situation other than meeting a German assault with massive firepower.

The means of communication, relaying orders down from the top of the command to the lower levels took time, too much time in the case of the French. Information that reached the front lines was often out-of-date; the Germans advanced so quickly that the real-time communication of the Allies could not keep up with it. The confusion at the front line was amplified by the unrealistic optimism channelled down from higher levels. To put it simply, front-line soldiers often mentioned that the order and the situation they confronted did not make sense. And yet, they were bound to that order. Their only alternative was to retreat.

Organisations, such as Volkswagen, may well have adopted the French approach of centralisation, and top managers may have made their workforce 'obedient' to their will. But it is folly to believe that top managers have all the 'right' answers. Most often, they believe they have but, driven by power struggles, isolation in 'knowing better' and a safe remoteness from tactical problems, they deprive the lower levels of a licence to think, even forbidding front-line employees from doing so. The top manager only has to be wrong once; no one else can or would want to step into the breach to sort out the problem.

In contrast, a decentralised way of making decisions offers the application of greater local knowledge and the exploitation of capabilities of 'front-line' soldiers that can make a difference at a local level. Nevertheless, a form of decentralisation requires commitment, the willingness of people to prioritise the strategic and operational objectives above their own individual interest (e.g. for glory). In the case of the Battle of Leyte Gulf in late 1944, the lack of commitment by senior figures led to local action that was not aligned to the shared direction, leading to a near disaster.

As such, organisations may find centralisation simpler to carry out and thus more efficient. However, history shows that the effort to decentralise is worth the long-term outcomes, if commitment and alignment is established (see Chapter 5 for more insights into Commitment and Alignment).

Reflection *To what extent does your work unit adhere to Centralisation or Decentralisation? For each item, select one box only that best reflects your conclusion.*

	Neutral	
We see 'front-line' employees as replaceable	○ ○ ○ ○ ○	We invest in 'front-line' people's response repertoire and leadership development
Rank and status defines who is defined as a leader	○ ○ ○ ○ ○	Everybody is considered a leader
We value hierarchy over experience	○ ○ ○ ○ ○	We value experience over rank
	Neutral	
We are task-oriented	○ ○ ○ ○ ○	Intent-orientation is most important
We are expected to carry out orders without knowing their purpose	○ ○ ○ ○ ○	Tasks are executed according to the intent set
We defer to those with greater rank or status	○ ○ ○ ○ ○	We defer to those most competent

Scoring: If your answers tend to the left, you are pursuing a more traditional, centralised approach to decision making. If your answers are more on the right, the concept of decentralisation – mission-oriented – seems paramount to your ways of working.

REFERENCES

BArch. "Bild 146-1972-066-03." Koblenz: Bundesarchiv.
———. "Bild 146-1974-113-59." Koblenz: Bundesarchiv.
———. "Bild 183-L05069." Koblenz: Bundesarchiv.
Development Concepts and Doctrine Centre. 2013. "Allied Joint Doctrine for Operational-Level Planning (+UK National Elements)."
Dunstan, S. 2005. *Fort Eben Emael: The Key to Hitler's Victory in the West*. Oxford: Osprey Publishing.
Guderian, H. 2000. *Panzer Leader*. London: Penguin Classics.
Klein, G. 1999. *Sources of Power: How People Make Decisions*. London, UK: MIT Press.
Kuhn, V. 1978. *German Paratroopers of World War II*. London: Ian Allan.
May, E. 2009. *Strange Victory: Hitler's Conquest of France*. London: I.B. Tauris & Co.
McNab, C. 2013. *The Fall of Eben Emael: Belgium 1940*. Oxford: Osprey Publishing.
North Atlantic Treaty Organization, and NATO Standardization Agency (NSA). 2010. "Allied Joint Doctrine AJP–01(D)."
Rava, G. 2015. *Leyte 1944: Return to the Philippines*. Oxford: Osprey Publishing.
Rear Adm, C.A.F. 2000. Sprague Report to COMINCH. "Action Against the Japanese Main Body off Samar." *SWPA Journal*.
Tzu, S. 2008. *The Art of War*. London: Penguin Books.
Von Clausewitz, C. 2011. *On War*. United States: Madison Park.

CHAPTER FIVE
Leadership

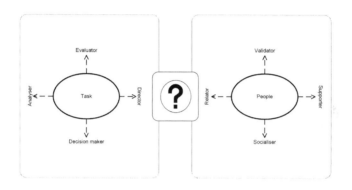

There are Five Pitfalls
For a general:
Recklessness,
Leading to
Destruction;
Cowardice,
Leading to
Capture;
A hot temper,
Prone to
Provocation;
A delicacy of honour,
Tending to
Shame;
A concern for his men,
Leading to
Trouble.

(Tzu 2008, 50)

CONTENTS

The story: May 13th–May 17th 1940	156
Adaptive versus administrative leadership	159
Limitations of Von Clausewitz and De Jomini: leadership as a trait	160
The challenge: breaking out	168
Deciding factors: direction, alignment and commitment	174
Command philosophy	175
Importance of a cohesive staff team – command of the German Africa corps	177
Von Clausewitz: boldness	180
Translation and explanation: adaptive leadership versus administrative leadership	181
Towards organisational resilience: the fallacy of order	184
Battle of Hürtgen forest	186
Wargaming	191
Outlook	194
Notes	196
References	196

This chapter focusses on an essential function that enables strategic, operational and tactical resilience: leadership. Leadership provides

- Vision, the ability to determine a future with imagination or wisdom
- Direction and the ability to change direction if necessary
- Alignment of resources and capabilities
- Commitment to allow dedication towards a common direction to flourish.

THE STORY: MAY 13TH–MAY 17TH 1940

The beleaguered Dutch could not withstand the continuous pressure. They capitulated on May 14th. The surrender of Holland hastened the retreat of the French 7th Army. In Flanders, the Luftwaffe took its toll on Blanchard's 1st Army. However, in the north, the thrust by German

Forces was contained for the moment. Despite the setbacks, the French Armoured divisions showed that they were more than a match for the Germans. During May 14th/15th, the Battle of the Gembloux Gap inflicted losses of up to 50 per cent on the German 3rd and 4th Panzer divisions.

An attack by Panzer IIs and IIIs near Gembloux on May 14th/15th

The Germans became disconcerted at seeing their tank rounds bounce off the heavy Char B1s and even the medium Somuas. They noticed, though, that the French had their own Achilles's heel: their tanks did not attack in force but tended to move in loose formations. French gunnery was revealed as imprecise and lacking coordination due to the fact that the role of French tank commanders included aiming, reloading and commanding their tank crews. Hence, the Germans were able to close the distance and aim their guns at weak points, such as the air intake of the CharB1.

Further south, the situation remained precarious. German armoured forces crossed the river Meuse in force at Dinant, Monthermé and Sedan. Counter-attacks by French armoured divisions were finally launched against the still vulnerable German bridgeheads but to little avail:

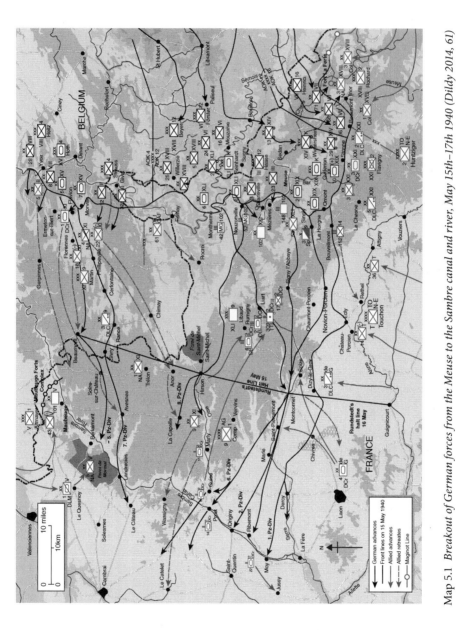

Map 5.1 *Breakout of German forces from the Meuse to the Sambre canal and river, May 15th–17th 1940 (Dildy 2014, 61)*

CHAPTER FIVE: LEADERSHIP

> About ten o'clock this morning Colonel de Villelume told us of the collapse of the army which was defending the Meuse between Sedan and Namur. Eight or nine divisions were in full retreat. The position is the more serious in that our armies in the north have not yet begun to fall back. We have a dozen divisions there without counting the English and the Belgians.
>
> The Prime Minister was unwilling to telephone direct to General Gamelin in order to avoid a breach with M. Daladier, who is hypersensitive in matters of this sort. He therefore rang up Daladier to ask him what were Gamelin's counter-measures, to which Daladier replied "He has none." I was standing in front of the Prime Minister's desk when, dumbfounded, he repeated the words he had just heard.
>
> (Baudouin 1948, 30)

It became clear that previous piecemeal attacks would not stop the Germans for good, but at least they bought some time to fall back to a second line of defence along the line Recroi-Signy l'Abbaye (see Map 5.1).

ADAPTIVE VERSUS ADMINISTRATIVE LEADERSHIP

The previous chapter looked at aspects of (de)centralisation and the breadth of decision-making, focussing on matters such as autonomy and intent. As it covers more the 'what' of leadership, this chapter aims to delve further into aspects of 'how' to lead. In other words, how can doctrinal concepts such as *Auftragstaktik* and *La Bataille Conduit* be brought to life through the human agency of culture and behaviour? What conditions of leadership need to be in place to activate tactical, as well as operational and strategic resilience?

From a modern management perspective, the Germans adopted an adaptive leadership style in their armed forces:

> A culture of adaptability is vital to survival in the armed services. As business executives cope with increasing unpredictability, they can take a page from the military's book:

- Create a personal link with every employee – individually or in gatherings. A direct connection reinforces your message.
- Act fast – don't shoot from the hip but don't wait for perfection. Make organizational interests your top priority – don't let others falter as you prosper.
- Set a direction but don't micromanage – give people the freedom to improvise.

(Useem 2010)

LIMITATIONS OF VON CLAUSEWITZ AND DE JOMINI: LEADERSHIP AS A TRAIT

Von Clausewitz and De Jomini tend to describe leadership as a trait: a distinguishing quality or characteristic, typically one belonging to a higher-ranked person, such as a general. First, leadership may be as much a trait as it is a state; leaders are not so much born as made. Despite extreme opposing views, research seems to indicate that leadership is up to 40 per cent in our genes and 60 per cent the result of lessons learned through life experiences, through conditioning. On many occasions, leadership has emerged partly because an individual did indeed have the necessary leadership qualities but mostly because the circumstances were right, because the context allowed and made them lead. It may be, though, that leadership is not so much evidenced through courage and bravery, as stated by Von Clausewitz and De Jomini, but is a predominantly individualistic exercise.

VON CLAUSEWITZ ARGUED

Military virtue is for the parts what the genius of the Commander is for the whole. The General can only guide the whole, not each separate and individual part, and where he cannot guide the part, there military virtue must lead. A General is chosen on the basis of reputedly superior talents: the chief leader of a large group following a careful probation. This element of probation diminishes as we descend in rank just as we may reckon less and less on the basis of individual talents lower down the hierarchy; what is wanting in this respect should be supplied by military virtue. Military virtue can be equated with the natural qualities of a warlike people: bravery, aptitude, powers of endurance and enthusiasm.

These properties may therefore supply the equivalent of military virtue and vice versa, from which the following may be deduced:

1. Military virtue is a quality of standing Armies, which is where it is most required. In national risings, its place is taken by natural qualities, which develop themselves there more rapidly.
2. Standing Armies can more easily dispense with military virtue than can a standing army opposed to a national insurrection; in the latter case, the troops are more scattered, and divisions are left more to themselves. But where an army can be kept concentrated, the genius of the General has a greater role to play and supplies what is wanting in the spirit of the army. Therefore, general military virtue is proportionately more necessary when the theatre of operations and other circumstances make the war complicated, and forces are scattered.

(Adapted from Von Clausewitz 2011, 79)

DE JOMINI STATED

The most essential qualities for a general will always be as follows: first, A high moral courage, capable of great resolution. Second, A physical courage which takes no account of danger. A general's scientific or military acquirements are secondary to these characteristics, though if great they are valuable auxiliaries.

It is not necessary to be a general of vast erudition. Knowledge may be limited, but it should be thorough, and the general should be perfectly grounded in the principles at the base of the art of war. Next in importance come the qualities of personal character. A person who is gallant, just, firm, upright, capable of esteeming merit in others instead of being jealous of it and skilful in making their merit contributory to their own glory will always be a good general and may even pass for a greatness. Unfortunately, the disposition to give credit to merit in others is not a common quality: mediocre minds are always jealous and inclined to surround themselves with persons of little ability, fearing that they will be perceived as followers and not leaders, and not realising that the designated commander of an army always receives almost all the glory of its success, even when least entitled to it.

The question has often been discussed whether it is preferable to assign command to a general with long experience in service with troops or to a staff officer who, usually, has little experience in the management of troops. It is beyond question that war is a distinct science of itself and that it is quite possible to combine operations skilfully without ever having led a regiment against an enemy. Peter the Great, Condé, Frederick and Napoleon are instances of this. It cannot, then, be denied that a staff officer may, as easily as any other, prove to be a great general, but it will not be because that person has grown grey in the duties of a quartermaster that he or she is capable of the supreme command but because they have a natural genius for war and possess the requisite characteristics. So, also, a general from the ranks of the infantry or cavalry may be as capable of conducting a campaign as the most profound tactician. So this question does not admit to a definite affirmative or negative answer since almost everything depends upon the personal qualities of individuals; however, the following remarks will be useful in reaching a rational conclusion:

1. A general, selected from general staff, engineers or artillery, who has commanded a division or a corps d'armée, will, all other things being equal, be superior to one who is familiar with the service of only one arm or special corps.
2. A general from the line, who has made a study of the science of war, will be equally fitted for command.
3. The character of the individual is more important than any other requisite in a commander-in-chief.
4. Finally, a good general is one in whom are united the requisite personal characteristics and a thorough knowledge of the principles of the art of war.

(Adapted from De Jomini 2008, 35)

A second limitation on leadership, according to Von Clausewitz and De Jomini, is the assumption that it comes with rank, that only individuals of the rank of senior officers – most notably generals – can exercise leadership. As this was a distinguishing factor of leadership – rank and status – during the eighteenth century (although Napoleon Bonaparte was a fierce opponent of inherited and conferred nobility and thus rank), the First World War (WWI) and in particular the Second World War (WWII) saw a rise in elevating non-commissioned officers (NCOs) to be leaders. In the true spirit of decentralisation (see Chapter 4), training and education in the German army typically included leadership and management as well as service-specific and combat training.

Officer candidates or cadets *(Kadetten)* in Germany were judged in terms of their character as potential leaders but not using criteria traditionally associated with a Prussian upbringing:

obedience, sense of honour, frugality, love of truth or love for the Kaiser:

> paramount among the capabilities were Willenskraft – willpower – which covered the will to become an exemplary officer, the will to succeed in any given task, the will to force a tactical decision. The will to speak his mind, and the will to remain steady under pressure. Verantwortungsbewusststein – sense of responsibility – covered another area and meant being aware of his responsibilities toward the officer corps and the *Wehrmacht* in his deeds and having the very important sense of responsibility towards his men, walking the fine line between a hard-ass superior in a crisis situation and taking care of his men like a father would his sons, in short, being a comrade. Last but not least, it meant the responsibility of learning his trade and excelling in his area of expertise. Finally, the candidate had to display a kämpferisches Wesen – a fighting spirit, going against any odds, possessing a longing for battle and leading from the front.
>
> (Muth 2011, 97)

The German manual for leadership states that even divisional commanders should stay close to their troops, maintaining close sensitivity to the front line and thus being credible to front-line troops. Zooming in and out, grasping the big picture and the minutiae of a battlefield, is facilitated by members of staff. It is no surprise that the casualty rate among German commanding officers as well as non-commanding officers was relatively high (Muth 2011, 101).

Student officers were trained to instil leadership in others in case designated leaders were unable to enact the leadership role. The schooling of junior officers included war games that required flexibility of mind to make them think on their feet while facing novel situations (Muth 2011, 165).

In this respect, creativity may be interpreted as disobedience:

> the German and Prussian officer corps are the officer corps with the greatest culture of disobedience – with maybe the exception of the French. The stories and events that kept alive the virtue requiring an officer – even in war – to disobey an order "when justified by honour and circumstances" were corporate cultural knowledge within the Prussian and German officer corps and it is therefore important to recount them there.
>
> (Muth 2011, 168)

EXCERPT FROM *TRUPPENFÜHRUNG* (HANDLING OF COMBINED-ARMS FORMATIONS), THE GERMAN ARMY FIELD MANUAL OF 1936

- Leadership in war demands leaders possessed of judgment, a clear understanding and foresight. They must be independent and firm in making a decision, determined and energetic while carrying it out, sensitive to the changing fortunes of war, and possessed of a strong consciousness of the high responsibility resting on them.
- The officer is leader and educator in every field. Besides a knowledge of men and a sense of justice, he must distinguish himself by superior knowledge and experience, moral excellence, self-control and high courage.
- The example of officers and men in commanding positions has a crucial effect on the troops. The officer who demonstrates cold-bloodedness, determination and courage in front of the enemy pulls the troops along with himself. He must, however, also find his way to subordinates' hearts and gain their confidence by understanding their feelings and their thoughts. His care for them must never cease.

Mutual confidence is the secure basis for discipline in times of need and danger.

- Every commander is to commit his entire personality in any situation without facing responsibility. A readiness to assume responsibility is the most important of all qualities of leadership. It must not, however, go so far as to lead to headstrong decisions without regard for the whole, or to the imprecise execution of orders, or to an I-know-better-than-you-attitude. Independence should not turn into arbitrariness. But independence which knows its limits is the foundation for great success…
- Commanders are to live with the troops and to share with them danger and deprivation, happiness and suffering. Only thus can they gain a real insight into their troops' fighting power and requirements.

  The individual man is responsible not merely for himself but for his comrades also. Whoever possesses more ability, is stronger, must aid and lead the inexperienced and the weak.

  On such information does the feeling of real comradeship grow. Its importance in relations between commanders and men is as great as among the men themselves.

- … It is every commander's duty to proceed against breaches of discipline, to prevent excesses, plundering, panic, and other harmful effects by using every means at his disposal, including even the most drastic ones.

  Discipline is the central pillar on which the army is built. Its strict maintenance is a blessing for all.

- The troops' strength must be conserved so that the highest demands can be made on them at the decisive moment. Whoever demands unnecessary chores sins against the prospect of success.

  The use of force in combat must be proportionate to the purpose at hand. Demands that are incapable of fulfilment are

> as harmful to the troops' confidence in their leaders as they are to their morale.
>
> - Personal influence by the Commanding Officer on his troops is of the greatest importance. He must be near the fighting troops.
>
> - The selection of a location for a corps headquarters is determined above all by the need to keep in close and constant touch with both the divisions and the rear. A corps commander is not to rely on technical means of communication alone.
>
>   In spite of the availability of advanced technological apparatus, staying far away from the front extends the distance orders and reports must travel, endangers communications and may cause reports and orders to arrive belatedly or not at all. It also puts difficulties in the way of obtaining a personal view of the country and of the state of combat.
>
>   On the other hand, the location of corps headquarters should be fixed in such a way as to make possible the orderly activity of the various services.
>
> - A divisional commander's place is with his troops … During encounters with the enemy seeing for oneself is best.
>
> (Van Creveld 1982, 128)

In contrast to adaptive leadership, encapsulating the capability of agility and creativity, administrative leadership is about orchestrating tasks and making people compliant in executing these tasks in a prescribed fashion in an efficiently consistent and transparent manner. Successful administrative leaders are able to establish systems (of rules and procedures) that protect and sustain essential operational functions to meet the needs of the organisation. Military staff (often referred to as general staff, army staff, navy staff or air staff within the individual services) and enlisted and civilian personnel are commonly tasked with managing administrative, operational and logistical needs.

In both the German armed forces and those of the French and their Allies, both adaptive and administrative leadership run in concert with each other, providing crucial contributions to the ability to wage war. However, while the Germans saw administrative leadership as a supporting function, in particular the French developed a strategic, operational system of rigidity, defined by strict timetables of movement and firepower. Hence, front-line officers in the French army were relegated to mere administrators of a methodical battle.

THE CHALLENGE: BREAKING OUT

During the night of May 13th, German engineers completed a first crossing of the Meuse. Getting heavy equipment across was another matter. Roads leading to the crossings were clogged, soldiers were fatigued, and the night sky made organising an effective crossing more challenging, cumbersome and slow. Hence, the bridgeheads on the west bank of the Meuse remained vulnerable for some time.

Their opposition was formidable. X Corps (French Second Army under Huntzinger) was made available to counter-attack along the Chéhéry–Bulson–Haraucourt axis (10–12 km south of Sedan) to strike at the Meuse bridgeheads. Their preparation to thrust the Germans back across the Meuse took shape on the morning of May 13th, roughly 24 hours before the Germans managed to get their first units to the opposite side of the Meuse. Despite that, valuable time was wasted. Delays in bringing up X Corps, hesitation and procrastination took their toll. A striking example of how obscure levels of hierarchy and depth of communication constrained the ability to respond quickly refers to the mobilisation of counter-attacks by the French 55th division (Lafontaine):

May 13th, 19:00 hours: Telephone discussion between Grandsard and Lafontaine about attachment of additional infantry and tanks for a counterattack.

19:30 hours: Telephone discussion between Grandsard and Lafontaine about moving command post of 55th Division.

After 19:30 hours: Movement of 55th's command post. Lafontaine meets Labarthe in Chemery.

After 19:30 hours: Lieutenant Colonel Cachou, who was the deputy Chief of Staff of the Xth Corps, meets Labarthe in Chémery. Approves Labarthe's decision not to move north.

After 19:30 hours: Cachou meets Lafontaine east of Chémery. Informs him of Labarthe's decision.

After 19:30 hours: Lafontaine calls Grandsard to discuss counterattack.

22:00–23:00 hours: Lafontaine definitely learns of the 205th Regiment and 4th Tank Battalion's being attached to 55th Division.

24:00 hours: Lafontaine departs for Xth Corps command post.

01:30 hours: Chaligne learns that counterattack would consist of two infantry regiments and two tank battalions.

03:00 hours: Lafontaine returns to Chémery without having reached Xth Corps.

04:15 hours: Lafontaine issues order for counterattack.

(Doughty 1990, 260)

It took the French a staggering nine hours to mobilise a counter-attack. By then, the situation on the ground had already changed considerably. Along the Meuse, some German units made it across the Meuse and moved inland towards the French second line of defence. At Sedan, the commander of the 1st Panzer Division moved the *Grossdeutschland* regiment, an elite infantry unit, as well as a tank battalion, towards Bulson and Stonne. It did not take long for the German forward units to run into trouble, although it was not of a magnitude they could not deal with:

> The *Grossdeutschland* Infantry Regiment closely followed the tanks in an excellent manner. Suddenly, reconnaissance revealed an enemy counterattack with tank support. The enemy's infantry were operating as if they were on a training exercise, and they were running directly into the fire of the company. Three enemy tanks were knocked out. The [German tank] company crossed over the road and continued attacking further toward the south. Close to the Chémery-Raucourt road east of Maisoncelle, the company occupied its position and secured the continued movement of the *Grossdeutschland* regiment.
>
> Suddenly, 10 French R-35 tanks, grouped together closely in a column, appeared on the edge of Maisonelle on the road to Raucourt. In a flash the [German tank] company opened fire with every gun tube. The enemy was completely surprised. He did not fire a single round. Three vehicles turned toward the south and, although hit, managed to escape. Four tanks remained in place, one of them burning in a fiery blaze. The last three vehicles could turn and drive back into the village. They were nevertheless so badly damaged that their crews abandoned them.
>
> (Doughty 1990, 209)

Intense fighting ensued at Bulson. The French were quickly routed. Yet the German High Command insisted on halting the advance to allow more infantry and panzer forces to catch up with the forward units that had been in battle for an excruciating three days without pause. As Guderian lacked sufficient and potent enough anti-tank weapons, a defensive stance would be foolish. Hence, he ignored this 'advice' and pushed further south towards the Stonne plateau, where French forces were massing, to aggressively disrupt any French attempt to counter-attack:

> From the headquarters of the 10th Panzer Division I drove to the headquarters of the Infantry Regiment 'G.D.' [*Grossdeutschland*] in Stonne. A French attack was actually in progress when I arrived and

CHAPTER FIVE: LEADERSHIP

I could not find anyone. A certain nervous tension was noticeable, but finally the positions were held. I then went to my new corps headquarters, which was a small town wood near Sapogne on the southern bank of the Meuse.

Contrary to expectations the night was one of confusion, not owing to the activity of the enemy but on account of command difficulties with our superiors. Panzer Group Kleist ordered a halt to all further advance and to any extension of the bridgehead. I neither would nor could agree to these orders, which involved the sacrifice of the element of surprise we had achieved. I therefore got in touch, personally, first with the Chief of Staff of the Panzer Group, Colonel Zeitzler and, since this was not enough, with General Kleist himself, and requested that the order to stop be cancelled. The conversation became very heated and we repeated our arguments several times. Finally, General von Kleist approved of the advance being continued for another twenty-four hours.

(Guderian 2000, 107)

Stonne is a small village with a dozen farms. Its position was of strategic importance. Elevated at 330m, a force could observe the approach of the enemy and rain down artillery and anti-tank fire. On the French side, around 15,500 troops were positioned in a fortified line, although these fortifications were nothing like the massive casemates of the Maginot Line but consisted mostly of an array of smaller bunkers, earthworks, barbed wire and mines.

On May 15th, the Germans attacked, again with the *Grossdeutschland* regiment as spearhead, supported by a range of PzKpfw IV and IIs at the front (10th Panzer Division). They were met by French anti-tank guns, knocking out three of the approaching German tanks. The Germans, though, swiftly found another path into the village and made the remnants of the French units abandon Stonne.

The loss of Stonne was of great concern to the French High Command. What followed is sometimes referred to as the 'Verdun of 1940', because of its viciousness and level of casualties. Attacks were followed by counter-attacks. In total, Stonne changed hands 16 times (see Table 5.1):

Table 5.1 Battle for Stonne (Frieser, 210)

Date	Time	Outcome
May 15th	08:00	German victory
	09:00	French victory
	09:30	German victory
	10:30	French victory
	10:45	German victory
	12:00	French victory
	17:30	German victory
May 16th	07:30	French victory
	17:00	German victory
Night to	Unoccupied	
May 17th	09:00	German victory
	11:00	French victory
	14:30	German victory
	15:00	French victory
	16:30	German victory
	17:00	French victory
	17:45	German victory

This photo was taken on June 13th 1940. It shows two destroyed Pz IV at Stonne (BArch)

CHAPTER FIVE: LEADERSHIP

At the end of May 17th, Stonne and the surrounding area were littered with knocked out tanks and abandoned equipment. The village of Stonne lay in ruins, obliterated by artillery fire and street fighting.

German casualties were immense: around 8,500 men, of whom 3,000 were assumed killed or missing. The *Grossdeutschland* regiment alone lost 570 men. The French suffered an assumed 1,200 killed or missing in action. This battle was a sound French tactical victory in terms of casualties inflicted.

Nevertheless, such tactical victories are in vain if the German advance cannot be stopped at Stonne or elsewhere at the Meuse front. Whereas the German front-line officers were opportunistic in their push forward, not allowing the French to solidify their defence, French officers showed hesitation that passed the baton of initiative to the Germans.

XXIst corps, under General Flavigny, was complemented by the 3rd Armoured Division, led by General Brocard. This division was set up in March 1940 and suffered from shortages in fuel and foremost preparedness. When Flavigny approached Brocard in regard to launching a counter-attack on the 14th, Brocard replied,

> We are not ready … We came to this area to continue training of the division.
>
> It is not a question of training; it is necessary to fight. This is urgent. Can you be at your departure position at 1100 hours?
>
> That is impossible. I am not resupplied with fuel, answered Brocard.
>
> What? asked Flavigny. If you were an infantryman, your men would have eaten. If you were a cavalryman, your horses would have received their oats … in the vicinity of the enemy. Your fuel tanks are not empty. How much time will it take to complete your refuelling?
>
> Four hours
>
> That's impossible

(Doughty 1990, 286)

While the French were throwing their units at the Germans in a piecemeal fashion, desperately catching up with a timetable that the Germans imposed on them, the Germans disrupted and destroyed their efforts for a successful counter-attack, one by one. A decisive, organised attack against the Meuse front would have likely led to a French strategic victory. Instead, three German corps – XV (Hoth), XLI (Reinhardt) and XIX (Guderian) – broke through just five days after the commencement of hostilities and were let loose to race towards the English Channel into the rear of the Maginot Line and the bulk of the Allied crack forces in the north.

DECIDING FACTORS: DIRECTION, ALIGNMENT AND COMMITMENT

Adaptive leadership is associated with three properties: Direction, Alignment and Commitment. Direction refers to a shared and collective agreement on the vision, mission, goals and aims. Direction implies change, a change from the current reality towards some future state. Alignment is defined as the coordination and integration of people, structures, skills, process and systems to produce collective work in service of the shared direction. The willingness of people to prioritise the success of the collective work above their own interests, to devote their time and energy in service of the shared direction, is a form of leadership commitment (McCauley and Fick-Cooper 2015).

The creation of Direction, Alignment and Commitment in 1940, though were defined by military doctrines:

> Both the French and German styles of leadership came from the two armies' doctrines. While one emphasised the management of men and material in methodical battles [administrative], the other emphasised rapid decisions and personal influences at decisive points in highly mobile battles [adaptive]. In other circumstances, the French approach of having commanders "on the handle of a fan" may have been appropriate, but in the dynamic battles of 1940, the approach appeared to be completely out of place.
>
> (Doughty 1990, 331)

DIRECTION

German commanders, often at a level down to Sergeant, made *ad hoc* decisions, within the boundaries of intent (see Chapter 4), without waiting for detailed orders from higher echelons. During the six-week campaign, commissioned as well as non-commissioned officers excelled in making operational and tactical decisions, changing direction as deemed necessary to adapt to a changing environment. In other words, direction was not produced by officers with rank and status but by those that were sensitive enough to understand what direction needed to be taken. In regards to the usefulness of intent, it provides lower-ranked troops with a responsibility to constantly direct, though less so by order and obedience to these orders but rather through personal commitment.

The Allies believed in the power of administrative direction. Men and material were directed, in line with strict timetables. Again, such an approach may be unsurprising, given the number of conscripts who, in default of experience, required detailed orders. Nevertheless, most crack units also fell under the spell of being ordered to be at a specific time and place. The leadership style of the French High Command was like that of a chessboard, moving around chess pieces without an appreciation that many of the front-line leaders' capabilities to lead were being subdued. As a result, operational and tactical leadership was characterised by hesitation, ignorance and at times panic with the absence of clear orders from a higher authority.

COMMAND PHILOSOPHY

Command is the authority vested in an individual to influence events and to order subordinates to implement decisions; command is exercised by, or on behalf of, commanders. It comprises three closely related elements: leadership, decision-making (including risk assessment) and control. The commander's role in command (employing the art of war) is critical, regardless of the technological and other improvements in control (the science of war).

Military command at all levels is the art of decision-making, motivating and directing to accomplish given missions. It requires a vision of the desired outcome(s), an understanding of concepts, mission priorities and allocation of resources, an ability to assess people and risks, and involves a continual process of re-evaluating the situation. A commander requires, above all, to decide on a course of action (COA) and to lead his command. Thus leadership and decision-making are his primary responsibilities. Command also involves accountability and control. However, control is not an equal partner with command but merely an aspect of it. The execution of control is shared between the commander and his staff.

Command is an intrinsically forceful human activity involving authority as well as personal responsibility and accountability. Command philosophy has four facets: a clear understanding of superior commanders' intent; a responsibility on the part of subordinates to meet that intent; the importance of making a timely decision; and a determination, on the part of the commander, to see the plan through to a successful conclusion. This philosophy requires a style of command that promotes decentralised command, freedom and speed of action, and initiative – but one which remains responsive to superior direction.

Effective employment and support of military forces is, however, dependent on the Command and Control (C2) arrangements established, from the highest to the lowest levels of authority. The balance of this Chapter describes the principles on which the C2 of Allied joint operations are based.

(North Atlantic Treaty Organization and NATO Standardization Agency (NSA) 2010)

CHAPTER FIVE: LEADERSHIP

ALIGNMENT

Traditionally, the role of military staff is defined as an administrative role to serve the operational demands of a unit, a division or regiment. This has included the administration of manpower, finance, logistics, military education and training. More modern views on administration emphasise a greater support of commanders on the battlefield.

As already seen on the battlefield in May 1940, German Chiefs of Staff (COS) were tasked to manage information, to filter information and to relay information to where it was needed. In essence, staff provided a commander with adaptive space, controlling information and dealing with smaller issues that do not require the attention of the commanding officer.

Many commanders also used their divisional or regimental staff to inform their decision-making. Ultimately, Guderian (or Rommel, see following textbox) asserted ultimate decision power, but involved corps and divisional staff; they frequently appreciated and also ignored their advice.

IMPORTANCE OF A COHESIVE STAFF TEAM – COMMAND OF THE GERMAN AFRICA CORPS

In 1940, the Italian army was defeated by the British in North Africa. Hitler agreed to send a German corps of three divisions to reinforce the Italians. The first element to arrive was Lieutenant General Erwin Rommel's Reconnaissance Staff. The German Army also formed a larger staff, originally called 'General Liaison Staff Italian Army Libya'. It was led by a highly capable staff officer, Colonel Alfred Gause. Once command relationships had been confirmed, Rommel became commander of 'Panzer Group Africa'. He had the German Africa Corps, the Italian XX Armoured and XXI Infantry Corps under command. Gause became Rommel's

COS of Panzer Group (subsequently Panzer Army) Africa. Before arriving in Libya, Gause's team had spent one month training in Bavaria. They had practised staff procedures and assessed the situation in Libya in detail. The team was small: 25 officers, including the political adviser, but not the attached artillery staff. It contained just four staff trained officers: Gause, Siegfried von Westphal (subsequently Chief of Staff to Rommel, Field Marshal Kesselring and then Field Marshal von Rundstedt), Friedrich von Mellenthin (subsequently COS of Fifth Panzer Army) and one other. Rommel had not attended staff college.

Rommel's staff was extraordinarily efficient. They operated under intense pressure, often with poor intelligence and minimal guidance from their commander. There were probably four factors behind their effectiveness. They:

- were all very capable individuals;
- all knew each other well – it was a socially cohesive team;
- had trained together before deploying; and
- had already researched and assessed the situation in North Africa before arrival.

(Development Concepts and Doctrine Centre 2013, 3–5)

Rommel noted in his diary,

In my view the duties of a commander are not limited to his work with his staff. He must also concern himself with details of command and should pay frequent visits to the fighting line, for the following reasons:

(a) Accurate execution of the plans of the commander and his staff is of the highest importance. It is a mistake to assume that every unit officer will make all that there is to be made out of his situation; most of them soon succumb to a certain inertia. Then it is simply reported that for one reason or another this or that cannot be done – reasons are always easy enough to think up. People of this kind must be made to feel the authority of the commander and be shaken out of their apathy. The commander must be the prime mover of the battle and the troops must always have to reckon with this appearance in personal control.

(b) The commander must be at constant pains to keep his troops abreast of all the latest tactical experience and developments, and must insist on their practical application. He must see to it that his subordinates are trained in accordance with the latest requirements. The best form of 'welfare' for the troops is first-class training, for this saves unnecessary casualties.

(c) It is also greatly in the commander's own interest to have a personal picture of the front and a clear idea of the problems his subordinates are having to face. It is the only way in which he can keep his ideas permanently up to date and adapted to changing conditions. If he fights his battles as a game of chess, he will become rigidly fixed in academic theory and admiration of his own ideas. Success comes most readily to the commander whose ideas have not been canalised into any one fixed channel but can develop freely from the conditions around him.

(d) The commander must have contact with his men. He must be capable of feeling and thinking with them. The soldier must have confidence in him. There is one cardinal principle which must always be remembered: one must never make a show of false emotions to one's men. The ordinary soldier has a surprisingly good nose for what is true and what false.

(Liddell Hart 1953, 226)

The French relied very much on their generalship to direct, and their staff to 'obediently' support such direction. Whereas on the German side, constructive conflict was encouraged and opinions at times fiercely contested, Allied leadership was defined by rank and status; administrative direction was reinforced, with often little or no mindful intervention by members of staff.

COMMITMENT

The degree of commitment to confront a life and death situation was exceptional. As much as ideology plays a role, it was one of leadership on both sides; a deep-seated feeling of commitment to the immediate commander in charge. In the case of the battle for Stonne, the Germans and their French foe knew about the importance of losing this battle, and attacks followed counter-attacks until the French were simply exhausted in men and material. In a true Von Clausewitz manner, purposeful boldness was shown that did not require obedience, but a true loyalty in purpose and immediate leadership.

VON CLAUSEWITZ: BOLDNESS

The higher the rank the more necessary it is that boldness should be accompanied by a reflective mind, that it may not be a mere blind outburst of passion to no purpose, for with increase of rank it becomes always less a matter of self-sacrifice and more a matter of the preservation of others, and the good of the whole. Where regulations of the service, as a kind of second nature, prescribe for the masses, reflection must be the guide of the General, and in his case individual boldness in action may easily become a fault. Still, at the same time, it is a fine failing and must not be looked at in the same light as any other. Happy is the army in which an untimely boldness frequently manifests itself; it is an exuberant growth which shows a rich soil. Even foolhardiness, that is boldness without an object, is not to be despised; in point of fact it is the same energy of feeling, only exercised as a kind of passion without any cooperation of the intelligent faculties. It is only when it strikes at the root of obedience; when it treats with contempt the orders of superior authority, that it must be repressed as a dangerous evil, not on its own account but on account of the act of disobedience, for there is nothing in War which is of greater importance than obedience.

(Adapted from Von Clausewitz 2011, 79)

Unfortunately, the gallant fight by the French was hampered by administrative shackles, imposed by a strategic, operational and tactical 'straightjacket'. In this regard, the commitment that front-leadership infused into their troops was bordering on foolhardy as the Germans continued to have the strategic and operational upper hand.

TRANSLATION AND EXPLANATION: ADAPTIVE LEADERSHIP VERSUS ADMINISTRATIVE LEADERSHIP

As with the other concepts in this book, this has many nuances. On leadership, many perspectives exist. For reasons of simplicity, the focus here will be on administrative versus adaptive leadership. As already introduced earlier in this chapter, administrative leadership refers to planning, coordinating and orchestrating tasks in line with a predefined direction. Successful administrative leaders are able to establish, maintain and improve operational functions.

Adaptive leadership is about the creation of operational functions, fostering learning and adaptive ideas, the development of new directions or simply the change in direction. Table 5.2 shows some key differences between these two styles of leadership.

Table 5.2 Key Differences between Administrative and Adaptive Leadership

Administrative Leadership	Adaptive Leadership
Focus	
The focus of attention is on tasks; how to realise task execution in an aligned manner. Policies, rules and procedures define how tasks are being carried out. Orientation is towards control, outlining what people can't do.	How to carry out tasks is secondary to defining and creating value-adding outcomes, through relationship-based leadership. As a result, policies, rules and procedures are defined to encourage a 'can-do' attitude among people.

(Continued)

Administrative Leadership	Adaptive Leadership
Superior-Subordinate Relationships	
In its most simple form, leadership in a centralised organisation is associated with the setting of clear instructions to be carried out by subordinates. Obedience is part of the relationship between superiors and subordinates, and this is (either tacitly or explicitly) acknowledged by both sides. The leader's authority may be characterised by the ability to issue some form of punishment for non-compliance. As a result, a personal relationship does not necessarily have to be established if the management style is primarily transactional in nature.	The latitude of decision-making power allows a subordinate to act in obedience to the intent, but also allows freedom to define how he or she accomplishes it. This requires a different form of development for subordinate leaders. The objective is not only to train subordinates, but to develop their capability to think on their feet, to assess and to be creative in addressing the situation at hand. As a result, such development may include a greater understanding of the broader organisational strategy and more focus on the 'why' to allow decisions to be taken with a greater knowledge of the wider context and with a longer-term view. The relationship between superiors and subordinates is less likely to be distinguished by hierarchical authority or rank but rather by a closer coaching-like relationship, building more on social commitments.
Culture	
Traditional values and cultures are reinforced. Such values may include obedience and loyalty.	Values such as conflict, criticism, creativity and responsiveness are emphasised and fostered (see Chapter 4).
Assessment	
Leaders are assessed by their ability to reinforce administrative structures; reward is driven by aspects of efficiency, transparency, consistency, continuous improvement and predictability. The inability to comply with a rule book is punished.	The reward to leaders is defined by their ability to innovate, learn, adapt and deal with change in the environment. The ability to move beyond a rule book, to think and act outside prescriptive rules and procedures. Creativity in 'disobeying', although with purpose, is encouraged and rewarded.

Direction, Alignment and Commitment

Direction and Alignment are established in the form of planning. Commitment to a prescribed direction is reinforced through compliance. The leader's key activity is to define direction and reinforce it. Alignment is predominantly carried out by support staff.	Direction and Alignment remain in a fluid state. Leaders constantly assess whether Direction and this Alignment have to be adapted. Commitment does not refer to obedience to a set direction; but to allowing changes to Direction to emerge. Although support staff provide constant Alignment, a leader's key activity is to foster and commit people to drive creativity and responsiveness in direction.

The main emphasis of administrative leadership is to control, and to maintain order that drives stability, predictability and efficiency. Adaptive leadership, though, drives fluidity, not chaos, in direction. In their own right, administrative and adaptive leadership provide a range of benefits (see Table 5.3).

Table 5.3 Advantages of Administrative and Adaptive Leadership

Benefits of Administrative Leadership	*Benefits of Adaptive Leadership*
Organising	Reorganising
Transparency	Opaqueness
Stability	Fluidity
Predictability	Variety
Consistency between options	Creation of options

The benefits of adaptive leadership appear to convey a negative connotation. Who wants to be a leader whose task is to confuse, to drive instability in management, as a mean to enable adaptability? As the next section will outline, it is equally detrimental to go for the other extreme of leadership: trying to establish order, standardisation, alignment, and control, maintaining the status quo. Ultimately, neither extreme is a desirable state of leadership.

TOWARDS ORGANISATIONAL RESILIENCE: THE FALLACY OF ORDER

The previous chapter revolved around the question of whether leadership should be centralised around a single person. It is tempting to believe that 'I' am central to decision making, that 'I' can make better decisions than anybody else. Nevertheless, 'I' am fallible insofar as how centralised leadership tends to be imposed on others in a mindless fashion.

The taxi business is one that may not be described as glamorous or one that yields exceptional profits. However, in recent years, a new competitor, Uber, has shaken up this industry like no other. They have provided customers with control of when and where a taxi is needed, giving them greater flexibility with lower fares.

The rise of Uber is largely attributed to two services. First, the Uber application (app). Using a mobile phone's GPS, a customer can summon a taxi to theoretically any location, and in return receive an accurate pick up time. Second, unlike most other taxi companies, Uber does not provide vehicles to its drivers or require its drivers to obtain an often pricey taxi licence.

The meteoric rise of Uber has recently been challenged by leadership issues. Its CEO, Travis Kalanick, found himself and his company in the press for the wrong reason. Referred to as a cutthroat meritocracy, the emerging culture at Uber started to hurt its reputation. To identify the leadership problems at Uber, a consultancy firm was hired to provide a greater degree of order to Uber's operation. Kalanick stepped aside as the CEO, supposedly for personal reasons.

Uber found itself at a crossroad. Adaptive leadership is certainly required to maintain a leading edge in this industry. Shaking up an industry is key to establish a leading role; notwithstanding, stability, transparency and predictability are necessary to stabilise the company. It is yet to be seen whether too much order is eroding that competitive lead that Uber created through his enigmatic, adaptive, if not disruptive, leadership.

LIMITATIONS OF BUREAUCRACY

The entrepreneurial system established by Uber provided a competitive advantage that led to a market dominance in several countries around the globe. It is only rational to 'tame' the entrepreneurial form of instability, and the variety of products and services and confusion that come along with a vastly growing business. A bias towards imposing greater order through bureaucracy, through greater administration, is a blessing as well as a curse. A system of governance provides long-term stability and an established system of rules and procedures that contains any excessive adaptive leadership. Unfortunately, stifling adaptive leadership also reduces a company's capability to continue adapting to a changing environment. It is not that administrative workings can be simply put aside, suspended or dismantled quickly if adaptive leadership is required.

LIMITATIONS OF AUTOMATION

As a follow-on criticism concerning moving towards administrative leadership, establishing a rule-book for day-to-day operations might again sound obvious in times of instability and resulting confusion. The aim is to reduce situated human cognition through consistency in action. Nevertheless, leadership is a profoundly social endeavour. In particular, commitment is driven socially. To believe that leadership can be enabled and reinforced by an administrative system alone is foolhardy, although leadership through the imposition of rules and procedures provides a compass for how to act; but it still needs to be embedded through social interaction.

ADAPTIVE RESPONSE BEING SUPPORTED BY ADMINISTRATION INSTEAD OF ADMINISTRATIVE RESPONSE STIFLING ADAPTATION

Reacting against administrative leadership *per se* and adopting a pure entrepreneurial, adaptive form of leadership is a folly in itself too. An organisation in its growth- and maturing-stage needs to maintain adaptive leadership as well as administrative leadership to provide stability and efficiency in day-to-day operations. It is important that administrative leadership supports adaptive leadership and does not stifle it. The extent of administrative leadership is defined by the degree to which strict rules and procedures, as well as people's routines, are adhered to. It is however the task of administrative leadership to continuously improve a 'rule-book' as well as constantly help adaptive leadership to challenge habitual routines, past-informed rules and procedures. It can enhance such support by providing adaptive leaders with real-time intelligence and facilitating communications throughout an organisation.

Nevertheless, as straightforward as this sounds, finding the right balance between administrative and adaptive leadership is very challenging, as the US 28th Infantry Division experienced in 1944 (see following textbox).

BATTLE OF HÜRTGEN FOREST

The Battle of the Hürtgen forest was fought between September 12th and December 16th 1944. Although it was the longest single, as well as one of the costliest, series of battles the US Army fought in WWII, it is often overshadowed by the Battle of the Bulge.

After the capture of the first major German city, Aachen, the primary objective of the Americans was to push towards Düren and the Ruhr river, crossing the Rhine south of Cologne. But in the south of their planned corridor was the Hürtgen forest. It is located on the Belgian-German border, and its northern borders lie between the cities of Aachen and Düren.

The dense conifer forest, littered with steep hills and valleys, is broken by few roads, tracks and firebreaks. Tank movements were severely restricted as ground conditions considerably worsened during October–December 1944. Some areas of the Hürtgen forest were incorporated into the *Siegfried* Line, also often referred to as the Westwall. Pillboxes, tank traps, trench systems, minefields with dreaded shoe-mines, box and teller mines turned the Hürtgen forest into a killing zone. There, the Germans intended to defend the Ruhr dams, and to use the surrounding area as an assembly point for the upcoming offensive, *Wacht am Rhein*, to be launched on December 16th 1944.

The Americans though, were initially not aware of the strategic importance of capturing the Ruhr dams. However, in order not to expose their flanks, they planned to clear the forest. The Battle of the Hürtgen forest commenced on September 12th with the attack of elements of the US 3rd Armoured Division and, shortly after, the 9th Infantry Division. By October 19th 1944, the 9th Infantry Division alone had suffered 4,500 casualties in the light of stiffening German resistance.

On October 21st, the 28th Infantry Division, commanded by Major General Cota, was to relieve the embattled 9th Infantry Division. When Cota received his orders, he was stunned. In detail, the orders said that his three regiments were to attack three separate objectives: the 109th Infantry Division to push north towards Hürtgen and the 112th to carry out the main attack through Vossenack, cross the Kall river gorge and capture Schmidt with its important road intersections. Finally, the 110th Infantry Division was to drive southwards to prevent the Germans from counter-attacking and taking control over the road networks leading to Schmidt. It was very similar to the attack that had been unsuccessfully carried out by the 9th Infantry Division.

On November 2nd, the attack was launched with a preparatory 60-minute artillery barrage into the Hürtgen forest. The three regiments moved towards their objectives, in full view of German artillery observers on the Brandenberg-Bergstein ridge.

Well-directed artillery shells rained down on the 28th, and all three regiments started to have casualties. Entrenched Germans slowed down the progress through the thickly forested area. Deteriorating weather stopped all aerial support, so much of the fighting was carried out by infantry in close quarters.

At the end of November 2nd, the Americans paid a terrible blood toll, but captured Vossenack, Kommerscheidt and Schmidt with a battalion size force in each of these villages. Cota remained for most of his time in his divisional headquarters, jubilant at the capture of Schmidt. However, he was oblivious of the state of his regiments. His troops were exhausted; little or no effort was made to send out patrols or to dig-in in anticipation of a counter-attack by the Germans. To make matters worse, the supply route through the Kall Trail came to a standstill. The first M10 tank destroyers, bound for Kommerscheidt and Schmidt, threw their tracks on the narrowly winding Kall trail or were disabled by mines. The trail would remain blocked until November 5th.

On November 3rd, the Germans – as expected – would counter-attack, with a force of Pzkpfw III, IV and V (Panthers). The beleaguered American defenders, under constant artillery fire, had not been supplied with anti-tank guns nor had any tank or tank destroyer made it to Schmidt. The Germans quickly routed Schmidt. They proceeded towards Kommerscheidt but were stopped by recently arrived Sherman tanks and fighter bombers that had used a favourable weather window.

What appeared to be a successful operation, turned out to be a nightmare. Schmidt had been recaptured by the Germans, the 109th failed to take Hürtgen, the 110th to achieve its objectives. Some battalions virtually ceased to exist; others were not battle worthy because of casualties, fatigue and lack of reinforcements and supply.

CHAPTER FIVE: LEADERSHIP

On November 5th, Cota assembled a ragtag force to get through the Kall trail to resume the attack on Schmidt. German units, however, infiltrated this narrow gorge of the Kall stream, inflicting serious casualties and interrupting the vital supply line.

November 6th saw Cota leaving his command post and visiting the Vossenack-Kommerscheidt-Schmidt battle line. He was visibly appalled to see the condition his troops were in, and the terrain of the Kall trail – constantly harassed by the Germans – that made a resumption of offensive actions so hazardous.

But again, the Germans took the initiative and attacked Kommerscheidt. Storming into the picturesque village, they inflicted heavy casualties on the depleted remains. The Americans withdrew their forces through the Kall trail, which was under constant pressure from the Germans, inflicting heavy casualties on the engineer units attempting to maintain this vital, solitary supply route.

Any aspiration of getting on the offensive and recapturing Schmidt turned into a hopeless undertaking. The 28th division was an empty shell. In the early hours of November 8th, Cota was greeted in his command post by General Eisenhower and General Bradley. Eisenhower was aware of the disaster that had unfolded and greeted Cota with *Well Dutch, it looks like you've got a bloody nose.*

The action for the 28th division was over, although the fighting continued in the Hürtgen forest, turning it into a killing field without precedence in WWII for the US army. The 28th Infantry Division alone suffered 6,184 casualties, a staggering 40 per cent of its full strength.

After the disastrous days in November 1944, the V Corps conducted an analysis of the attacks on Vossenack, Kommerscheidt and Schmidt. First, poor weather prevented effective close air support, and hampered operational movement of armoured vehicles. Second, there was reliance on a narrow dirt track, the Kall trail, which was under constant pressure from the *Wehrmacht*. Third was German resistance and the effectiveness of artillery on the Brandenburg-Bergstein ridge.

Some leadership lessons were learned. The orders given to Cota were deemed too complex, and detailed and thus allowed him too little latitude. Nevertheless, Cota agreed to carry out these orders and did not stand up to his superiors. In addition, once the offensive operation commenced, Cota had too little oversight of the combat readiness of his regiments as he spent most of his time in the division command post. In this respect, it was surprising that too few patrols had been sent out to enhance understanding of German intentions.

As for every commander, it was necessary to maintain freedom to act, not allowing superiors or staff to take over directional leadership. But directional leadership is not heroic leadership, when the circumstances clearly indicate that the current direction cannot be maintained. Regimental and divisional staff need to support their commanders in directing by aligning regimental and divisional directions, and administering men and material. WWII has shown over and over again that balancing administrative and adaptive leadership is an extremely difficult undertaking, with only fine margins of error.

FLEXIBILITY OF MIND INSTEAD OF MERE OBEDIENCE

Traditional leadership is often seen as a means of imposing one's will on others. In regard to the previous chapter, this implies that the person imposing leadership on others must be infallible (see Chapter 4), an approach with minimal margin of error. It is also troubling to see that many organisations still opt to eliminate situated human cognition as a source of error through administrative leadership, stifling the very capability that allows people to adapt to novel situations.

A more progressive perspective on leadership though is one that drives adaptiveness in others, in a decentralised manner but nonetheless within the boundaries of an administrative system. Decision power migrates to a person who is close to a problem and can deal with it before it escalates to a crisis. Those close to the problem, though, need to deal with it, always in line with the big picture, the intent (see Chapter 4). Such a leadership approach requires a culture of 'letting go', supporting and guiding 'front-line' employees and mindfully adapting to a situation.

Adapting to a situation, never mind improvising, is a skill in itself, and needs preparation. If people are supposed to slip into the shoes of a leader, they need a specific form of training that is less based on obedience and more on establishing an approach of mindful flexibility. In the armed forces, as well as in management, the importance of wargaming cannot be overstated. Forms of wargaming, scenario planning and 'real-life' exercises are not only tools and techniques to provide direction to an organisation at a strategic level (see Chapter 2) but can also help and empower those at a tactical level to establish situated human cognition, and thus to assume adaptive leadership.

WARGAMING

WARGAMING THE COURSES OF ACTION (COAS)

Wargaming is a flexible instrument designed to develop, compare, and improve COAs. It should be used, whenever time permits, in order to evaluate the potential of the COA to accomplish the mission against foreseen opposition with respect to the different opposing

COAs as well as to identify and correct deficiencies. However, the real value is its ability to permit the JFC[1] and his staff to visualise the conduct of operations and gain insight into opposing capabilities and actions as well as conditions in the operational environment. Wargaming should help them anticipate possible events and foster the mental agility to deal with them. The war game should also help identify potential risks and opportunities, which may drive the need for branches and sequels to counter or exploit such situations, as well as decision points for the commander to take action. Ideally, each own-force COA should be war gamed against the 'most likely' and 'most dangerous' opposing COAs. Wargaming is regularly conducted in OLPP Step 4 to compare COAs. Additionally, it can be used in other steps. Then, however, its purpose would not be comparison but development, improvement or revision of COA. Besides being used in operational planning, wargaming can also be applied as a dry run in mission rehearsals.

GENERAL PRECONDITIONS

Some preconditions have to be met, without which wargaming will fail or only achieve biased results:

- Well-trained staff must be available when setting up the JOPG[2] for wargaming. Especially, a coordinator has to be appointed. He will be responsible for the preparation and the conduct of wargaming in terms of contents and organization.
- Constraints and restraints for the friendly conduct of operations as well as for the opposing forces (OPFOR) COAs assumed conduct of operations have to be identified, made available for wargaming and followed.
- Operational analysis (OA) includes not only the development and application of mathematical models, statistical analyses and simulations but also the application of expertise and experience for the determination of quantitative factors for friendly and

opponents' COAs. Mathematical models and simulations, and the interpretation of their results, form the core of OA. The results indicate trends and tendencies and as such are only one factor to be considered in decision-making. The quality of these trends and tendencies depends on the quality of the initial factors. These models simplify reality, which is especially true for asymmetrical scenarios. The scope of OA has to be agreed upon between the coordinator, the head of JOPG, and the OA experts. If available and time allows, wargaming can benefit from OA support from the very beginning, whether it is conducted in a computer-based or manual manner.

PREPARING AND CONDUCTING WAR GAMES

This involves determining the desired type of outcome; the method and scope of the game; and the participants of the game, including subordinate commands, friendly, opposing and, eventually, neutral players (Blue, Red and Green Teams), referees, expert arbitrators and recorders. In addition, the operational situation must be prepared, tools for manual or computer-assisted simulation and analysis, and rules need to be established.

While there are benefits to a war game, it must be noted that preparing a joint staff war game may be cost, manpower and time-intensive. The conduct of a war game is determined largely by the desired outcomes, selected method and the scope. War games will include:

- Setting conditions. An introduction to set the strategic and operational conditions affecting the operation, including political considerations, threat conditions, environmental conditions, civil conditions, information and media conditions, etc.

> - Game moves. A series of 'game turns' considering the action – reaction – counter-action of opposing actors, starting with the opposing actor deemed to have the initiative.
>
> ASSESSMENT AND RECORDING
> OF OVERALL RESULTS
>
> An assessment of probable results of any action – reaction – counteraction typically follows each game turn within a cognition phase and is used to set conditions for the succeeding game turns. Observations and conclusions drawn from the war game are recorded in line with the purpose.
>
> (Development Concepts and Doctrine Centre 2013, 3–52)

OUTLOOK

During the fateful days in May 1940, the French relied very much on a centralised, administrative manner of leadership. This may have been a logical response to having a largely citizen army at their disposal. Nevertheless, their officers were far from being laymen, or ill-equipped to make situated decisions. There are countless accounts where the right decisions were made, but due to administrative shackles, could not be carried out on time. On a range of other occasions, with the lack of sensitivity that came with the absence of out-of-date intelligence, a confusing picture emerged so that commanders could only do the obvious: following the initial order, whatever the costs, or opting to fill the void of lack of orders with the opposite extreme – falling back.

Adaptive leadership is crucial in a battle as well as in an organisation. In an organisation it may be tempting to 'tame' people by the strict imposition of standard-operating procedures and make them compliant to rules and procedures. In the case of Uber, aggressive leadership

CHAPTER FIVE: LEADERSHIP

needed to be 'tamed'. It is, however, worth considering whether the initial disruptive entrepreneurial spirit of Uber will be controlled to an extent that is stifling, and ultimately eradicates the adaptive leadership that any organisation needs maintained.

Reflection — *To what extent does your work unit adhere to Centralisation or Decentralisation? For each item, select one box only that best reflects your conclusion.*

Left		Right
Situated cognition is being eliminated as a source of error	○ ○ ○(Neutral) ○ ○	Situated cognition is being fostered as an answer to problems
Consistency of action is paramount	○ ○ ○ ○ ○	We provide people with the freedom to act
Consistency, transparency and stability are paramount	○ ○ ○ ○ ○	Creativity, agility are most important
Leadership is a non-social function	○ ○ ○(Neutral) ○ ○	Leadership is dependent on social interactions
Decision power migrates to the person with rank and status	○ ○ ○ ○ ○	Decision power is deferred to the people with the greatest expertise
Compliance drives the execution of tasks	○ ○ ○ ○ ○	Responsibility and empowerment drive the execution of intent

Scoring: If your answers tend to the left, you are pursuing a more administrative leadership approach. If your answers are more on the right, the concept of adaptive leadership seems more applicable to your ways of working.

NOTES

1 Joint Forces Command.
2 Joint Operations Planning Group.

REFERENCES

BArch. "RH 82 Bild-00059." Koblenz: Bundesarchiv.
———. "RH 82 Bild-00097." Koblenz: Bundesarchiv.
Baudouin, P. 1948. *The Private Diaries of Paul Baudouin*. London: Eyre & Spottiswoode.
De Jomini, A.H. 2008. *The Art of War*. Kingston Legacy Books Press.
Development Concepts and Doctrine Centre. 2013. "Allied Joint Doctrine for Operational-Level Planning (+UK National Elements)."
Dildy, D. 2014. *Fall Gelb 1940 (1): Panzer Breakthrough in the West*. Oxford: Osprey Publishing.
Doughty, R.A. 1990. *The Breaking Point: Sedan and the Fall of France*. Hamden, CT: Archon.
Frieser, K.-H. 2005. *The Blitzkrieg Legend: The 1940 Campaign in the West*. Annapolis, MD: Naval Institute Press.
Guderian, H. 2000. *Panzer Leader*. London: Penguin Classics.
Liddell Hart, B.H., ed. 1953. *The Rommel Papers*. New York: Da Capo Press.
McCauley, C., and L. Fick-Cooper. 2015. *Direction, Alignment, Commitment: Achieving Better Results Through Leadership*. Greensboro, NC: Center for Creative Leadership.
Muth, J. 2011. *Command Culture*. Denton: University of North Texas Press.
North Atlantic Treaty Organization, and NATO Standardization Agency (NSA). 2010. "Allied Joint Doctrine AJP–01(D)."
Tzu, S. 2008. *The Art of War*. London: Penguin Books.
Useem, M. 2010. *"Spotlight on Leadership Lessons from the Military."* HBR Spotlight Article Collection. November.
Van Creveld, M. 1982. *Fighting Power: German and U.S. Army Performance, 1939–1945*. Westport, CT: Greenwood Press.
Von Clausewitz, C. 2011. *On War*. United States: Madison Park.

CHAPTER SIX
Logistics

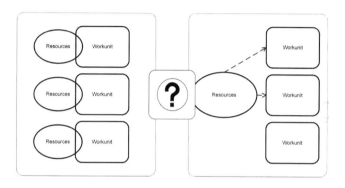

Supplying an army
At a distance
Drains the public coffers
And impoverishes
The common people

(Tzu 2008, 9)

CONTENTS

The story: May 18th–May 25th 1940	198
Logistical independence versus dependence	201
De Jomini: a few remarks on logistics in general	202
North Atlantic Treaty Organization (NATO): logistics planning	206
The challenge: racing to the channel	207
Deciding factors: abundance of resources, operational availability and logistical autonomy and cohesion	213
Continuous logistics	214
Translation and explanation: JIT versus JIC	217
Towards organisational resilience: the fallacy of 'pure' just-in-time	219
The Africa campaign	222
NATO: logistic planning considerations	228
Outlook	230
Notes	232
References	232

This chapter looks at logistics as a supporting function for strategic, operational and tactical management. It revolves around

- Procurement of resources, such as men and material
- Planning, organising, movement and stationing of resources.

THE STORY: MAY 18TH–MAY 25TH 1940

In northern Belgium, the Germans were still hammering away at the Gembloux Gap, sustaining considerable losses. News of the breakout of the Meuse bridgeheads was trickling through. In the centre, the *Wehrmacht's* armoured divisions moved 200 km inland (see Map 6.1), threatening to encircle the battered Allied forces in the north. Consequently, the Allies started a methodical withdrawal as the pressure became too much. The diary of Lieutenant General Brooke (BEF) mentioned,

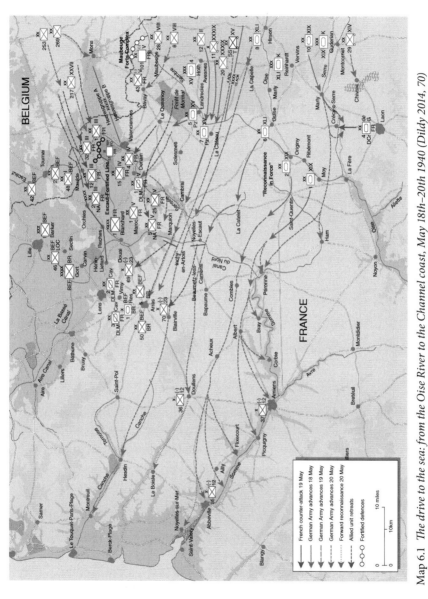

Map 6.1 *The drive to the sea: from the Oise River to the Channel coast, May 18th–20th 1940 (Dildy 2014, 70)*

> I was too tired to write last night, and now can barely remember what happened yesterday. The hours are so crowded and follow so fast on each other that life becomes a blur and fails to cut a groove in one's memory.
>
> (Horne 1990, 507)

May 16th saw a renewed attempt by the German chiefs of staff, in particular Rundstedt, supported by Hitler, to put a brake on Guderian's advance as they feared their flanks were overexposed. Despite clear and unmistakeable orders to halt the advance, Guderian disobeyed, continuing what he referred to as a reconnaissance in force. After a very brief respite, the Panzer forces were on the move again. The forwardmost units risked being out of step with their motorised infantry units, offering the Allies a window of opportunity to strike.

The situation was not hopeless for the Allies (see Map 6.1). The rapid advance by the Germans created a large salient. This presented an opportunity for the Allies to counter-attack, stop the German's westernmost approach towards Amiens and Arras, break through their lines and cut off considerable German forces.

On May 16th, Winston Churchill met Daladier and Reynaud in the French Foreign Ministry at the Quai d'Orsay. After Gamelin provided the British and French politicians with a situational assessment, the focus of attention was on the emerging 'bulge' at Sedan. Churchill asked in his nonchalant manner, in bad French, *Où est la masse de manoeuvre?* (Where is the strategic reserve?). Gamelin replied in a similar and sobering manner: *Aucune* (None). The strategic reserve was committed to the north of Belgium as part of the Dyle-Breda Plan and currently relentlessly engaged by the German forces.

To make matters worse, the British started disengaging from what they believed to be a lost battle. The French soon noted British intentions:

> At 10:30 General Weygand came into the Prime Minister's room, and found Marshal Pétain already there. I remained throughout this meeting, which lasted until a quarter to one.
>
> On entering, the General whispered to me, "The situation is very serious, for the English are falling back on the ports instead of

attacking to the south." He told the Prime Minister that according to a telegram from the French liaison office with the King of the Belgians, actually the only means of communication between the British Army and General Blanchard, the English had abandoned Arras without being compelled by the Germans to do so, and appeared to be retreating in the direction of the ports. This was contrary to the formal instructions given by General Weygand to the British army according to the plans shown on Wednesday the 22nd to the British Prime Minister and approved by him.

General Weygand declared that this strategy on the part of the British Army did not surprise him, for on the previous evening he had been struck by General Ironside's tone over the telephone. "I would willingly have boxed his ears", said General Weygand, and then went on, "It is impossible to command an army which remains dependent on London in the matter of military operations. All this is the more regrettable in that yesterday and during the night Besson's army group, coming from the south, reached the Somme, while Colonel de Gaulle's armour is at Boves, ready to issue forth to assist the southern army to move north."

(Baudouin 1948, 43)

May 17th saw one of the first planned counter-attacks by the French from the north and south. These French efforts would be complemented by British attempts to disrupt the advance of the Germans coming from the east at Arras. These counter-attacks would pose the last chance to turn the tide, to free the Allied forces from encirclement and utter defeat.

LOGISTICAL INDEPENDENCE VERSUS DEPENDENCE

The importance of logistics cannot be overstated: *Logistics governs the battlefield, not only at the lowest levels of strategy, where it determines whether or not soldiers receive food and bullets, but at the highest, where it determines what armies can do* (Kane 2001, 32).

DE JOMINI: A FEW REMARKS ON LOGISTICS IN GENERAL

1. The preparation of all the material necessary for setting the army in motion or, in other words, for opening the campaign. Drawing up orders, instructions and itineraries for the assemblage of the army and its subsequent launching upon its theatre of operations.
2. Drawing up in a proper manner the orders of the general-in-chief for different enterprises as well as plans of attack in expected battles.
3. Arranging with the chiefs of engineers and artillery the measures to be taken for security of the posts which are to be used as depots as well as those to be fortified in order to facilitate the operations of the army.
4. Ordering and directing reconnaissance of every kind and procuring in this way, and by using spies, as exact information as possible of the positions and movements of the enemy.
5. Taking every precaution for the proper execution of movements ordered by the general. Arranging the march of the different columns so that all may move in an orderly and connected manner. Ascertaining with certainty that the means requisite for the ease and safety of marches are prepared. Regulating the manner and time of halts.
6. Giving proper composition to advanced guards, rearguards, flankers and all detected bodies, and preparing good instructions for their guidance. Providing all the means necessary for the performance of their duties.
7. Prescribing forms and instructions for subordinate commanders or their staff officers, relative to the different methods of drawing up the troops in columns when the

enemy is at hand, as well as their formation in the most appropriate manner when the army is to engage in battle, according to the nature of the ground and the character of the enemy.

8. Indicating to advance guards and other detachments well-chosen points of assembly in case of their attack by superior numbers and informing them what support they may hope to receive in case of need.

9. Arranging and superintending the march of trains of baggage, munitions, provisions and ambulances, both with the columns and in their rear, in such a manner that they will not interfere with the movements of the troops and will still be near at hand. Taking precautions for order and security, both on the march and when trains are halted and parked.

10. Providing for the successive arrival of convoys of supplies. Collecting all the means of transportation of the country and of the army, and regulating their use.

11. Directing the establishment of camps and adopting regulations for their safety, good order and policing.

12. Establishing and organising lines of operations and supplies as well as lines of communications with these lines for detached bodies. Designating officers capable of organising and commanding in the rear of the army; looking out for the safety of detachments and convoys, furnishing them with good instructions and looking out also for preserving suitable means of communication of the army with its base.

13. Organising depots of convalescent, wounded and sickly men; movable hospitals; and workshops for repairs, and providing for their safety.

14. Keeping accurate record of all detachments, either on the flanks or in the rear; keeping an eye upon

> their movements and looking out for their return to the main column as soon as their service on detachment is no longer necessary; giving them, when required, some centre of action and forming strategic reserves.
> 15. Organising marching battalions or companies to gather up isolated men or small detachments moving in either direction between the army and its base of operations.
>
> (Adapted from De Jomini 2008, 202)

The Germans followed a principle of logistical independence (Frieser 2005). It posits that in operational terms, the *Schwerpunkt* is equipped with an abundance of supplies being made permanently and continuously available to a fighting force. Oberst Zeitzler (Chief of Staff, *Panzergruppe Kleist*) relied on what he called the *Rucksack-Prinzip* (backpack principle). It implies that a force has to have its own logistical capabilities to 'carry with it' (hence backpack) resources, not to have resources delivered to a moving force. This principle was operationalised through the following measures:

> In addition to its organic supply elements, the Panzer Group was given three truck transport battalions with a total cargo capacity of forty-eight hundred tons.
>
> All 41,140 vehicles used were loaded to the limit of their cargo capacity with ammunition, rations, and above all fuel.
>
> So-called march movement tank depots were spaced along the planned march movement routes from the assembly areas all the way to the border.
>
> Abundantly stocked supply depots were set up near the border so that the units could draw on them during the operation's first phase.

CHAPTER SIX: LOGISTICS

The required ration, fuel, and ammunition convoys were ready for the advance supply base, planned in Luxembourg, before the start of the offensive.

(Frieser 2005, 107–8)

One invention, like no other, epitomises logistical independence: the *Wehrmacht-Einheitskanister* (also labelled by the Allies as a jerrycan). It is a steel liquid fuel container holding 20 litres. To increase the speed of filling and draining it was fitted with a large spout and flip-top closure. Its shape made it easily stackable, and two of them could be carried by one soldier. More importantly, they could be attached to motorised units and, when empty, replaced quickly or discarded altogether.

This image shows the refuelling process, most likely of a Panther in France 1943 (BArch)

As a result of such logistical foresight and independence, the Germans did not face a single major supply crisis during the campaign in the west. In contrast, French operational readiness was too often compromised by a sluggish logistical system. Motorised units ran out of fuel and remained stationary for too long until a refuelling unit made its way up clogged roads to the forward units. Precious time and thus movement were wasted in the process of requesting resupplies, having them approved, and then ultimately having them delivered.

NORTH ATLANTIC TREATY ORGANIZATION (NATO): LOGISTICS PLANNING

Logistic standards and doctrine are the key elements of logistic planning. They provide the common basis for both the force planning and operational planning activities of NATO and national logistic planners. They are the means to ensure that national plans support NATO objectives and Strategic Command (SCs') missions. These logistic standards supplement and further define Ministerial Guidance and other planning documents.

(a) Strategic Mobility. Strategic mobility is the capability to move forces and their sustainment in a timely and effective manner over long distances to the place of their intended employment. This could be between Joint Operations Area (JOAs), between regions (interregional) or beyond NATO's Area of Responsibility. The Defence Requirements Review (DRR) is key to strategic mobility planning by identifying the requirements for sealift and airlift assets to deploy forces and sustainment to support operations envisioned in the Ministerial Guidance. Additionally and outside of the DRR, planners must determine the reception assets that are needed. Through the force planning process, the requirements for strategic mobility are then identified to nations. The shortfall in capability between the overall requirement and what nations commit via the Defence Planning Questionnaire (DPQ) must be made up by other means, such as through contracting or arrangements with commercial transport interests.

(b) Sustainability. Logistic planning in this area focusses on ensuring that personnel, equipment and other material

> is available in sufficient quantity and quality for NATO operations. The main logistic elements to be covered are:
>
> > Mission decisive equipment
> > Munitions
> > Petroleum, Oil and Lubricants (POL)
> > Maintenance
> > Medical support
> > Movement and transportation
> > Rations/water
>
> (c) Stockpile Planning. In accordance with MC 55/3, the SCs establish, in consultation with the nations, requirements for the provision of logistic resources. In this respect both SCs provide the biennial Bi-Strategic Command (Bi-SC) Stockpile Planning Guidance (SPG), which applies to Land, Air and Maritime Forces, and which covers all classes of supply as well as pharmaceuticals and medical material. However, it focusses on the requirements for battle decisive munitions. The Bi-SC SPG provides national authorities of NATO nations with generic guidance, required tools and planning data to calculate the stockpile requirements to support NATO's military mission regarding the Planning Situations as specified in the DRR.
>
> (NATO Standardization Agency 2003, 2–4)

THE CHALLENGE: RACING TO THE CHANNEL

Hitler's constant flank panic led to a brief halt in the German advance from the bridgeheads in the area of Sedan. Notwithstanding, they covered considerable ground once the first halt-order was lifted. The race to the channel, sealing the encirclement of the Allies, would not only lead to the breakdown of Allied operational latitude but also to their' destruction.

On May 17th, the 4th Armoured Division, under the command of Colonel Charles de Gaulle, was dispatched to finally put a halt to the enemy's intentions. Georges told him, *There, de Gaulle! For you who have for so long held the ideas which the enemy is putting into practice, here is the chance to act.*

Such commitment could not have come at a worse time as it dawned on de Gaulle that it was already too late to turn the tide, with only some elements of a motorised division at his disposal. By dawn of May 17th, he could only muster three tank battalions, of which two were equipped with light Renault R35s; only one included heavy Char-Bs as well as a company with modern D-2 light (16 tons) tanks, both types mounting a potent 75 mm gun. In light of his meagre forces, he commented,

> Miserable processions of refugees crowded along all the roads coming from the north. I saw, also, a good many soldiers who lost their weapons. They belonged to the troops routed by the panzers during the preceding days. Caught up, as they fled, by the enemy's mechanised detachments, they had been ordered to throw away their arms and make off to the south so as not to clutter up the roads. "We haven't time" they had been told, "to take you prisoners!" ... Then, at the sight of those bewildered people and those soldiers in rout, at the tale, too, of the contemptuous piece of insolence of the enemy's, I felt myself borne up by a limitless fury. Ah! It's too stupid! The war is beginning as badly as it could.
>
> (The Complete War Memoirs of Charles de Gaulle 1972, 39)

The attack by De Gaulle's 4th Armoured Division took the Germans by surprise. They managed to punch into the rear echelons of the German 1st Panzer and started to create mayhem as de Gaulle was approaching Montcornet. Graf von Kielmansegg, a supply officer in 1st Panzer, recounted,

> Leaving Montcornet and continuing along the main highway – the Division's only route of advance – I saw several Germans running

CHAPTER SIX: LOGISTICS

back toward me. They were engineers who said that there were French tanks coming after them! I did not want to believe that because the direction in which they pointed was the direction of our own front line.

(Von Kielmannsegg 1941, 164)

The Germans improvised a mine-barrier as they noticed in horror that the French made their way into the streets of Lislet. Kielmansegg rushed back to Guderian's headquarters to warn him of the impending disaster. On his way, he stumbled across some German tanks that had just left their repair depot, which he requestioned. He also mustered a few light anti-aircraft guns, which he deployed even though they could not penetrate the armour of the French main battle tanks:

> In spite of the fact that my light flak guns (which I had brought up in the interim) could not penetrate their thick armour, by firing at the tracks of the French machines they forced them to turn about.

(Von Kielmannsegg 1941, 166)

A 31.5t Char B1. They were deployed most often only in single units, with the purpose of supporting infantry. The coordination between tank and infantry, as well as with close air support, was woefully inadequate (BArch)

Some French tanks were finally shot up, but the defence at Montcornet and Lislet was woefully inadequate. The French attacked again in the afternoon, but a familiar picture of operational and logistical ineptitude made them disengage before they could fully exploit their surprising raid on the German rear. Captain Idée noted,

> 19:00 hours: Petrol is running low. The 'B' [Char B] tanks have just turned about. They are leaving Lislet. The infantry had not been able to follow them, and what can we do without them? There must be some infiltration at our rear. The enemy platoon commanders have a terribly enterprising air about them.
>
> (Horne 1990, 494)

De Gaulle resumed his attack two days later but was increasingly pounded from the air and worn down by the 10th Panzer Division that had been redirected from the Battle of Stonne. The pressure mounted. The French counter-attack fizzled out.

The counter-attack from the south (see Map 6.1) did not bring a breakthrough, failing to punch through the German communications line. From the north, though, the BEF, under the command of General Lord Gort planned an attack southwards from Arras on May 21st. Their available strength was as pitiful as what was at de Gaulle's disposal: two infantry divisions and the 1st Army Tank Brigade, mustering a total of 58 Mark I and 16 Mark II (later christened 'Matilda') infantry tanks, slow, but with a 2-pounder gun that could knock out most of their German counterparts, although only at relatively close range. The plan was to bolster the British with French armour, but a good part of the French 1st Light Mechanised Division had been committed to support de Gaulle's attack, and other motorised units were destroyed in the bitter fighting with the Germans. Gort decided not to wait for any further reinforcements and instructed General Martel to proceed with an attack southwards.

On May 21st, Rommel's 7th Panzer was to proceed around the flank of Arras, while the 5th Panzer Division advanced to north-east of it.

CHAPTER SIX: LOGISTICS

Rommel's flanks were protected by the *Waffen-SS* Division *Totenkopf* (deathhead) and rifle regiments. Not long after, the forward sections of General Martel's 'Frankforce' got in contact with the Germans. Rommel commented,

> The enemy tank fire created chaos and confusion among our troops in the village [Wailly, south of Arras] and they were jamming up the roads and yards with their vehicles, instead of going into action with every available weapon to fight off the oncoming enemy. We tried to create order. After notifying the divisional staff of the critical situation in and around Wailly we drove off to a hill 1,000 yards west of the village. We found a light AA [anti-aircraft] troop and several anti-tank guns located in hollows and a small wood, most of them totally under cover. About 1,200 yards west of our position the leading enemy tanks, among them one heavy, had already crossed the Arras-Beaumetz railway and shot up one of our Panzer IIIs. At the same time several enemy tanks were advancing down the road from Bac du Nord and across the railway line towards Wailly. It was an extremely tight spot, for there were also several enemy tanks very close to Wailly on its northern side. The crew of a howitzer battery, some distance away, now left their gun and swept along the retreating infantry. With Most's [Lieutenant Most] help, I brought every available gun into action at top speed against the tanks. Every gun, both anti-tank gun and anti-aircraft, was ordered to open rapid fire immediately and I personally gave each gun its target. With the tanks so perilously close, only rapid fire from every gun could save the situation. We ran from gun to gun. The objections of the gun commanders that the range was still too great to engage tanks effectively were overruled. All I cared about was to halt the enemy tanks by heavy gunfire.
>
> (Liddell Hart 1953, 30–1)

The deployed anti-tank guns plastered British tanks with shells, but likewise with French medium and heavy tanks, their fire bounced off their front armour. Rommel ordered some divisional artillery to open up and a few 88 mm anti-aircraft guns to fire over their open sights to engage the British armour. Artillery and incessant fire from 88 mm guns finally silenced the heavy Matildas.

A British Mark II Matilda. An officer points towards the entry point of a German shell. Given the thickness of front armour of the Matilda, it appears to be an 88 mm shell that knocked out this tank (BArch)

The counter-attack by Martel's 'Frankforce' sent panic waves through the German High Command, although it only achieved a tactical victory; despite this, Rommel was optimistic that a favourable outcome was inevitable. He wrote to his wife,

> Dearest Lu
>
> With a few hours' sleep behind me, it's time for a line to you. I am fine in every way. My division has had a blazing success. Dinant, Philippeville, break-through the Maginot Line and advance in one night 40 miles through France to Le Catâu, then Cambrai, Arras, always in front of everybody else. Now the hunt is up against 60 encircled British, French and Belgian divisions. Do not worry about me. As I see it the war in France may be over in a fortnight.
>
> (Liddell Hart 1953, 34)

CHAPTER SIX: LOGISTICS

DECIDING FACTORS: ABUNDANCE OF RESOURCES, OPERATIONAL AVAILABILITY AND LOGISTICAL AUTONOMY AND COHESION

The failure of the Allies to successfully counter-attack was due to numerous reasons already touched on in previous chapters. Among others, strategic reserves were prematurely committed to the wrong centre of gravity (COG). As so often, logistical shortcomings additionally constrained the operational movement of forces. In contrast, the Germans could rely on logistical independence: abundance of resources, operational availability and cohesion.

ABUNDANCE OF RESOURCES

The Germans concentrated most of their elite units on the *Schwerpunkt*, the COG. They structured these resources around the formation of Panzer Group Kleist, a temporarily formed and largely operational independent formation, true to Guderian's maxim of *Klotzen, nicht kleckern* (Boot them, don't spatter them). Under its command, significant air forces were placed to provide close ground support. In order to operate without any delays and downtime, the Germans pursued a 'push' effort of logistics, ordering more than enough fuel, spare parts, lubricants and other material that keeps an army moving and operational. Essentially, the operating area of Panzergruppe Kleist was flooded with material, stored in depots or being carried along (see the backpack principle, introduced earlier in this chapter).

The Allies, in particular the French, ran short of supplies. Movements, attacks and counter-attacks had to be postponed as machines were not refuelled or resupplied, because resources were simply not available or not made available. The French artillery was supplied with an abundance of shells as the envisaged way of fighting was to saturate the enemy with artillery fire. The more mobile forces, destined to 'plug' a breach in the front line, learned the hard way what it meant to ration movement and firepower as the fixed amount of resources allocated to a mobile unit was far from enough to keep the Germans in check.

OPERATIONAL AVAILABILITY

The operational availability of an army is defined by the length of downtime, non-operational periods associated with reliability, maintenance and logistics. This may include time to maintain tanks and vehicles as well as time to obtain spare parts or have an army unit resupplied. There is plenty of anecdotal evidence of the Germans keeping their units operational, despite the need to replace destroyed tanks and material or to retrieve broken down or knocked out tanks from the battlefield and have them serviced in a nearby repair depot. Unlike the Germans, the French were plagued by downtime, although not all down to logistical constraints. Some armoured units could not move due to lack of operational readiness. They were still in training and/or simply did not have sufficient continuous logistics allocated to them (see textbox).

CONTINUOUS LOGISTICS

Recalling our physical view of warfare, we said that classical warfare is best expressed by the laws of solid mechanics. Modern warfare on the other hand is best expressed by the laws of fluid mechanics. Fluids represent two states of matter: liquids and gases. Units engaged in distributed battle are analogous to liquids under the dynamics of extreme heat and pressure. Formations conducting a distributed campaign are analogous to gases undergoing similar force dynamics. If we are to maintain the validity of this particular physical analogy, we must show how these fluids maintain their density.

> Under the classical paradigm, Von Clausewitz characterised the strategic level of war in terms of space, time and mass. In terms of space, strategy is concerned with the expanse of a theatre of operations; in terms of time, with the duration of a campaign; and in terms of mass, with the density of an army as a whole.
>
> Under modern conditions the army as a whole can be visualised as flowing or percolating distributively through the depth of the theatre of operations. At this level the army projects force by virtue of its rate of flow: its tempo and density. Because of the significance of this physical relationship we can see why it becomes critical to view operational manoeuvre as relational movement to achieve and deny freedom of action. Fundamentally, the denial of freedom of action drives military forces and pressure to zero. Since pressure is proportional to density (mass) and tempo (acceleration), the ability of the attacker to mass and continue his momentum must be maintained. But tempo is not only practically a function of freedom of action, it is also a function of movement. And movement brings us to the issue of logistics.
>
> Logistics is concerned with the movement and sustainment of armies in the field. Not only does logistics sustain the movement tempo of an army, it also sustains its force density. Without operational logistics an army would, by analogy, simply evaporate. In order for a modern industrial army to maintain a militarily effective presence, its logistics system must be continuous.
>
> (Schneider 2015, 41-2)

LOGISTICAL AUTONOMY AND COHESION

The abundance of resources made available in a continuous manner was down to logistical autonomy and cohesion on the side of the Germans. Aligned with the motto of decentralised decision-making, local decision makers, such as a tank commanders, autonomously decided, on the basis of their military intelligence, what their demands for logistical support should be. They decided what quantity of supplies could be carried in the 'backpack' and how much logistical support was needed from higher logistical echelons. The range and variety of these individual logistical demands was managed by staff members of the unit, who made decisions about short-term and long-term supply. Long-term requirements included the provision of substantial contingencies, abundant static and mobile resources beyond the immediate request to anticipate shortfalls and potential bottlenecks.

As a result, forces could be supplied whenever and wherever and in whatever situation they found themselves. Logistical autonomy required logistical cohesion, harmonising the procurement, movement, storage and means to make diverse resources (equipment, supplies, etc.) available in a continuous manner. Again, German logistical staff excelled in establishing such cohesion between the *Wehrmacht*, *Waffen-SS* and *Luftwaffe*.

Due to these deciding factors, it is no surprise that the Germans did not face any major bottlenecks and had relatively little operational downtime, so that they kept their units moving and ready to encounter the next battle. A logistical after-action-report of Panzer Group Kleist stated,

> Between May 10th and the capture of Calais, there was not a single supply crisis that could not be resolved with the resources of the Group van Kleist, without in any way interfering with command functions.
>
> (Frieser 2005, 107)

On the Allied side, logistical constraints amplified strategic and operational as well as tactical shortcomings in mobility. An example of French lack of cohesion (as well as potential lack of military intelligence and inept central coordination) highlights what logistical incohesion the Allies had to deal with:

> As if things could not get any worse [for the French], most of the supply elements with the fuel trucks and the repair units were in the

south, whereas the French tanks were cut off from the farther north. A number of Char B1 battle tanks were standing on the railroad flatcars, almost without gas, in the unloading stations, when they were surprised by Reinhardt's panzer.

(Frieser 2005, 263)

TRANSLATION AND EXPLANATION: JIT VERSUS JIC

The role of logistics serves a different purpose in war than it does in most commercial organisations. In war,

> Logistics governs the battlefield, not only at the lowest levels of strategy, where it determines whether or not soldiers receive food and bullets, but at the highest, where it determines what armies can do.

(Kane 2001, 32)

Hence, logistics enables movement of an army and its battle effectiveness; how and when to move resources to the places of military conflict. In business, it is less a question of how armies can be moved, but of how customers' needs and wants can be served. In this regard,

> Business logistics is the part of supply chain management that plans, implements, and controls the efficient, effective forward and reverse flow and storage of goods, services, and related information between the point of origin and the point of consumption in order to meet customers' requirements.

(Adapted from Council of Supply Chain Management Professionals 2017)

Germany as well as the Allies in WWII applied a principal logistical philosophy that is known in management speak as Just-in-Case (JIC) logistics. JIC entails maintaining large inventories of supplies, parts and resources to buffer uncertainties in the supply chain. Stocks are reordered when these meet a minimum level.

Just-in-Time (JIT) is an inventory philosophy that builds on the premise of decreasing waste by receiving goods when they are needed in the production process. Hence, in comparison to JIC it tries to eliminate stock buffers.

The following table (see Table 6.1) delves to a greater extent into key properties of JIC and JIT:

Table 6.1 Key Differences between Just-in-Case and Just-in-Time

Just-in-Case	Just-in-Time
Contingencies	
The supply chain, the sequence of processes involved in the production and distribution of a product or service, can rely on excess inventory and backups. Inventory is restocked at specific levels.	Excess inventory is being eliminated. Inventory is only restocked when needed.
Ordering time	
Inventory is reordered before supplies reach the buffer or minimum level to allow for it to be produced/sold while the suppliers are resupplying the goods. Minimum buffer is defined by potential spikes in demand.	Inventory is recorded only as it is needed and not before. This means that no safety stocks are held. Production operates with low inventory levels.
Location	
Inventory is located and stored as close as possible to where it is needed.	Inventory is delivered to where it is needed.

The major difference between JIC and JIT is in the responsibility for logistics. With JIC, the producer takes responsibility for ordering and storing inventory. The sole duty of the supplier is to deliver stock when requested. With JIC, the supplier needs to provide storage (even mobile storage as in trucks or freight cars), has to maintain depots and is required to supply a producer on a much shorter notice. As a consequence, the producer is less dependent on a contentiously functioning supply chain than he would be under JIT. Such difference in logistical dependence is associated with distinct advantages (see Table 6.2).

Table 6.2 Advantages of Just-in-Case and Just-in-Time

Just-in-Case	Just-in-Time
Less planning required	Less waste
Less vulnerable to sudden spikes in demand	Less vulnerable to sudden changes in customers' wants and needs
Less dependent on suppliers to ensure supply	Less dependent on production to ensure supply
Longer lead time	Shorter lead time

A major advantage in pursuing a JIC philosophy is greater operational robustness in enabling continuous logistics. With contingent stock in place, unexpected sudden hikes in demand or potentially abrupt drops in supply can be accommodated for longer periods of time than are possible under JIT.

Nevertheless, JIT provides greater logistical efficiency and enables more production flexibility. Regarding the former, waste is reduced to a minimum. Storage, for example, does not need to be maintained. Reduced inventory costs go hand in hand with better use of cash flow. Shorter lead times also allow production flexibility as new stock imperatives for producing novel products and services can be introduced quickly.

TOWARDS ORGANISATIONAL RESILIENCE: THE FALLACY OF 'PURE' JUST-IN-TIME

The importance of logistics has been associated in modern management theory largely with the emphasis on increasing efficiency gains by reducing inventory. JIT inventory management, also at times referred to as lean-manufacturing or Toyota Production System (TPS), also has a dark side in that it tends to be ill-prepared for disruptions in the supply chain.

In April 2004, Boeing announced that All Nippon Airways (ANA) would be the launch customer for the new revolutionary 787 Dreamliner. On July 8th 2007, the first was unveiled at Boeing's Everett assembly factory. At that time, 677 orders had already been received.

The delivery of this aircraft was thereafter plagued by delays in production, on-board fires and emergency landings. In July 2013, Qatar airways grounded their whole fleet due to issues with an electrical panel. Air India followed suit with the problem of an overheated oven and launched an investigation. In 2016, ANA decided to ground all aircrafts due to complications with their Rolls-Royce engines. All these posed disruptions to the supply chain and Boeing had failed to set up adequate logistics to enable a fast and reliable delivery of their new aircraft.

It emerged that Boeing is rather unconventional (by airline industry standards) in its management of the supply chain. First, it outsourced 70 per cent of the production and development, thereby increasing the need for coordination and collaboration between suppliers while levering the expertise of these suppliers. Second, to expand delegation down the supply chain, Boeing reduced the number of strategic suppliers it dealt with directly. These strategic key suppliers were to deliver entire sections to Boeing, meaning that they, not Boeing, would in turn have to deal with the procurement of raw materials and components. This increased dependence on a few suppliers, over which Boeing had no immediate control. Finally, a risk-sharing agreement was implemented. Strategic suppliers would only get paid when the first Boeing 787 was delivered to ANA.

LIMITATIONS IN FORECASTING

Modern products and services become ever more complex as they are required to fulfil an increasing range of customer needs and wants. Hence, delivering a product such as an airplane has become a daunting challenge. Without a doubt, experience in engineering has led to greater reliability, but pushing the envelope of innovative, complex products and services limits the ability to forecast demand, restricting an organisation's capability to predict when and where to have what, and how much, inventory available.

One of many delays at Boeing was triggered by an aircraft component that one may not tend to associate with a shortage: aerospace fasteners, bolts, rivets and washers; all components that hold an aircraft together. The backlash of the terrorist attack on September 11th 2001 led to a consolidation of fastener makers, going hand in hand with a reduction in production capacity.

Boeing was aware of potential shortages and in response launched a new system, called Fastener Procurement Model (FPM). It offered a centralised demand and procurement system. Boeing and its partners would update their inventory on fasteners daily. Partners also had to provide preliminary pricing information and other information such as about lead times. Soon problems emerged. Partners were confused about what kind of information to feed into this system. In addition, they could not provide information in real-time or simply provided false information to conceal their own logistical shortcomings.

Other events at Boeing, as unpredictable as they might be, had a knock-on effect on their suppliers. Because of Boeing's aim to outsource 70 per cent of its work, the labour force of 25,000 employees launched a strike in September 2008. In the light of potential delays or cancellations of orders, key suppliers reduced their work schedule and thus reduced the availability of key parts to the 787. The impact of the strike could not have been predicted, but key suppliers started to protect their own interests: not producing any stock that might remain in their own inventory for too long. Unfortunately, although key suppliers reduced their output relatively quickly in anticipation of delays or cancellation, they could not compensate for an unexpected increase in demand in the same speedy manner as freed up work capacities had already been rerouted to other clients.

Such limitations at Boeing in forecasting exactly what was needed were just as prevalent 70 years ago (see following textbox).

THE AFRICA CAMPAIGN

In September 1940, the Italians, part of the Axis forces, launched an attack on the British (and Commonwealth) forces who were stationed in Egypt. Their numerical superiority did little to impress their enemy. On December 9th, the British launched a counteroffensive during operation Compass. Encouraged by initial successes they pressed on, pushing the Italians back into Libya. They soon captured the fortified port of Tobruk. A reconnaissance in force outflanked the Italians in the desert and cut off their retreat. The Italian Tenth Army ferociously tried to break out at the Battle of Beda Fomn but to no avail. It subsequently surrendered, with 130,000 prisoners of war.

To support one of his key Allies, Hitler formed an expeditionary force, later to be christened the Afrika Corps, under the command of Erwin Rommel. He was initially put in charge of a 'blocking force' designed to stop the British from advancing further into Libya. Once arrived, the Africa Corps did not stand still but launched immediate offensive actions against the Commonwealth troops. By the end of April 1941, they pushed the British back into Egypt, where Rommel took a defensive stand as his forces were considered not strong enough to capture Tobruk, a strategically important port.

The Allies soon launched a series of counter-attacks and a disastrous counteroffensive, Operation Battleaxe. It took place on the Egyptian-Libyan border. The passage the Allies had to take was very narrow, composed of a short coastal strip. Rommel fortified his garrisons, such as those at Fort Capuzzo, Sollum and Musaid.

The battle commenced on June 15th. Soon after, British armoured forces ran into a well-planned anti-tank screen, consisting of mines,

CHAPTER SIX: LOGISTICS

tank trenches and carefully concealed 88 mm guns. The British Matilda and Crusader tanks were easily picked off. On June 17th, the Allies were in retreat, having lost 220 tanks.

The following months saw events moving back and forth, without any party gaining the upper hand. In November 1941, Operation Crusader was launched. The Axis forces fell back again to where they started, at El Agheila. Notwithstanding, after receiving supplies and reinforcements from Tripoli, they resumed their offensive actions, defeating the Allies at Gazala and capturing the port at Tobruk in June 1942. Rommel wrote to his wife,

> Dearest Lu,
>
> Tobruk! It was a wonderful battle. There's a lot going on in the fortress area. I must get a few hours' sleep now after all that's happened. How much I think of you.
>
> (Liddell Hart 1953, 231)

By now, the logistical shortcomings were becoming obvious. The weeks following the capture of Tobruk revealed the precarious logistical situation the Germans found themselves in. Rommel noted in his diary,

> My panzer army had now been five weeks in battle against superior British forces. For four of those weeks the fighting had raged backwards and forwards before Tobruk. We had succeeded partly by attacks with limited objectives, partly in defence, in wearing down the British forces. After the fall of Knightsbridge and Gazala we stormed Tobruk. The British had retired first to Mersa Matruth and then to El Alamein.
>
> This series of engagements brought the strength of my Army to the point of exhaustion. With our reserves of material –

including the immediately usable booty – beginning to run out, it was only the men's amazing spirt and will to victory that kept them going at all. Not only had no replacement material arrived, but, with an almost unbelievable lack of appreciation of the situation, the supply authorities had actually sent only three thousand tons to Africa during June, as compared with our real requirement of sixty thousand tons, a figure that was never in fact attained. Captured stores certainly helped to tide us over the expected crisis in our supply situation after the fall of Tobruk, but it was urgently necessary that this should have been followed up by adequate supplies from our own sources.

In Rome one excuse after the other was found for the failure of the organised supply which was supposed to maintain my army. It was easy enough back there to say: "It can't be done", for life and death did not depend on finding a solution. If everybody had pulled together in a resolute search for ways and means, and the staff work had been done in the same spirit, the technical difficulties could without any doubt have been overcome.

(Liddell Hart 1953, 243)

Rommel already foresaw that at this stage, he would not be able to launch major offensive operations in the light of the constant build-up by the British. The following month witnessed an attempt by the Germans to breakthrough at El Alamein, only to be halted by a stiffening defence. The British, now outnumbering the Germans 2:1 drove the Germans back during the second battle of El Alamein in late October 1943.

Operation Torch, the American landings in Vichy-held French North Africa on November 8th 1942, was the beginning of the end, although Rommel continued to inflict heavy losses (e.g. at the Battle of Kasserine Pass in February 1943). The Axis forces surrendered on May 13th, with 275,000 soldiers made prisoners of war.

In direct contrast, Operation Yellow, the invasion of the Low Countries and France in May 1940, was undertaken under favourable logistical conditions. By comparison, the North African Campaign suffered from a range of logistical shortcomings. First, the distances to be covered until the next local storage with available resupplies were immense. Hence, the Africa Corps had to rely to a great extent on the 'backpack principle', carrying everything with it along the vast distances through the Libyan Desert. The capture of Tobruk brought some relief, but the port was too small and under constant air attack.

Second, the great dependence on the Italian Navy left the Axis forces at the mercy of shipping lanes in the Mediterranean that were also constantly harassed by the Royal Air Force (stationed at Malta).

Third, the COG in Hitler's strategic vision was not North Africa, but Russia, where the *Wehrmacht* was in a critical situation in late 1942. Something had to give, and in this case that meant curtailing supplies to the Africa Corps.

Finally, German and Italian equipment became ever more complex. New arrivals, such as the Tiger I tank, required different maintenance compared to the PzKpfw IV. Desert conditions meant that, in some eyes 'overengineered' German battle tanks broke down very quickly. The lack of spare parts, lubricants and in particular fuel added to the downtime of armoured vehicles.

Rommel commenced the North Africa Campaign in a logistical straitjacket. His tactical brilliance could not offset what logistical constraints prevented him from doing. In this regard, strategists should always start by arguing the extent of the logistical independence necessary to enable strategic objectives to be achieved.

LIMITATIONS IN BUYER-SUPPLIER RELATIONSHIPS

Shorter lead times reduce cost. But the delegation of shortening lead times to suppliers also increases the risk of the supplier not being committed to such lead times. In a 'tug-of-war', a supplier often realises that his own objectives may be incompatible with those of the organisations who 'depend' on stated lead times. Flexibility in modifying lead times, in satisfying the customer's demand for a fast-changing inventory, available wherever and whenever, strips the supplier of planning certainty and may well erode its own financial viability.

With Boeing, the risk sharing contract implemented to commit suppliers to a better performance actually resulted in the opposite. Being on time meant that a supplier was penalised for being too early or being too late. But if a strategic supplier sees that other suppliers may be late too, he can slow down his production. Hence, even the slightest delay can have a ripple effect through the supply chain. The aim of increasing production without any additional costs to Boeing ultimately produced the opposite outcome, enticing suppliers to operate to the lowest common denominator in the entire supply chain.

MANAGING SUPPLIERS INSTEAD OF DELEGATING RISK

Logistical dependence on external suppliers is a matter of relationship. Demanding variable 'continuous' logistics from a supplier for the sake of reducing one's own inventory necessitates a collaborative relationship. The main factor in a relationship is trust, a mutual belief in the logistical capabilities and limitations of a partner. Hence, planning must include consideration of uncertainty and the ability of all parties to provide continuous logistics. Nevertheless, continuous logistics come at a price. At Boeing, costs should not have been unilaterally delegated down the supply chain, with any imperfection in adapting to uncertain events being penalised. Instead, suppliers need to be incentivised as well as penalised with modern gain/pain sharing agreements. Given the power of incentives, on-time delivery should enable a supplier to maximise his profits (within reason).

Trust is driven by belief and manifested in an appropriate contractual agreement. Beyond, continuous logistics require cross-functional/organisational teams that enable social interaction and thus partnering. These cross-functional/organisational teams thrive under conditions of openness, visibility and transparency. Although they might contain conflicting objectives and ways of working, such conflict can be turned into critical reflection on how continuous logistics are enabled and also constrained by the suppliers and clients involved.

In the Boeing 787 Dreamliner Project, the following alternative strategies for mitigating risk were suggested (see Table 6.3):

Table 6.3 Alternative Strategies for Mitigating Program Risks (Tang and Zimmerman 2009, 82)

Risk Factor	Proactive Actions
Supply chain visibility	Use IT to ensure transparency of entire supply chain
Strategic partner selection and relationship	Use proper vetting of all strategic partners to determine their capability of completing tasks
Management	Establish proper working teams with expertise in supply chain logistics
Labour	Reach out and communicate with union heads about sourcing strategies
Demand (customer)	Treat customers as partners and ensure better communication of the potential for missing delivery deadlines

SAFETY STOCKS INSTEAD OF 'NONE-AT-ALL'

The approach of JIT may well reduce waste and excessive inventory costs. Nevertheless, in recent years, a reverse trend towards JIC can be seen, although not to the extent to which the Germans practiced it in 1940. A little extra inventory is starting to be seen as a good thing because reserve (safety) stocks can protect against unexpected changes in demand, compensating for natural inaccuracies in forecasting. It also provides a buffer for disruptions in the supply chain. In sum, safety stocks can be maintained in order to provide continuous logistics, of crucial importance in warfare just as they are in organisations for which continuous production makes or breaks a competitive advantage. If there is one aspect of behaviour that ruins an organisation's reputation, it is to not deliver a product or service on time.

The question is thus what safety stock should be maintained? One may argue that commodities such as nuts and bolts for a plane do not need to form part of reserve stock. However, such supposedly insignificant parts had a significant effect on Boeing's production of the 787 Dreamliner. For each service and product, one can define what parts and components are essential for the whole of the service and product to be produced. It is all a matter of planning (see following textbox).

> ## NATO: LOGISTIC PLANNING CONSIDERATIONS
>
> Planners will need to determine generally the overall logistic support requirements for an operation in order to prepare a coherent plan. Further, planners will need to determine specifically the JOA level support requirements in order to place accurate requests for logistic support force contributions from participating nations at the beginning of the force generation process. The following considerations, which apply to all logistic functional

CHAPTER SIX: LOGISTICS

areas and particularly so to supply and maintenance, will assist planners in determining the JOA level support and sustainability requirements.

(a) Mission Analysis. Mission analysis defines the operational tasks to be performed and the resultant logistic requirements. Some tasks are specified, while others are implied. If the mission analysis only notes the specified task, then the resources necessary to perform the implied tasks will be understated. Once the specified and implied tasks are identified, the logistic planner must consider the tasks in relation to the environment in which they are to be executed.

(b) Logistic Planning Factors. These are a listing of relationships between two or more variables, e.g. kgs/man/day, which can be used to plan resource needs in detail. If they are not readily available, they should be developed and applied when planning a specific mission.

(c) Determination of Logistic Requirements. This is accomplished by applying the logistic planning factors against the tasks outlined in the mission analysis. The gross logistic requirements can then be used by the planner to determine the most cost effective and efficient method of providing the required support.

(d) Sources of JOA Level Logistic Support. NATO will seek to satisfy JOA level support requirements from the following sources: NATO force structure assets; logistic forces from participating nations, to include contributions to MILUs/MIMUs[1] or as LN[2] or RSN[3]; HNS[4]; and contractor support, either *ad hoc* or pre-planned.

(e) Determination of Logistic Shortfalls. Once the level of participation is determined, the planner can assess whether any capability shortfalls exist. If identified shortfalls cannot be resolved through additional participating nation solicitations, the planner should look to the host nation and/

> or the possibility of contractor support. If shortfalls remain, the logistic planner must make appropriate recommendations to the operational planning staff to include an assessment of how the shortfall in OA level logistic support will impact on the accomplishment of the mission.
>
> (NATO Standardization Agency 2003, 2-9-2-10)

OUTLOOK

The defeat of the Allied forces in the Battle of France was partially down to their ill-defined approach to JIC. Bureaucratic hurdles and logistical shortcomings in making supplies available to the Allied forces as needed played their part in delaying movements of men and material and reducing operational availability, in being able to react quickly enough to the German operations. The Germans, in contrast, also relied on JIC, but with more cohesive, logistical independence of the COG. Where it mattered – Panzer Group Kleist – supplies were made available, in abundance. Logistical challenges such as the number of roads in the staging area of the Ardennes were prioritised and, if necessary, improvisation replaced a bureaucratic logistical planning system. The jerrycan may have done its bit. Mobile forces who were cut off from continuous logistics for whatever reason, were able to 'carry' safety stocks of fuel with them.

In business, a trend towards JIT has received extensive attention and certainly provided organisations with efficiency gains that would not otherwise be possible. Considering all the supply chain disruption in modern times, for example due to climate change, a reverse trend to safety stocks is observable and customer satisfaction is increasingly defined by dependable and reliable delivery of services and goods, so that bottlenecks such as in the case of Boeing's production of the 787 Dreamliner do not turn into major delays in a world where a competitive advantage is defined by JIT.

Reflection — *To what extent does your work unit adhere to Logistical in-dependence? For each item, select one box only that best reflects your conclusion.*

Neutral

The organisation defines for us how much inventory we are allowed to have	○	○	○	○	○	We define how much inventory we need
We delegate most responsibility and accountability for disruptions in the supply chain to our suppliers	○	○	○	○	○	We are jointly responsible and accountable for disruptions in the supply chain
Our aim is to reduce safety stocks	○	○	○	○	○	Our aim is to maintain safety stocks that cover even major disruptions

Neutral

We demand that inventory is delivered where and when it is needed	○	○	○	○	○	We 'carry' some inventory with us
Our primary purpose is to be efficient in logistics	○	○	○	○	○	Our primary aim is to provide continuous logistics
The customer demands the cheapest product and service	○	○	○	○	○	The customer demands a continuous supply of products and services

Scoring: If your answers tend to the left, you are pursuing a more JIT approach to logistics. If your answers are more on the right, the concept of JIC seems more appropriate to your ways of working.

NOTES

1 Multinational Integrated Logistic/Medical Unit.
2 Lead Nation.
3 Role Specialist Nation.
4 Host Nation Support.

REFERENCES

BArch. "Bild 101I-127-0399-16A." Koblenz: Bundesarchiv.
———. "Bild 101I-296-1652-0.8." Koblenz: Bundesarchiv.
———. "GNMX6703_018." Koblenz: Bundesarchiv.
Baudouin, P. 1948. *The Private Diaries of Paul Baudouin*. London: Eyre & Spottiswoode.
Council of Supply Chain Management Professionals. 2017. "CSCMP Supply Chain Management Definitions and Glossary." *Publicity Material from CSCMP*. www.csmp.org.
De Jomini, A.H. 2008. *The Art of War*. Kingston, ON: Legacy Books Press.
Dildy, D. 2014. *Fall Gelb 1940 (1): Panzer Breakthrough in the West*. Oxford: Osprey Publishing.
Frieser, K.-H. 2005. *The Blitzkrieg Legend: The 1940 Campaign in the West*. Annapolis, MD: Naval Institute Press.
Horne, A. 1990. *To Lose a Battle: France 1940*. London: Penguin Books.
Kane, T. 2001. *Military Logistics and Strategic Performance*. New York: Routledge.
Liddell Hart, B.H., ed. 1953. *The Rommel Papers*. New York: Da Capo Press.
NATO Standardization Agency. 2003. "AJP-4JA Allied Joint Logistic Doctrine." 4 (December).
Schneider, J. 2015. *Vulcan's Anvil: The American Civil War and the Foundations of Operational Art*. New York: Scholar's Choice.
Tang, C., and J. Zimmerman. 2009. "Managing New Product Development and Supply Chain Risks: The Boeing 787 Case." *An International Journal* 10: 74–87.
The Complete War Memoirs of Charles de Gaulle. 1972. New York: Simon Schuster.
Tzu, S. 2008. *The Art of War*. London: Penguin Books.
Von Kielmannsegg, J. 1941. *Panzer Zwichen Warschau Und Atlantik*. Berlin, Germany: Verlag "Die Wehrmacht."

CHAPTER SEVEN
Roads to resilience

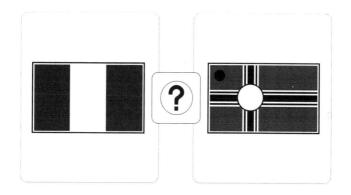

*There are Five Essentials
For victory:
Know when to fight
And when not to fight;
Understand how to deploy
Large and small
Number;
Have officers and men who
Share a single will;
Be ready for the unexpected
Have a capable general,
Unhampered by his sovereign.*

(Tzu 2008, 16–17)

CONTENTS

The story: May 26th–June 20th 1940	234
Roads to resilience	240
Why and what can be learned?	241
Erosion of resilience	243
The fallacy of hindsight	249
The five fallacies: some thoughts on British military thinking	250
Reversing the erosion of resilience	252
Red Teaming	254
Epilogue	262
Comment on De Jomini and Von Clausewitz	262
Notes	265
References	266

THE STORY: MAY 26TH–JUNE 20TH 1940

The moment the first German forces reached the Channel coast, the bulk of the British, French and Belgian land forces were encircled. Some Allied forces had already embarked at Calais, Boulogne and Cherbourg when these ports were overrun by the Germans. Only the deep-sea port of Dunkirk remained as a gateway to safety.

The Belgian High Command sent the following message to the head of the British Military Mission:

> The Belgian Command begs you to inform the Commander-in-Chief that the plight of the Belgian army is serious. The Belgian Commander-in-Chief means to go on fighting until his resources are entirely spent. At present the enemy is attacking from Eecloo to Menin. The limits of Belgian resistance are very close to being reached.
>
> (Benoist-Méchin 1956, 160)

The message remained unanswered. The British Expeditionary Force (BEF) made up its mind. The plans relayed by the British War Office focussed on the evacuation of the remaining Allied forces; a defensive perimeter around Dunkirk was established on May 27th (see Map 7.1). On May 28th, Belgium surrendered.

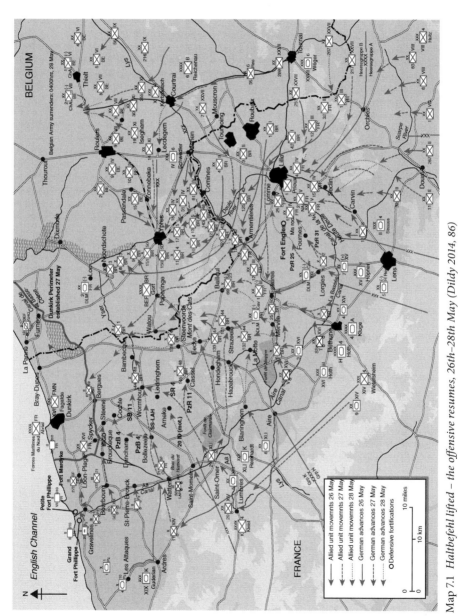

Map 7.1 *Haltbefehl lifted – the offensive resumes, 26th–28th May* (Dildy 2014, 86)

Operation Dynamo, the evacuation of the encircled Allied Armies, was completed on June 4th. Around 400,000 troops made it back to Britain.

Vast amounts of equipment had to be left by the evacuating British and French (BArch)

A further 110,000 French soldiers were repatriated to the south via the Normandy and Brittany ports to bolster the Weygand line. The line of fortified positions running along the river Somme was manned by a depleted French army, consisting of some 40 divisions plus the remains of three armoured divisions. To offset the weakness of a continuous line, the French Command switched to a 'hedgehog' strategy of mobile defence in depth. For that purpose three *groupements de manoeuvre* were established.

At 04:00 on June 5th, the German offensive - *Fall Rot* (Operation Red)- started with preparatory artillery fire and aerial attacks. Its aim was to turn south and eliminate the remnants of the French army. By noon, the German armoured divisions were 10 km ahead of their infantry units and were greeted by fierce resistance from the French defenders. Captain Jungenfeld, 1st Battalion, 4th Panzer described the events:

> Our tanks were greeted with truly hellish gunfire. In a trice the first of them, caught in the cross-fire, were in flames. The position was far from heartening ... Now it was up to our artillery to deal with the French; their defence was really very strong, and we had very little ammunition for the guns on our tanks. It was exactly noon – 11:00, French time. A long day still lay ahead of us, and there was no telling how much longer the enemy's blocking fire would keep us from our supply line.
>
> (Benoist-Méchin 1956, 243)

The next three weeks were characterised by successful rearguard actions by the French in that they inflicted substantial losses on the Germans. Nonetheless, despite the sustained attrition to German armour and men, the end was near:

> **Memorandum for the Prime Minister**
>
> The enemy may succeed in seizing the crossings of the lower Seine and in advancing on the Paris area from the south; his armour may break through in Champagne on a wide front; it may be that our divisions, worn out by fatigue and reduced in strength by their losses, will, under pressure of an enemy three times as strong, no longer be able to hold the Paris-Marne sector of the line.
>
> If any of these contingencies materialize our armies will go on fighting until the means and their strength are exhausted, but it will only be a question of time before their cohesion is at an end.
>
> (Signed) Weygand (Baudouin 1948, 92)

On June 10th, Paris was declared an open city; it was occupied by June 14th.

The Parisian population watches the arrival of the German occupiers in disbelief (BArch)

Prime Minister Paul Reynaud resigned on June 16th to be succeeded by Marshal Philippe Pétain. The French government sought to negotiate an armistice. Adolf Hitler, disdainful of a defeated enemy, selected the Forest of Compiègne as the site for the negotiation. Compiègne had been the site of the 1918 armistice which marked the end of the First World War (WWI) and Germany's defeat.

The French emissaries received the conditions for a ceasefire. The proceedings took place in the same railway carriage in which the surrender of Germany was signed in 1918 (BArch)

The armistice was signed on June 22nd by General Keitel for Germany and General Huntziger for France. It went into effect at 00:35 on June 25th, once the Franco-Italian Armistice had also been signed at 18:35 on June 24th near Rome:

> The armistice is signed. It has averted the total occupation of the country, and it maintains a Government whose duty it is to defend the French people against the enemy. It saves North Africa, and it leaves us the custody of our colonies, and of our fleet. It authorizes the maintenance of a small army, and it prevents the greater part of the adult male population from being made prisoner. It permits the restoration of order in the country by the return to their homes of several million refugees who are scattered on the roads, and by the rapid demobilization of two million men.
>
> The armistice was not an act of renunciation. It was a mournful deed, accomplished with the faith of a son bent over his wounded mother. It was to allow us to take in hand once again a country that had collapsed; to defend it against its own weakness and against the enemy in occupation; to nourish in secret new military forces; and to prepare patiently and clandestinely for better days. This was part of the policy of General Weygand and of myself, and the greater part of our colleagues shared our hopes. It was our intention to follow this programme without faltering, and we took the risks it involved clear-sightedly and without fear.
>
> (Baudouin 1948, 144)

Vast swathes of France and the Low Countries lay in ruins. The collapse of the Allies was as sudden as it was unexpected. Indeed, five days into the campaign, at the time when the Germans broke through the Sedan front, the fate of France was already sealed.

With France having surrendered, Britain was left on its own. Its struggle to keep the Germans at bay lasted four years until their troops set foot in France on June 6th 1944, this time with overwhelming firepower and on their side an economic and military juggernaut: the United States of America. The liberation of Paris took place on August 25th 1944. Germany capitulated on May 8th 1945.

A destroyed Dunkirk. (BArch)

ROADS TO RESILIENCE

In the previous chapter, we evaluated two opposing archetypal approaches from a strategic, operational and tactical (leadership) as well as a logistical perspective. In essence, the French pursued an approach of defensive consistency (see Figure 7.1), relying on consistency in action and protection of the status quo. In contrast, the Germans predominantly relied on a form of progressive flexibility while trying to maintain a minimum of defensive consistency.

The French vision was not to lose a war; its goals and objectives were to keep Germany at bay while avoiding the mass-slaughter of WWI. It is unsurprising that they played to their strengths by continuously optimising the capabilities and bolstering the defensive capacities that ultimately led to a victory in 1918. The attempt to repeat this success in 1940 was predominantly defined by a linear strategy, a dispersion of resources to prepare for all eventualities, and a decentralised way of managing a largely citizenarmy. In this respect, they defined a logical means-to-an-end approach to Organisational Resilience.

Likewise, the Germans had to surprise the French and their Allies as a repeat of WWI had to be avoided at all costs. Their strategic perspective was one of being adaptive for the purpose of continuously outmanoeuvring and outsmarting their enemy, triggering a collapse of France's morale and ability to maintain a continuous frontline. The

CHAPTER SEVEN: ROADS TO RESILIENCE

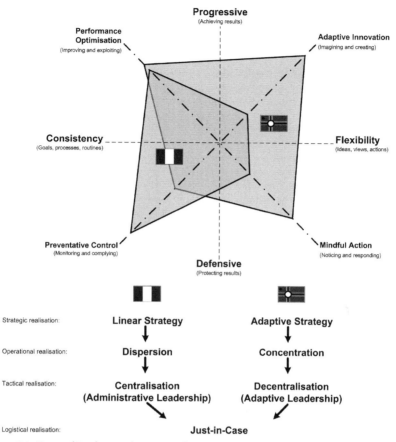

Figure 7.1 *Focus of Resilience of France and Germany in 1940 (adapted from Denyer 2017)*

Germans could only achieve such a level of adaptation by providing a local 'hammer-blow' that was surprising and disruptive enough for the Allies to lose their composure.

WHY? AND WHAT CAN BE LEARNED?

The fact that Germany could achieve such a complete surprise is, more than anything else, evidence that in Germany, in 1937–1940, even with Hitler as leader, the processes of executive judgement worked better than in France or Britain. Or, to put it the other way around, however much more civilised their judgements of values and objectives, leaders in France and Britain exhibited much less common sense in appraising their circumstances and deciding what to do.

This is obviously not to say that the Germans showed greater wisdom – far from it. The basic values that governed German choices were Hitler's – mad cravings to gain land and glory, to exterminate Jews, to enjoy a killing war. But neither do I mean to say only that Germany succeeded, while France failed. German processes of executive judgement – the ways in which the German government decided how to act – worked better than those in the French and British governments, a truth Marc Bloch touched on when he commented in *The Strange Defeat* that the German victory had been a 'triumph of intellect' and observed in a letter to his sometime collaborator, Lucien Febvre, that the victory owed much to Hitler's 'methodical opportunism'.

At any time, executive judgement involves answering three sets of questions: 'what is going on?', 'so what?' (or 'what difference does it make?'), and 'what is to be done?'. The better the process of executive judgement, the more it involves asking the questions again and again, not in the set order, and testing the results until one finds a satisfactory answer to the third question – what to do (which may be, of course, nothing).

The tests for 'what is going on' include distinguishing what is actually known from what is presumed to be true, then probing the strength and reliability of the presumptions. The tests for action choices also have additional questions: 'exactly what is to be done?' ('what to do?' becomes 'what to do?'), 'how will success or failure be recognizable?', and 'why is the particular action under consideration likely to lead to success so conceived?' In other words, 'what is the theory of the case?'

In the German government in 1937–1940, these questions were asked, re-asked and re-asked, but in the French and British

> governments they were hardly asked at all. French and British political and military leaders – Churchill not excepted – answered for themselves the question 'what is going on?' The almost inevitable answer was based on those pieces of information most consistent with their preconceptions. They did not test or even identify critical presumptions. They believed what they needed to believe in order to do what they thought either desirable or expedient. General Bock (Fedor von Bock, commander of Army Group B) had it right when, after learning that Group Kleist had crossed the Meuse river, he wrote in his war diary, *The French seem really to have lost all common sense! Otherwise they could and would have stopped us.*
>
> (May 2009, 458–59)

EROSION OF RESILIENCE

The French and their Allies remained complacently static and linear in their approach towards defensive consistency as their prevalent mode of resilience. Nevertheless, the weakness of a focus on preventative control should have been blatantly obvious to the French and their Allies in light of the Polish campaign in September 1939: *her [France's] army and its leaders lacked the proper flexibility and responsiveness to reply to the unexpected* (Doughty 1990, 4).

The sole focus on preventative control and performance optimisation as a form of organisational resilience does provide distinctive advantages, and yet distinctive signs of weakness (see Table 7.1) could provide the necessary warnings to refocus and recalibrate a profile as well as breadth and depth of resilient operating. Although a range of dissenting voices in French politics and higher military echelons were raised, voices concerning the erosion of resilient capabilities were in the minority and remained unheard until it was too late.

Organisational Resilience is permanently under the threat of erosion, whether that be because of complacency, perception, uncritical satisfaction with one's organisation's performance, or the need to reduce costs in the short term, undermining the very capability of resilience in the long run.

Table 7.1 Preventative Control: At Its Best; Signs of Weakness; France Pre-1940

At Its Best	Signs of Weakness	France, Pre-1940
Known problems are solved using proven techniques	Systems and people are impractical and rigidly 'go by the book'	Fixed line of fortifications, firmly maintained expectations of where the enemy's *Schwerpunkt* is to be expected, and predefined timetables of movement and firepower reaffirmed expectations and created blind spots for dealing with the unexpected
Standard ways to do things are perfected by fine tuning	Local practice has taken over from written procedure and has become 'normal'	
Redundancy through design and diversification has a stabilising effect	Inefficient and complex systems and processes; analysis paralysis	
Disturbances are quickly counteracted by planned responses	Prearranged corrective actions are unclear or impracticable	

Source: Adapted from Denyer (2017).

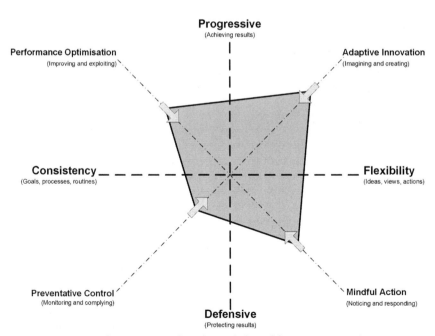

Figure 7.2 *Erosion of Organisational Resilience (adapted from Denyer 2017)*

CHAPTER SEVEN: ROADS TO RESILIENCE

The following tables provide a glimpse of what constitutes resilience, what warning signals indicate, the erosion of resilience and those indicators prevalent pre- and post-1940.

A clear sign of the inadequacy of preventative control ought to have been visible in the focus of training of some front-line divisions. This included digging trenches and guard duties, with less emphasis on training in the adequate defence of a fortified position. Local practice reinforced the need to defend an area at all costs but did not provide an alternative for when such an expectation was not met.

And so a defensive stance of 'digging in' gradually embeds itself in the organisational mainframe. The weakness inherent in lack of breadth of preventative control amplifies the corrosive need to optimise the status quo (see Table 7.2).

The need to optimise capabilities to withstand an invasion by German forces started to dissipate during the years between WWI and WWII.

Table 7.2 Performance Optimisation: At Its Best; Signs of Weakness; France Pre-1940

At Its Best	Signs of Weakness	France, Pre-1940
Performance improvement – 'do what we do better'	Lack of novel ideas on how to 'do better things'	Rigid thinking, driven by 'proven' methods in WWI, prevailed in the Allied Forces pre-1940
Known solutions are implemented quickly – even by edict	Overconfidence in 'best practice'; viewpoints of non-experts are excluded	
A clear sense of direction, goals, roles and responsibilities	People's individual identities and motives are at odds with the organisational goals	
A strong individual leader who people can relate to	Lack of leadership at all levels; lack of devolved ownership and responsibility	

Source: Adapted from Denyer (2017).

Long periods of success or the absence of failure validated the 'proven' approach taken in WWI. Such proof was not challenged as the French and their Allies did not engage in major combat activities between 1918 and 1940. As a consequence, changes to doctrinal thinking were few and far between.

The lessons of WWI led to a different executive judgement by the Germans during the interwar years. The development of the *Siegfriedstellung* (the *Siegfried* Line, commonly referred to as the Westwall), a fortified line of defensive forts and tank defences built in 1916–1917 and expanded in the interwar years, indicated a similar preventative control approach to resilience. Nevertheless, this was a mere precaution in case of an attack by the western Allies. Innovations in technology went hand in hand with the development of new thinking on how to exploit such technology to offer greater power of destruction (e.g. hollow charge) and movement (e.g. the further development of the tank). These means were transformed into 'new'[1] strategic doctrinal thinking and experimented with during the initial campaigns in Poland, to a more limited extent in Norway, as that was a predominantly amphibious invasion and in France.

Notwithstanding, the German military machine also experienced a similar erosion of resilient capabilities post-1941. The successes of the early war years were followed by major crises, among them the defeats of the Afrika Corps in Tunisia and the 6th Army at Stalingrad in 1943, each of which had an erosive impact on the degree of adaptive innovation applied (see Table 7.3).

In times of crises, adaptive innovation tends to come to a standstill as short-term incremental changes are made to recover quickly from impending disaster. In other words, organisations cannot afford lengthy periods of innovation when faced with imminent catastrophe. Hence, only incremental changes may be carried out to avoid and reduce operational downtime.

In this respect, of being able to innovate, organisations require sufficient 'space' (e.g. time) to innovate, implement and operationalise innovations; this 'space' (and the desire to innovate) is what the Germans had between

Table 7.3 Adaptive Innovation: At Its Best; Signs of Weakness; Germany Post-1940

At Its Best	Signs of Weakness	Germany, Post-1940
Productive tension disrupts existing patterns and generates a search for new possibilities	Entrenched thinking; people often resist even when acknowledging adaptive challenges	The Germans experienced major setbacks, reducing their desire and 'space' to innovate
Creative thinking and problem-solving by people drawing on multiple perspectives and taking risks in a safe environment	Lack of diversity of people and outlooks; nonconforming voices are ignored; people are too frightened to try something new	
Collective strategic action with rich interactions, coalition forming, negotiation and compromise	Silos; people refer to 'them' and 'us'; resources or ideas are not shared	
Systems-wide changes across borders and boundaries; multidimensional and fundamental changes	Quick fixes; local changes; reinventing the wheel	

Source: Adapted from Denyer (2017).

1918 and 1940. Post-1940, the constant pressure of the Allies stifled Germans' ability to radically rethink their approach.

Thus, being stripped of 'space' to innovate, the Germans could at least have incrementally optimised their ways of working, adapting their approach to resilience to the emerging threat at the western and eastern fronts (see Table 7.4).

In technological terms, the Germans incrementally optimised their machines and material; in 1940, their doctrinal approach over the French was critical. Gradually, the Germans lost this advantage to the Russians and western Allies. The erosion of this dominance was driven by an illusory overconfidence that what had worked in the past would work as well in the

Table 7.4 Performance Optimisation: At Its Best; Signs of Weakness; Germany Post-1940

At Its Best	Signs of Weakness	Germany, Post-1940
Performance improvement – 'do what we do better'	Lack of novel ideas on how to 'do better things'	Rigid thinking, driven by 'proven' methods applied during the Polish and French campaigns in 1939/1940
Known solutions are implemented quickly – even by edict	Overconfidence in 'best practice'; viewpoints of non-experts are excluded	
A clear sense of direction, goals, roles and responsibilities	People's individual identities and motives are at odds with the organisational goals	
A strong individual leader who people can relate to	Lack of leadership at all levels; lack of devolved ownership and responsibility	

Source: Adapted from Denyer (2017).

future. This rigidity in thinking came to a climax in the Battle of the Bulge in 1944. The Allies innovated and optimised their doctrinal thinking; the Germans did not due to overconfidence in their capabilities and the lack of 'space' that would have allowed them to innovate and optimise.

The erosion of adaptive innovation and performance optimisation goes hand in hand with an erosion of mindful action (see Table 7.5); the erosion of a single approach to resilience tends not to happen in isolation but in conjunction with remaining approaches to resilience.

Mindful capabilities in the German armed forces eroded over time due to complacency and the lack of 'space' and desire to innovate. The resulting indoctrination of 'best' practice led to the silencing of visionaries. The pressure exercised by the Allies and subsequent failures and losses sustained by the Germans led to greater centralisation, to an 'I know better' mentality. Constructive conflict was stifled, and responsibility diffused. Key decision makers became increasingly mindless, 'blindly' following authority, rank and status.

Table 7.5 Mindful Action: At Its Best; Signs of Weakness; Germany Post-1940

At Its Best	Signs of Weakness	Germany, Post-1940
People are wary about what could go wrong	People are too certain of how things are	The early successes in the Polish and French campaigns in 1940 led to the doctrine of the lightning war. In the light of subsequent failures, such as in North Africa and Russia in 1941–1945, critical voices were subdued by an ever-growing centralisation of decision making power.
Opportunities and problems are noticed, understood and addressed quickly	Signs of problems are missed; people who raise issues are ignored; people don't report errors	
People exercise judgement, discretion, and imagination when faced with challenges	People disperse responsibility for resolving problems and defer decision making and action to others	
People are empowered to act when they recognise a problem	People are blamed quickly if they make errors or fail to follow procedures	

Source: Adapted from Denyer (2017).

THE FALLACY OF HINDSIGHT

It is an old saying that military leaders tend to fight the previous war as long as they emerged as a winner. Hindsight in this respect is a double-edged sword. It enables managers to replicate a winning formula, yet it drives rigidity that is counterproductive for managing a future that is anything but like the past.

The winning formula in many organisations, such as Kodak, British Airways, Volkswagen and Uber, appeared to rely on 'best practice': professional ways of working that are accepted or prescribed as having been self-evidently correct or most effective in the past. Each fallacious belief, self-evidently correct but ultimately a mistaken belief based on unsound arguments, tends to be reinforced over time, particularly in the absence of failure. Hindsight bias implies that organisations tend to recall information that confirms what they believe to be true and ignore or discount information that might challenge this 'easy-to-hold' belief.

THE FIVE FALLACIES: SOME THOUGHTS ON BRITISH MILITARY THINKING

By the mid-1930s, what had started out as a most praiseworthy attempt to wrench British military thought back to the path where modern scientific developments, mobility, imagination, and above all, intellect were to have free play, had become distorted, and five fallacies had become accepted as substitutes for the genuine laws of war.

The first of these may be called 'miniaturism' or the 'David and Goliath' fallacy. No truth has been more resolutely ignored in British thinking than that a big good army will always beat a small good army.

The second is closely allied to the first, and is the fallacy of the magic weapon, and there have been signs of tactical or battlefield nuclear weapons elevated to this position.

The third is the 'chess' fallacy. Here we have the clearest example of not merely a valid but essential approach to the study of war becoming distorted by wishful thinking. The object of grand tactics; that is to say the direct or indirect approach, the attack on the rear or the flank, surprise, the concentrated attack on separate fractions of the enemy, infiltration, and so on, is to give one's own soldiers the best possible chance in the decisive combat that must be the culmination of manoeuvre. The 'chess' fallacy elevates the manoeuvre to the decisive factor as if wars were won by shadow-boxing. (Like that degenerate art of Malay self-defence called 'bersilat', which appears to consist of agile moves and menacing gestures.)

The fourth is dependent on the third and is the fallacy of the bloodless operation. Nothing is more disgusting to read of than the slaughter in the breach at Badajoz or in front of, say, Thiepval in 1916, and no British commander could, or would, dare to sacrifice troops on the scale which would be unhesitatingly accepted by a Russian or an American army. It is, however, mere self-deception to believe that a hard fight can be anything but costly.

The fifth, which is also dependent on the third, is the fallacy of a passive enemy. Why should it be assumed in the face of all military history that good troops whose headquarters has been captured or neutralised, whose supply line has been cut, who have been outflanked or surrounded or who have been faced with some novel method of war, will tamely give in? A Beda Fomm can be pulled off against poor and irresolute commanders whose troops can see no good reason as to why they are fighting at all, but against others the riposte may well be one version or other of the 'mot de Cambronne', accompanied by a good kick in the teeth. What, one wonders, would have been the reaction if, say, the garrison commander at Kohima or the surviving officers of the Irish Guards on Bou Ficha had sent back an appreciation based on the theories of the 'mobile school' to the effect that any resistance was, in view of the disposition of the enemy forces, futile and that the correct solution was to surrender? Why should not the enemy be equally brave or equally ingenious in thinking up countermoves and counter-weapons? One of the mysteries of the interwar years is why the advocates of armoured warfare did not display equal energy in urging the development of suitable anti-tank guns. The ballistics were simple and the costs, compared with a tank, low.

(Bidewell 1967, 54–5)

REVERSING THE EROSION OF RESILIENCE

Due to the 'dark side' of hindsight and the paradoxical nature of approaches to resilience, it is easier said than done to build and maintain organisational resilience in a holistic manner, producing consistency and flexibility, and progressiveness and defensiveness simultaneously. The following stepwise process may be of use:

STEP 1: CHALLENGING COGNITIVE BIASES AND HEURISTICS

As a first step, organisations may examine closely whether successes involve universal success factors, factors that can be used in any given (future) situation or environment; problematic, given the plethora of cognitive biases and heuristics that clouds a key decision maker's rational thought. The following table (see Table 7.6) offers a few:

Table 7.6 Cognitive Biases and Heuristics

Definition	Manifestation from an Allied Perspective
Ambiguity effect	
The tendency to avoid options that are deemed uncertain	WWI provided a sense of certainty about what had worked in the past. More ambiguous options were deemed uncertain and thus rejected
Anchoring effect	
The tendency to manifest expectations by relying too heavily on a single piece of information	The expectation of a German attack in the north was 'anchored' by the Mechelen Incident (see Chapter 2)
Bandwagon effect	
The influence of group-think and herd behaviour	The predominant perception of defensive action prevailed. The immense costs associated, for example, reinforced a common perception of invulnerability

Confirmation bias		
The tendency to have one's preconceptions confirmed		The initial successes by the French in the north confirmed their preconception of the centre of gravity (COG). 'Framed' information from the front line in the south (see Framing effect) did not fit this preconception and thus was largely ignored
Conservatism		
The tendency to revise one's preconception insufficiently in the light of new information. Related to Anchoringbias		The initial indications of a German breakthrough at Sedan were ignored as their 'anchored' expectation was constrained to an attack in the north
Courtesy bias		
The tendency to provide opinions that are socially correct and acceptable		The military system is largely defined by rank and status, and the need to pay courtesy to it
Curse of knowledge		
The tendency to belief that with more knowledge, one 'knows better'		The Allied High Command received information from the front line, although it was often outdated and unreliable. The perception, though, of having access to more information, was constructed as 'We know better'
Focussing effect		
The tendency to pay too much attention to a singular event		The focus of the Allied command was predominantly on a single stretch of front line in the north; assuming that a breakthrough by the Germans at the Centre or in the South was 'impossible'
Framing effect		
Drawing different conclusions from the same information, depending on how that information is presented		*There has been a rather serious hitch at Sedan* is a piece of information that was presented to the French High Command in the form of a situation report; framed as something non-urgent (see also confirmation bias)
Illusion of control		
The tendency to overestimate's one's influence over external events		A perception of control persisted in the Allied High Command, despite receipt of contradictory information

Normalcy bias

A refusal to plan for or to react to abnormal events — The norm in WWI was to entrench oneself against to the power of artillery fire. This norm was manifested with the construction of the Maginot Line

Ostrich effect

Ignoring an obvious (negative) situation — Refusal to accept that a breakthrough had occurred in a very vulnerable section of the front line persisted until the Allied forces were encircled

Sunk cost fallacy

Increased investment in a decision 'justifies' a decision — The building of the Maginot Line came at an immense cost to the French economy. It was a manifestation of France's defensive stance

These biases and heuristics were prevalent on both warring parties in 1940 and can be expected in any organisation. Left untreated, they may well lead to an erosion of resilience over time; to a mode of resilience that has been identified as the 'norm', that has been already invested in, one that has been 'anchored' as an irrefutable, self-evidently correct doctrine.

Nevertheless, to counter such bias and its unfortunate impact on eroding resilience, a process of scrutiny needs to be started: this tends to be referred to in the military as 'Red Teaming'. Red teaming is based on constructive conflict: an open, honest and critical discourse that aims to resolve the multiplicity of the most important and diverse conflicting perspectives.

RED TEAMING[2]

BENEFITS

The red team provides the end user with an independent capability to critically consider concepts, projects, plans and operational designs, thereby leading to improved decision making. Although red teaming can be readily used to challenge assumptions based on quantitative factors (structures, capabilities, geography and so on) it is uniquely useful in helping to identify and understand the impact of qualitative factors (attitudes, reactions, perspectives and so on).

> Plans are based on assumptions…
>
> …assumptions are based on understanding…
>
> …the better the understanding, the better the plan.

The specific benefits of red teaming include:

- broader understanding of the operational environment;
- filling gaps in understanding;
- identifying vulnerabilities, opportunities, risks and threats;
- identifying bias, group-think, flawed assumptions and the tendency to jump to conclusions;
- revealing how external influences, adversaries or competitors could affect plans, concepts and capabilities;
- identifying second- and third-order effects and unforeseen consequences;
- identifying further or improved measures of effectiveness;
- identifying the need for contingency plans;
- and more focussed intelligence collection and improved information requirements.

The ultimate benefit of red teaming is that it assists the end user to make a better informed decision or to produce a more robust product. However, despite its many advantages, red teaming is not a silver bullet; its credibility hinges on the:

- quality and experience of the team;
- approach and toolset; and
- support of the leadership.

An uninformed, overconfident or biased red team is unlikely to add value and may be detrimental to the project. Furthermore, the product of a successful red team will be of no benefit if it is rejected or not considered by the end user.

SUCCESSFUL RED TEAMING

Red teaming is important but it is neither easy nor often done well. It has attracted a 'buzzword' status and is often reduced to a box-ticking exercise rather than the robust intellectual challenge activity that it should be.

Red teaming activities range from scrutinising and challenging emerging thoughts, ideas and underpinning assumptions to considering the perspectives of adversaries, competitors or outsiders. Our analysis should enable the end user to make choices and select preferred options. The end user should also be more cognisant of the threats, alternatives, weaknesses and downstream consequences associated with each option that they are considering.

THE ROLE OF THE END USER

A red team needs a scope, charter and reporting relationship with the end user that fit both its role and the overarching task. End users should fully support the red team and intend to use its products as part of their decision-making process. Red teaming can only thrive in an environment that tolerates and values internal criticism and challenge.

To make sure we use red teaming successfully, the end user needs to:

- appoint a red team leader who has been exposed to red teaming techniques;
- establish the red team as a discrete entity without broader tasking in the project to protect their impartiality;
- provide all the required information to complete the task successfully;
- give clear objectives, defining the scope, timeframe and delivery mechanism for the task;

- develop a good working relationship, including regular contact with the red team leader;
- be accessible to the team leader throughout the task;
- engage with, and listen to, the red team;
- give due weight to the red team's findings and use them where appropriate;
- protect the red team from unwarranted criticism and negative reaction;
- ensure that the red team findings are heard, and acted on, by senior decision makers; and
- give constructive feedback on how the red team has performed in terms of its analysis and delivery of the outcomes.

GUIDELINES FOR GOOD RED TEAMING

The art of good red teaming is founded on the following guidelines being applied by the end user:

1. Plan red teaming from the outset. It cannot work as an afterthought.
2. Create the right conditions. red teaming needs an open, learning culture, accepting of challenge and criticism.
3. Support the red team. Value and use its contribution to inform decisions and improve outcomes.
4. Provide clear objectives.
5. Fit the tool to the task. Select an appropriate team leader and follow their advice in the selection and employment of the red team.
6. Promote a constructive approach which works towards overall success.
7. Poorly conducted red teaming is pointless; do it well, do it properly.

End users should use the following steps to make sure that they do all of the aforementioned tasks.

STEPS FOR THE END USER

 Step 1 – Identify the specific task that they are to undertake
 Step 2 – Identify an appropriate red team leader and potential red team
 Step 3 – Task and empower the red team leader

 Step 1 – Identify the specific task that they are to undertake. This may range from scrutinising underpinning data and assumptions through to considering the project or plan in its entirety.

 Step 2 – Identify an appropriate red team leader and potential red team. The team must possess the right mix of skills and expertise necessary to address the problem. It is likely to comprise a combination of:
 - critical and creative thinkers;
 - subject matter experts;
 - analysts;
 - cultural advisors; and
 - role players.

 To achieve such a team, the end user may require a reachback capability through which they can call on wider expertise. Most importantly, the size and membership of the red team should match the task in hand. Red teaming should not be considered a 'one-size-fits-all' activity.

 Step 3 – Task and empower the red team leader. The end user needs to provide the red team leader with guidance, clear objectives and terms of reference, where necessary. The red team leader should be allowed to run the team, employing the techniques that the leader feels are appropriate to the task. This may involve endowing the red team with a degree of latitude to explore the problem on a broad base and spend time thinking in areas not originally specified.

> (Development Concepts and Doctrine Centre 2013, 1-6-1–7; 2-1-2–3)

CHAPTER SEVEN: ROADS TO RESILIENCE

Getting red teaming right requires the right choice of a red team. The red team needs to consist of specialists who know the organisation inside-out; they also need to have knowledge beyond the organisational boundaries so that they can truly target the organisation's thinking as a knowledgeable and competent adversary. The red team should have a breadth of expertise but should not be bigger than 8–10 people and should not be emotionally or structurally attached to the problem in question.

Setting up red teaming is crucial to the success of problem-solving. All parties involved (Blue and Red Teams) need to be briefed about the purpose of red teaming as an exercise not to undermine people, their passion or their competence, but to help them make more informed decisions about key problems within the organisation. The process of red teaming, though, is hampered by common fallacies, such as:

> Ad hominem attack: Criticising the person making the argument rather than the argument itself (e.g. "That's ridiculous. What do the factory guys know about engineering?"
>
> Appeal to age or tradition: Based in argument on the assumption that previous generations were wiser or knew more that the current generation (e.g. "James has been here since the Old Man was running the show, so I think we should do as he suggests").
>
> Appeal to emotion or fear: Playing on people's heartstrings or anxieties instead of arguing the merits of a position (e.g. "If we don't approve this plan, we'll all be looking for jobs next month").
>
> (Hoffman 2017, 145–8)

Challenged with the previously mentioned fallacies, the red team confronts the Blue Team with opposing views. Consequently, the blue team is tasked to 'protect' its domain, whatever that might be related to (e.g. cyber-security, emergence of a new competitor, etc.).

Both roles, the roles of the red and the blue teams will be stressful, but the ultimate outcome is constructive conflict, with the purpose of opening communications (questions are being asked that otherwise would not be asked), encouraging debate (addressing deep-seated biases), enhancing collaboration and producing high-quality ideas and informing high-quality decisions. An essential quality of red teaming is that it fosters the questioning of hindsight, habitual thinking and acting, and triggers foresight, an essential process for keeping resilience from eroding over time.[3]

STEP 2: ESTABLISHING FORESIGHT

Constructive conflict through red teaming reveals blind spots in an organisation and triggers scanning beyond what an organisation believes it knows, beyond what an organisation thinks it should do, beyond what an organisation has tended to do in the past.

Scanning beyond the knowable, the 'used to', the past ways of working can be facilitated with a range of tools. The most widely used in organisations is Scenario Planning (see Chapter 2). The use of foresight provides decision makers with imaginative power to envisage how resilient they need to be and how resilient they used to be – the basis for organisational insight.

STEP 3: CREATING INSIGHT

The previous two steps help an organisation to gain an accurate and deep intuitive understanding of how resilient an organisation is and about how vulnerable it still remains to the environmental challenges. Foresight is established in order to move an organisation forward in light of the past and multiple, still unrealised, futures.

Looking at insight from an organisational resilience perspective (see Figure 7.2), raises questions such as

- How much do we need to enhance our resilience repository?
- How do we need to manage the tensions between opposing poles of resilience?

CHAPTER SEVEN: ROADS TO RESILIENCE

An insight-driven organisation may well shape such a discourse by relying on a few experts, just as the French relied predominantly on their generals, who turned out to be human beings, flawed in their decision-making. Instead, an insight-driven organisation may spread the degree of responsibility out towards those at an operational, tactical level, exploiting the mindset of all those in an organisation, and not just of a few individuals.

Reflection *To what extent does your work unit foster constructive conflict as a trigger to (re)define resilience? For each item, select one box only that best reflects your conclusion.*

	Neutral	
Because we respect rank and status, we restrain ourselves from confrontation	○ ○ ○ ○ ○	We are free to explore contrary views
We tend not to be challenged	○ ○ ○ ○ ○	We have dedicated red teaming exercises in our organisation
We are confident that we are not vulnerable to the external environment	○ ○ ○ ○ ○	We are aware of our vulnerabilities to the external environment
	Neutral	
We focus on a very narrow definition of resilience	○ ○ ○ ○ ○	We tend to focus on more than one dimension of resilience
We are unaware of paradoxical tensions between opposing poles of resilience	○ ○ ○ ○ ○	We are aware of paradoxical tensions between opposing poles of resilience
We don't know how to reconcile opposing poles of resilience in our daily work (see Figure 7.1)	○ ○ ○ ○ ○	We understand how to reconcile opposing poles of resilience in our daily work (see Figure 7.1)

Scoring: If your answers tend to the left, you tend to produce fewer insights into organisational resilience. If your answers are more on the right, your process triggers greater recalibration of resilience in your organisation.

EPILOGUE

In social as well as military science, managers and commanders tend to be portrayed as rational human beings, able to rely on well-oiled organisational structures, procedures and processes; incredibly farsighted and efficient in their ability to adapt to an ever-changing environment. What is missing from this mosaic are the emotive dimensions of human beings, whether they are operating in military institutions or in commercial organisations.

In the time leading up to WWII, the French may have been less forsighted, and thus less resilient in their ability to repulse a German invasion which was in itself a high-risk undertaking. Ultimately, fighting on the ground was down to the 'grunt' (a term often used to describe a low-level worker), the front-line infantry soldier and his survival instinct, and his ability and willingness to kill.

COMMENT ON DE JOMINI AND VON CLAUSEWITZ

The Jominian *Weltanschaung* has had an unfortunate impact on the effectiveness of those military services that embraced it. When military doctrine aims at a simplicity and a clarity possessed only by the clean red and blue arrows of post-war military histories, it leaves the landscape littered with smashed aircraft and the burnt-out hulks of tanks, not to mention dead and mutilated human beings. Unfortunately, narrowly-educated wartime commanders have often attempted to make reality fit doctrinal preconceptions, for example, the experiences of Eighth Air Force and Bomber Command in the WWII. In the former case, Eighth Air Force Commanders threw large unescorted formations of B-17s against German fighter defences until their command came close to destruction in the skies over Germany in October 1943. Similarly,

Arthur Harris in 1944 nearly destroyed Bomber Command in the Battle of Berlin in his effort to prove that independent 'strategic' bombing could win the war by itself. Don Bennett, the commander of the Pathfinder force in Bomber Command, has suggested that the best method for avoiding such unwillingness to face reality in the upper levels of command of the air forces would be to make senior air commanders fly on active operations: *For every Air Vice Marshall lost, the RAF would save 200 air crews.*

This Jominian view of war has spilled over into the area of command and control, where it holds that, despite the spread of military operations over wider and wider areas, advances in technology will allow commanders to cope ever more effectively. Such views, despite the US failure in Vietnam, are unfortunately still alive and well in the US military. The 1980 edition of US Air Force Manual 1-1, the basic doctrinal manual of that service until 1984, suggested that the Airborne Warning and Control System (AWACS) *allows commanders to comprehend the total air-surface battle.* This belief that a centralised command and control system is the best approach to war is a basic theme in twentieth-century military history. And for the most part its impact has been unfortunate, whether one recounts military operations on the Somme in 1916 or in Market Garden in 1944.

Unfortunately, for their enemies, the Germans have generally avoided the Jominian view of military operations in favour of the Clausewitzian one. Above all, *On War* raises the dark, bloody, fearful qualities of combat:

> We are not interested in generals who win victories without bloodshed. The fact that slaughter is a horrifying spectacle must make us take war more seriously, but not provide an excuse for gradually blunting our swords in the name of humanity. Sooner or later someone will come along with a sharp sword and hack off our arms.

> Von Clausewitz' depiction of war not only records its horror but notes the difficulties of acting and thinking under such circumstances. In Chapter 4 of Book I he describes the movement of the novice on to the battlefield. From the first terrifying sounds of battle to the *sight of men being killed and mutilated*, Von Clausewitz sets out, in a brilliant and still-relevant passage, the fearful impressions that assault the new recruit. *It is'*, he tells us, *'an exceptional man who keeps his powers of quick decision intact if he has never been through this experience.* And while exposure to combat may mitigate some of its impact, the ordinary man can never achieve a state of perfect unconcern in which his mind can work with normal flexibility. Here again we recognise that ordinary qualities are not enough: Headlong, dogged or innate courage; overmastering ambition; or long familiarity with danger – all must be present to a considerable degree if action in this debilitating element is not to fall short of achievement that in the study would appear as nothing out of the ordinary.
>
> Real war has little in common with the clear, concise depictions that appear in military histories, little to do with the Jominian clarity: it is blood, and fear and terror.
>
> (Handel 1986, 272–4)

We can learn a lot from military science. Modern armed forces tend to be very progressive in their doctrinal thinking whereas many commercial organisations are still 'stuck' in traditional, rigid, ways of operating. Organisational resilience is indeed an art, with no prospect of a 'Holy Grail': an approach that is universal to all environments, and thus per se self-evidently correct. As such, an art is very difficult to master given the need for a holistic form of resilience, and the paradoxical tensions on the roads to resilience. What is your organisation's road to resilience?.

CHAPTER SEVEN: ROADS TO RESILIENCE

A Wehrmacht soldier in the ruins of a French village. The destruction throughout villages in France was immense. It is evidence that the French forces defended their homeland with tenacity and courage. (Kutsch)

NOTES

1 As outlined in Chapters 1 and 2, the concept of Blitzkrieg was not one that was purposefully developed. Most concepts that the Germans adopted originated in the experiences of the late WWI years. Hence, they cannot be considered as revolutionary and new, but rather as evolutionary and progressive.
2 The name of red teaming originated in the wargames by the Prussian army in the early 1800. They tended to indicate the enemy as red. As the Prussians' uniforms were predominantly of a blue colour, their military units in wargames were also coloured blue.
3 More insights into red teaming can be gained from Development, Concepts and Doctrine Centre (2013). Red Teaming Guide.

REFERENCES

BArch. "Bild 101I-126-0349-08A." Koblenz: Bundesarchiv.
———. "Bild 101II-MW-1160-38." Koblenz: Bundesarchiv.
———. "Bild 116-483-078." Koblenz: Bundesarchiv.
———. "Bild 183-L11621." Koblenz: Bundesarchiv.

Baudouin, P. 1948. *The Private Diaries of Paul Baudouin*. London: Eyre & Spottiswoode.

Benoist-Méchin, J. 1956. *Sixty Days That Shook the World – The Fall of France: 1940*. New York: Putman.

Bidewell, R. 1967. "The Five Fallacies: Some Thoughts on British Military Thinking." *Journal of the Royal United Service Institution* 112: 53–57.

Denyer, D. 2017. "Organizational Resilience A Summary of Academic Evidence, Business Insights and New Thinking." BSI and Cranfield School of Management.

Development Concepts and Doctrine Centre. 2013. "Red Teaming Guide." Ministry of Defence.

Dildy, D. 2014. *Fall Gelb 1940 (1): Panzer Breakthrough in the West*. Oxford: Osprey Publishing.

Doughty, R. A. 1990. *The Breaking Point: Sedan and the Fall of France*. Hamden: Archon.

Handel, M. I. 1986. *Clausewitz and Modern Strategy*. London: Frank Cass and Company.

Hoffman, B. 2017. *Red Teaming: Transform Your Business by Thinking like the Enemy*. London: Piatkus.

Kutsch, L. "Frankreichfeldzug." Private Collection.

May, E. 2009. *Strange Victory: Hitler's Conquest of France*. London: I.B. Tauris & Co.

Tzu, S. 2008. *The Art of War*. London: Penguin Books.

INDEX

NUMBERS
10.5 cm Leichte Feldhaubitze gun 27
37 mm anti-tank guns 27–28
47 mm Atelier de Puteaux (APX) gun 27
88 mm multipurpose Flak gun 27
1940 west campaign: air forces 32–34; Allies COG 113; armoured warfare 25–26; Battle for Stonne 168–174; Belgium surrender 236; Blitzkrieg 24–25; British betrayal of France 29–30; capturing Fort d'Ében-Émael 124–130; casualty rates 40; crossing the Meuse river 88–94; Fort d'Ében-Émael 119–120; fronts 20–22; Holland's surrender 156–157; human suffering 41–43; infantry 26–27; May 10th-May 11th 118–120; May 10th-May 12th German invasion 82–85; May 13th-May 17th 156–159; May 18th-May 25th 198–201; May 26th-June 20th 234–239; morale 28; need for resilience 10–14; order of battle 22; Panzer attacks near Gembloux 157–158; Position Fortifiée de Liège I 119; racing to the channel 207–212; Schwerpunkt 85–86; superior numbers 26; tanks 30–32; Verdun of 1940 171–174

A
abundance of resources 213–214
accountability: centralisation 140–141

Achtung Panzer 59
ad hominem attacks 259
adaptability: strategic management 61
adaptive innovation 9; Germany post-1940 247
adaptive leadership 158–160, 194–195; administrative leadership comparison 181–183; administrative leadership support 185–186; advantages 183; alignment 174, 177–179, 183; assessment 183; balancing with administrative leadership example 186–190; bureaucracy 185; commitment 174, 180–183; culture 183; direction 174–175, 183; focus 182; mindful flexibility 190–191; superior-subordinate relationships 182; Uber 184
adaptive strategy 64–67
administrative leadership 167–168; adaptive leadership comparison 181–183; advantages 183; alignment 177–179, 183; assessment 183; automation 185; balancing with adaptive leadership example 186–190; bureaucracy 185; commitment 180–183; culture 183; direction 175, 183; focus 182; French 194; mindful flexibility 190–191; superior-subordinate relationships 182; supporting adaptive leadership 185–186

adversarial relationships: COGs 96
Africa: German Africa Corps 177–179;
  North Africa campaign 222–225
agility: limitations 105; Sedan river
  crossings 98
air forces: quality 32–34
airborne raid on Fort d'Ében-Émael
  125–126
Airborne Warning and Control System
  (AWACS) 263
Albert Canal 119
alignment 177–179; administrative *versus*
  adaptive leadership 183; defined 174
Allies: adaptability 61; administrative
  direction 175; air forces 33; ambiguity
  effect 252; anchoring effect 252;
  bandwagon effect 252; Battle of the
  Bulge 107–112; casualty rates 40;
  COG 113; confirmation bias 253;
  conservatism 253; courtesy bias 253;
  curse of knowledge 253; defensive
  resilience 15–16; evacuation via
  Dunkirk 236; focussing effect 253;
  framing effect 253; illusion of control
  253; immovable defensive shield
  12–13; JIC logistics 230; liberation
  of Paris 239; logistical constraints
  216–217; mission command 121–123;
  normalcy bias 254; North Africa
  campaign 222–225; order of battle xiv;
  ostrich effect 254; sunk cost fallacy
  254; supply shortages 213–214; tanks
  32; tightly coupled defense 12
ambiguity effect 252
amphibious crossings 10–11
anchoring effect 252
antigoals: intent 142
anti-tank guns 27–28
appeals to age or traditions 259
appeals to emotion or fear 259
APX (Atelier de Puteaux) gun 27
Argentinian invasion of Falkland Islands 97
Armageddon 43

armistice: French surrender 238–239
armoured warfare 25–26
art of war 5
The Art of War: defensive battle tactics 17;
  offensive battle tactics 18–20; origins 4
artillery: French *versus* German 27
assembly of forces in space: De Jomini
  86–87; Von Clausewitz 88
assessment: administrative *versus* adaptive
  leadership 183; wargaming 194
Atelier de Puteaux (APX) gun 27
Auftragstaktik *see* mission-oriented tactics
authority: centralisation *versus*
  decentralisation 135; command
  175–176; infallibility of centralisation
  140; subordinates 131–132
automation: leadership 185
autonomy: centralisation *versus*
  decentralisation 136; logistics 215–217;
  tactics 131–132; undermining
  operational intent 144–149
availability: operational 214
AWACS (Airborne Warning and
  Control System) 263

B

BA (British Airways) IT meltdown
  102–103
back office functions 106
backpack principle 204–205
balancing: adaptive and administrative
  leadership 186–190
bandwagon effect 252
La Bataille Conduit *see* methodical
  battle tactics
Battle for Stonne 168–174
Battle for Verdun 48–49
Battle of Hürtgen forest 186–190; capture
  of Vossenack, Kommerscheidt,
  and Schmidt by Americans 188;
  commencement 187; General Cota
  visiting battle line 189; General Cota's

orders 187; German counter-attack 188; ground conditions 186–187; leadership lessons 190
Battle of Kursk 70–73
Battle of Leyte Gulf 144–149; American hierarchical communication 144–146; Halsey's fixation on sinking carriers 147–148; Kurita's assault on Leyete Gulf 148; Kurita's withdrawal 149; mapped approach 145; South Force 147
Battle of the Bulge 107–112; Allies moving defense 112; attacks on La Gleize 110–111; massacre of American prisoners of war 109; Operation Bodenplatte 108; Operation Market Garden 107; Operation Wacht am Rhein 107; slowing German advances 111
battle tactics: defensive 17; offensive 18–20
Baudouin, Paul: British betrayal 29
Belgium: casualty rates 40; Chasseurs Ardennais 26; surrender 236
best practices 249
Bewegungskrieg *see* Manoeuvre Warfare
blame culture 150
Blitzkrieg 24–25
Bloch, Marc: *The Strange Defeat* 242
bloodless operations fallacy 251
Boeing 787 Dreamliner project 220–221; buyer-supplier relationships 226; risk mitigation 226–227
boldness 180
border fortifications: post-WWI 51–52
Breda Variant 59
Breguet 693 assault aircrafts 33
Britain: Argentinian invasion of Falkland Islands 97; betrayal 29–30; casualty rates 40; executive judgement 242–243; fallacies of military thinking 250–251; liberation of Paris 239; Matildas 212; North Africa campaign 222–225; tanks 32
British Airways (BA) IT meltdown 102–103
British Mark II Matilda 212
bureaucracy: limitations 185
business logistics 217
buyer-supplier relationships 226
buy-in: contingency planning 76

C

capabilities: dispersion 104, 113; dispersion *versus* concentration 98–102; diverting to plug gaps 105; dynamic 73, 76; erosion of mindful 248–249; Lean 106; protecting everything at minimal costs 102–104; refocusing 106–107; thinning out until value-adding functions break 113; tying down in defensive stance 113; value 106
Central front 20–21
centralisation 135; accountability limitations 140–141; advantages 138; authority 135; autonomy 136; command and control system 263; decentralisation comparison 136–137; decision-making 151–152; hierarchy 136; infallibility limitations 140; initiative 137; Piëch's leadership at Volkswagen 139; sensitivity 137; top managers making workforces obedient to their will 152
centre of gravity *see* COGs
certainty: linear strategies 77
Char B1 tank 31–32
Chasseurs Ardennais 26
chess fallacy 250
Churchill, Sir Winston: message to defeated France 23–24
Citadel 70–73
civilians: human suffering 41–43
Clausewitzian view of war 263–264
COA (course of action): wargaming 191–194
cognitive biases 252–254; ambiguity effect 252; anchoring effect 252; bandwagon

effect 252; confirmation bias 253; conservatism 253; countering with Red Teaming 254–260; courtesy bias 253; curse of knowledge 253; focussing effect 253; framing effect 253; illusion of control 253; normalcy bias 254; ostrich effect 254; sunk cost fallacy 254

COGs (centre of gravity) 85–86; abundance of resources 213–214; Allies 113; determination 95–96; disruptive power 112; refocusing 106; South Atlantic 97

cohesion: logistics 215–217; teams 177–179

command 175–176; Jominian view of war 262–263

commitment 180–181; administrative *versus* adaptive leadership 183; defined 174

communication: centralised decision-making 152; complexity 144–149; intent 143; real-time 132; tactical sensitivity 132–134; Von Clausewitz's information in war 134

complexity 6–7; communication 144–149; mapping 13; methodical battle tactics 124

compliance 39

compulsory enlistment 38–39

concentration *versus* dispersion 98–102; advantages 101–102; defensively 100; differences 100; progressively 101

confirmation bias 253

conservatism 253

consistency: defensive 240–241; defensive resilience 15–16

constraints: intent 142

contingencies: JIC *versus* JIT logistics 218; planning 76

continuous logistics 214–215; risk mitigation 226–227

control 69; illusion of control 253; Jominian view of war 262–263

costs: dispersion limitations 104; saving by watering down critical functions 102–104; sunk cost fallacy 254; thinning out resources and capabilities until value-adding functions break 113; value 106

Cota, General 187

courtesy bias 253

creeping crisis 7

Cremers, Maréchal de logis 127

critical functions: value 106; watering down by cutting costs 102–104

crossing the Meuse river 88–94; armoured support crossing 93; Dinant 90–91

culture: administrative *versus* adaptive leadership 183

curse of knowledge 253

Curtiss Hawk 33

D

data identification 75

David and Goliath fallacy 251

De Jomini: army experience 4; art of war 5; assembly of forces in space 86–87; defensive battle tactics 17; Jominian view of war 262–263; leadership as a trait 161–163; logistics 202–204; offensive battle tactics 18–20; rank and status and leadership 163; strategy 63–64; surprising the enemy 15

decentralisation 135; advantages 138; authority 135; autonomy 136; centralisation comparison 136–137; decision-making 152–153; hierarchy 136; initiative 137; intent 141–143; logistics 215–216; sensitivity 137

decision-making: centralised 151–152; command 175–176; decentralised 152–153, 215–216

defense: battle tactics 17; consistency of France 240–241; digging in stance 244; dispersion and concentration

100; French preparations of German threats 58–59; resilience 15–16; tying down resources and capabilities 113
Delphi method of forecasting 69
Deployment Directive Yellow 54
desired outcomes: intent 141
determination: COGs 95–96; Sedan river crossings 95
digging in defensive stance 244
direction 174–175; administrative *versus* adaptive leadership 183
dispersion: advantages 101–102; concentration comparison 98–102; defensively 100; limitations 104; progressive 101; thinning out resources and capabilities until value-adding functions break 113
disruptive power: COGs 112
dive bombers 33
doctrine: defined 35
Dornier 17Z 33
downtime 214
drivers: uncertain industry/project identification 74–75
Dunkirk 240; Allied forces evacuation 236
dynamic capabilities: adaptive strategies 73; contingency planning 76

E
east offensive of Germany 70–73
Eastman, George 68
ecological resilience 7
environments: changes exceeding organisation's robustness 77; communicating intent 143; controllability 69; linear *versus* adaptive strategies 66–67; uncertainty 67–68
erosion of resilience 243–249; adaptive innovation 247; bloodless operations fallacy 251; chess fallacy 250; magic weapon fallacy 250; mindful capabilities 248–249; miniaturism 250; passive enemy fallacy 251; performance optimisation 245, 248; preventative control 245; Red Teaming 254–260; reversing 252–261
executive judgement: Allies WWI lessons 244–245; France pre-1940 243–245; Germans *versus* French and British 242–243; Germany interwar years 246; Germany post-1940 246–249

F
Fairey Battles 33
Falkland Islands invasion 97
fallacies of military thinking 250–251
fast bombers 32–33
Fastener Procurement Model (FPM) 221
Flak gun 27
flexibility: buyer-supplier relationships 226; operations planning 151
flow: lean thinking 99
fluid mechanics 214–215
focus: administrative *versus* adaptive leadership 182; France *versus* Germany 241
focussing effect 253
forecasting 69; Boeing example 221; limitations 220–221; North Africa campaign example 222–225
foresight: reversing erosion of resilience 260
Fort d'Ében-Émael 12, 119–120; capturing 124–130
fortifications 11–12; borders post-WWI 51–52
FPM (Fastener Procurement Model) 221
framing effect 253
France: air force 33; armistice after fall of Paris 238–239; artillery 27; border fortifications post-WWI 51–52; British betrayal 29–30; casualty rates 40; defensive consistency

240–241; determination 95; executive judgement 242–243; focus of resilience 241; fortifications 11–12; immovable defensive shield 12–13; liberation of Paris 239; logistical constraints 216–217; logistics 205; morale 28; operational reliability 214; overconfidence 60; Paris occupation 237–238; preparing for German threat 58–59; redundancy 95; sensitivity 61; supply shortages 213–214; tanks 31–32
France pre-1940 243–245
Frankforce 211–212
fronts 20–22

G
Gaulle, Colonel Charles de 208–210
Gause, Colonel Alfred 177–178
Gembloux Panzer attacks 157–158
Germany: 1914 and 1940 campaign comparison 55; abundance of resources 213; adaptability 61; adaptive leadership 158–160; Africa corps 177–179; air force 32–33; amphibious crossing obstacles 10–11; armoured warfare 25–26; artillery 27; Battle of the Bulge 107–112; Blitzkrieg 24–25; capturing Fort d'Ében-Émael 124–130; casualty rates 40; determination 95; east offensive 70–73; executive judgement 242; focus of resilience 241; French fortification obstacles 11–12; German Army Field Manual of 1936 165–167; Grossdeutschland regiment 26; imagination 59–60; infantry 26–27; interwar years 246; JIC logistics 230; logistical autonomy and cohesion 215–216; logistical independence 204–205; Manstein Plan 57–58; NSDAP 52; officer candidates 163–165; operational availability 214; operational management of surprising the Allies 57; order of battle xv; Paris occupation 237–238; progressive resilience 15–17; rearming and expansion post-WWI 52–53; redundancy 94; Schwerpunkt 85–86; strategic management of surprising the Allies 54–56; superior numbers 26; tactical sensitivity 61; tanks 30
Germany post-1940 246–249; adaptive innovation 247; mindful capabilities 248–249; performance optimisation 248
Gort, General Lord 210–212
Grossdeutschland regiment 26

H
Halsey, Admiral William F. Jr.: Battle of Leyte Gulf 144–149
Hawker Hurricanes 33
heuristics: reversing erosion of resilience 252–254
hierarchy: centralisation *versus* decentralisation 136
higher-level goals: intent 141
hindsight 249–250
Hitler: executive judgement 242
Holland: casualty rates 40; surrender 156–157
hollow charge effects 127
Hotchkiss 25 mm semi-automatique modèle 1934 gun 27
human suffering 41–43
Huntziger, General 239
Hürtgen forest *see* Battle of Hürtgen forest

I
identifying: COGs 95–96; data for decision making 75; uncertain industry/project drivers 74–75
ideology 39
illusion of control 253

imagination: strategic management 59–60
immovable defensive shield 12–13
incidents: sudden *versus* creeping crisis 7
infantry 26–27
information in war 124
initiatives: centralisation *versus* decentralisation 137; operations planning 151
insight: creating 260–261
intent: antigoals 142; autonomy undermining 144–149; communicating 143; constraints 142; definition 141; desired outcome image 141; higher-level goals 141; just culture 150; key decisions 142; leadership direction 175; rationale for plan 142; sequence of steps in plan 142
interwar years 48–53; Allies 243–245; Battle for Verdun 48–49; border fortifications 51–52; France 243–245; German lessons from WWI 246; German rearming and expansion 52–53; legacy of victory 48–52; Phoney War 56
Italy: German Africa Corps reinforcement 177–179; North Africa campaign 222–225

J
Japan: Battle of Leyte Gulf 144–149
jerrycans 205
JIC (Just-in-Case) logistics 217–219; advantages 219; Germans *versus* Allies 230; JIT comparison 218; safety stocks 228
JIT (Just-in-Time) logistics 218–219; advantages 219; business trends 230; disadvantages 219–220; JIC comparison 218
JOA logistical support 229
Jominian view of war 262–263
Jottrand, Major 125

Junkers 87 Sturzkampfflugzeug-Stuka 33
Junkers 88A Schnellbombers 32–33
just culture 150

K
Kalanick, Travis 184
Keitel, General 239
key decisions: intent 142
Kinkaid, Vice Admiral Thomas C: Battle of Leyte Gulf 144–146
Klein, G.: intent 141–142
Kodak 68
Kurita, Admiral Takeo: Battle of Leyte Gulf 146–149

L
La Gleize attacks 110–111
land-ships 32
leadership: adaptive 158–160; adaptive *versus* administrative 181–183; administrative 167–168; administrative leadership supporting adaptive leadership 185–186; alignment 174, 177–179; automation 185; balancing administrative and adaptive 186–190; boldness 180; bureaucracy 185; cohesive team 177–179; command 175–176; commitment 174, 180–181; direction 174–175; focus 182; Germany Army Field Manual of 1936 165–167; mindful flexibility 190–191; officer candidates in Germany 163–165; rank and status 163; superior-subordinate relationships 182; as a trait 160–163; wargaming 191–194
lean thinking 99: operations 106; restructuring resources and capabilities 106–107
lean-manufacturing 219–220
learning culture 150
legacy of victory 48–52; Battle for Verdun 48–49; border fortifications 51–52

LeO 451 day bombers 33
light artillery howitzer 27
linear strategy 64–66; certainty 77; controllability 69; Operation Zitadelle 70–73; uncertainty 67–68
location: JIC *versus* JIT logistics 218
logistical independence 204–205: abundance of resources 213–214; backpack principle 204–205; operational availability 214
logistics: abundance of resources 213–214; Africa campaign 225; autonomy and cohesion 215–217; backpack principle 204–205; business *versus* war 217; buyer-supplier relationships 226; continuous 214–215; De Jomini 202–204; forecasting limitations 220–221; importance 201; JIC by Allies and Germany 230; JIC *versus* JIT 217–219; JIT disadvantages 219–220; JIT trends 230; JOA level support 229; logistical independence of Germans 204–205; mission analysis 229; NATO 206–207; operational availability 214; planning factors 229; requirements 229; risk mitigation 226–227; safety stocks 228; shortfalls 229–230; stockpile planning 207; strategic mobility 206; sustainability 206–207
loose coupling 6–7

M

MacArthur, General: Battle of Leyte Gulf 144–147
magic weapon fallacy 250
Maginot Line 11, 50–51
maintenance of morale: operations planning 151
management levels 35–36
manoeuvre warfare (Bewegungskrieg) 53–54; Germans surprising the Allies 54–58
Manstein Plan 57–58

mapping: uncertainty and complexity 13
Martel, General 210–212
massacre: American prisoners of war 109
Matildas 32, 212
May 10th-May 11th 1940 118–120
May 10th-May12th 1940 German invasion 82–85
May 13th-May 17th 1940 156–159
May 18th-May 25th 1940 198–201
May 26th-June 20th 1940 234–239; armistice 238–239; Belgium's surrender 236; evacuation of Allied forces 236; Paris occupation by Germans 237–238; Weygand line defense 236–237
Mechelen Incident 59
methodical battle tactics 53–54, 124; capturing Fort d'Ében-Émael 124–130; French preparations of German threat 58–59
mindful action 8–9
mindful capabilities: erosion 248–249
miniaturism fallacy 250
mission command 121–123
mission-oriented tactics 120–123; capturing Fort d'Ében-Émael 124–130; logistics 229; mission command 121–123; operational intent 144–149; origins in Prussian Army 120–121
morale 28, 151
multinational environments: communicating intent 143

N

NATO (North Atlantic Treaty Organization); logistics planning 206–207
need for resilience in 1940 campaign 10–14; amphibious crossings obstacles 10–11; French fortifications 11–12; immovable defensive shield 12–13

Netherlands: casualty rates 40; surrender 156–157
normalcy bias 254
North Africa campaign 222–225
Northern front 20–21
NSDAP (National Socialist German Workers' Party) 52

O

obedience 39
offensive battle tactics 18–20
officer candidates in Germany 163–165
On War: origins 4
Operation Battleaxe 222
Operation Bodenplatte 108
Operation Dynamo 236
Operation Market Garden 107
Operation Torch 224–225
Operation Wacht am Rhein 107
Operation Yellow 24
Operational Order No. 6 70–73
operations 35–36; agility 98, 105; assembly of forces in space 86–88; availability 214; crossing the Meuse river 88–94; determination 95; dispersion limitations 104; dispersion *versus* concentration 98–102; identifying COGs 95–96; Lean 106; planning 151; protecting everything at minimal costs 102–104; redundancy 94–95; refocusing 106–107; Schwerpunkt 85–86; sensitivity 61; surprising the Allies 57; value-adding 106
order of battle 20–22
ordering time: JIC *versus* JIT logistics 218
organisational resilience 8–9; adaptive innovation 9; complexity 6–7; mindful action 9; performance optimisation 9; preventative control 9; resilience engineering, compared 7; uncertainty 6
ostrich effect 254

outcomes: intent 141–142
overconfidence: French strategy 60

P

Pacific: Battle of Leyte Gulf 144–149
Panzer attacks near Gembloux 157–158
Paris: ceasefire armistice 238–239; fall 237–238; liberation 239
passive enemy fallacy 251
performance optimisation 9; France pre-1940 244–245; Germany post-1940 248
Pétain, Marshal Philippe 238
Phoney War 56
Piëch, Ferdinand: leadership at Volkswagen 139
planning operations 151
plans: intent 142
Position Fortifiée de Liège I 119
pre-May 10th 1940 *see* interwar years
preventative control 9; France pre-1940 243–245; Germany interwar years 246
progressive: dispersion and concentration 101; resilience 15–17
propaganda 39
protecting everything at minimal costs 102–104
Prussian army: mission-oriented tactics 120–121
pull: lean thinking 99; refocusing 106–107
PzKpfW III tanks 30
PzKpfW IV tanks 30–31

Q

quality: air forces 32–34; tanks 32

R

racing to the channel 207–212; counter-attack from the south 210–212;

de Gaulle's attacks at Montcornet and Lislet 208–210
rationale for plans: intent 142
real-time communication 132
Red Teaming 254–260; benefits 254–255; Blue Team role 259–260; common fallacies 259; end user role 256–257; end user steps 258; guidelines 257; outcome 260; Red Team selection 259; successful 256
redundancy 94–95
refocusing: COGs 106–107
Reid, Leonard: centralisation 138–139
Reinberger, Helmuth 56–57
Reinhardt, Georg-Hans: XLI Panzer Corps 89, 94
requirements: logistics 229; mission command 122; scenario planning 74
resilience: defensive 15–16; ecological 7; engineering 7; erosion 243–249; need for in 1940 campaign 10–14; progressive 15–17; socioecological 7
resources: abundance 213–214; backpack principle 204–205; buyer-supplier relationships 226; defensively dispersing or concentrating 100; dispersion 104, 113; dispersion *versus* concentration 98–102; diverting to plug gaps 105; jerrycans 205; Lean 106; protecting everything at minimal costs 102–104; refocusing 106–107; safety stocks 228; supply shortages 213–214; thinning out until value-adding functions break 113; tying down in defensive stance 113; value 106
restructuring: resources and capabilities 106–107
reversing erosion of resilience 252–261; cognitive biases 252–254; creating insight 260–261; foresight 260; Red Teaming 254–260
Reynaud, Prime Minister Paul 238
risk mitigation: logistics 226–227

rivers: amphibious crossings 10–11
Rommel, General Erwin: 7th Panzer 90–91; Afrika Corps 222–225; Martel's Frankforce 211–212
Rucksack-Prinzip 204–205

S

safety stocks 228
Saint-Exupéry, Antoine de 2–3
saving costs: watering down critical functions 102–104
scenario planning 73–75; data identification 75; requirements 74; responses to uncertain drivers 75; uncertain drivers identification 74–75
scepticism: contingency planning 76
Schlieffen plan 55
Schoemaker, P.: scenario planning 73–74
Schwerpunkt *see* COGs
Sedan river crossings 88–94; agility 98; aerial photograph 89; armoured support crossing 93; determination 95; Dinant 90–91; redundancy 94–95
sensitivity: centralisation *versus* decentralisation 137; contingency planning 76; strategic management 61; tactics 132–134
sequence of steps: intent 142
Sichelschnitt *see* Manstein Plan
Siegfried Line 187, 246
Smyth, Sir John: German air forces 34
socioecological resilience 7
Somua S35 32
South Atlantic COGs 97
Southern front 21–22
SPG (Stockpile Planning Guidance) 207
spreading resources and capabilities 102–104
static warfare: border fortifications 51–52
stockpile planning 207
Stonne battle 168–174
The Strange Defeat 242
strategic mobility 206

strategy 35–36, 48; adaptability 61; Battle for Verdun 48–49; border fortifications 51–52; COGs 96; contingency planning 76; controllability 69; De Jomini 63–64; defined 35; environment uncertainty 67–68; forecasting 69; French defensive preparations of German threats 58–59; imagination 59–60; linear *versus* adaptive 64–67; manoeuvre warfare (Bewegungskrieg) 53–54; methodical battle 53–54; overconfidence 60; scenario planning 73–75; sensitivity 61; surprising the Allies 54–58; Von Clausewitz 62–63
Student, Kurt 124
subordinate authority 131–132
sudden crisis 7
sunk cost fallacy 254
superior numbers 26
superior-subordinate relationships 182
supplier-buyer relationships 226
surprising the enemy: De Jomini 15; defensive resilience 15–16; French defensive preparations for German threat 58–59; operations 57; progressive resilience 15–17; strategy 54–58; Von Clausewitz 14
sustainability: logistics planning 206–207
Sutcliffe, K.: mindfulness 8

T

tactics 35–36; accountability limitations of centralisation 140–141; adaptability 61; autonomy 131–132; capturing Fort d'Ében-Émael 124–130; centralisation *versus* decentralisation 135–137; centralised decision-making 151–152; COGs 96; defensive battles 17; defined 35; infallibility limitations of centralisation 140; information in war 134; intent 141–143; just culture 150; methodical battle 124; mission command 121–123; mission-oriented 120–123; offensive battles 18–20; operations planning 151; sensitivity 61, 132–134
tanks: British Mark II Matilda 212; French 31–32; German 30; quality 32
tasks 141
taxi industry 184
technology: watering down critical functions 103–104
temporality: dispersion *versus* concentration 100
tightly coupled defense: Allies 12
timeline xi–xiv
TPS (Toyota Production System) 220
Treaty of Versailles 52

U

Uber 184
uncertainty 6; environments 67–68; industry/project drivers identification 74–75; mapping 13; methodical battle tactics 124
unwanted outcomes: intent 142
US: Air Force Manual 1-1, AWACS 263; Battle of Hürtgen forest 186–190; Battle of Leyte Gulf 144–149; Jominian view of war 263; liberation of Paris 239; Operation Torch 224–225; prisoners of war massacre 109

V

value: costs 106; lean thinking 99; thinning out resources and capabilities until value-adding functions break 113
value stream: lean thinking 99
Verdun 48–49, 171–174
victory explanations: air forces 32–34; armoured warfare 25–26; Blitzkrieg 24–25; British betrayal of French 29–30; infantry 26–27; morale 28; superior numbers 26; tanks 30–32

INDEX

Volkswagen emission scandal 139
Von Clausewitz, Carl: army experience 4; art of war 5; assembly of forces in space 88; boldness 180; information in war 134; leadership as a trait 160–161; rank and status and leadership 163; space, time, mass of strategic warfare 215; strategy 62–63; surprising the enemy 14; tactics and strategy 35; view of war 263–264

W

Wack, P.: scenario planning 73–74
wargaming 191–194; assessment 194; conducting 193–194; preconditions 192–193; preparations 193
watering down: critical functions 102–104
Wehrmacht-Einheitskanister 205
Weick, K.: mindfulness 8
west campaign *see* 1940 west campaign
Westwall 187, 246
Weygand line 236–237
WWI (World War I): Allied lessons 24, 243–245; Battle for Verdun 48–49; border fortification 51–52; German lessons 246; German rearming and expansion 52–53; legacy of victory 48–52; liberation of Paris 239
WWII (World War II): Battle of Hürtgen forest 186–190; Battle of Kursk 70–73; Battle of Leyte Gulf 144–149; Battle of the Bulge 107–112; North Africa campaign 222–225

Z

Zitadelle 70–73